Best Wishes!

[signature]

Best Wishes!
Ellen

FRANK McKENNA

BEYOND
POLITICS

FRANK
McKENNA

Harvey Sawler

Foreword by The Right Honourable Paul Martin

Douglas & McIntyre
D&M PUBLISHERS INC.
Vancouver/Toronto

Douglas & McIntyre
An imprint of D&M Publishers Inc.
2323 Quebec Street, Suite 201
Vancouver BC Canada V5T 4S7
www.douglas-mcintyre.com

Library and Archives Canada Cataloguing in Publication

Sawler, Harvey, 1954–
Frank McKenna : beyond politics / Harvey Sawler.

Includes index.
ISBN 978-1-55365-490-2

1. McKenna, Frank J. 2. Prime ministers—New Brunswick—Biography.
3. Ambassadors—Canada—Biography. 4. Canada—Politics and government—1993–. I. Title.

FC636.M39S38 2009   971.07′2092   C2009-904796-9

Editing by Barbara Berson
Jacket design by Peter Cocking
Text design by Ingrid Paulson
Printed and bound in Canada by Friesens
Printed on acid-free paper that is forest friendly
and has been processed chlorine free.

We gratefully acknowledge the financial support of the Canada Council for the Arts,
the British Columbia Arts Council, the Province of British Columbia through
the Book Publishing Tax Credit and the Government of Canada through the Book Publishing
Industry Development Program (BPIDP) for our publishing activities.

Mixed Sources
Cert no. SW-COC-001271
© 1996 FSC
FSC

For Charlotte

FOREWORD
by **THE RIGHT HONOURABLE PAUL MARTIN**

IN 1987, I was working as president of Canada Steamship Lines in Montreal. I had never met Frank McKenna, but I had certainly heard of him. That year truly was his, as he swept New Brunswick in an unparalleled electoral victory and went on to become one of Canada's great political leaders.

Far better than most, Frank McKenna embodied two realities: the social conscience and deep compassion of a Liberal, and the no-nonsense, get-on-with-it approach of a businessman. I believe that it was his ability to act decisively, always balancing this social consciousness and his business instincts, that was responsible for his remarkable success as New Brunswick's twenty-seventh premier.

When I became finance minister, it did not take long before the premier asked to meet me and I encountered the pleasure, and truth be known the challenge, of dealing with his relentless pursuit of New Brunswick's best interests. What struck me immediately, however, was that he sought not only the best for his province, but also the well-being of Canada, and in so doing never backed down from his belief that good government fosters good jobs, that economic growth provides the strongest base for progress, and that pride and hope are essential components of a successful society, and of a successful people.

It was this perception that made him realize the importance for New Brunswick of becoming a knowledge-based economy, putting learning at the forefront of its priorities, and he pushed that discourse long before it became part of the mainstream.

After ten highly successful years in office as premier, Frank resigned, upholding the promise he made in 1987 to step down after a decade. When I became prime minister, I tried to entice him back into elective office—but to no avail.

I was luckier, however, when I asked him to become Canada's ambassador to the United States. The argument that won the battle was that he owed it to Canadians to put his skills, knowledge and talent at their service. Representing Canada's interests in an America consumed by the war in Iraq was not a task for the faint of heart. Canada's relationship with the United States is its most important, and it was strained because of the softwood lumber dispute, mad cow, the Devils Lake flood diversion project and ballistic missile defence. I knew our country could have no better advocate in Washington than Frank McKenna.

His ability to get along with the Bush administration yet speak frankly was crucial. As a former premier, he was also ideally suited for the job of manoeuvring through the political minefield of the United States Congress. Frank understood the dynamics of his mission well, and excelled at bridging the gap between the executive and legislative branches of the U.S. government. Publicly through the media and privately where it counted, he tackled some of the most challenging Canada-U.S. issues in recent history. In short, he went to Washington and he delivered. Had he been given a longer mandate, he certainly would have redefined the diplomatic relationship between Canada and the United States.

Since returning to private life, he continues to be a success, and our friendship has grown, as has that of our wives, Julie and Sheila.

There are so many ways to sum up Frank McKenna. His intelligence is to be admired; his wry humor is to be enjoyed. He is a family man who bets it all on honesty. His love of competition continues to stand out. He strives to be the best at everything he does, whether it is politics, business or even golf. Here too, he and I have laboured together. Is he any good? Well, those who have seen his swing will tell you that golf is about the only activity where Frank McKenna can't shoot straight.

With Frank McKenna as a great friend and a greater Canadian, I know you'll enjoy this book.

INTRODUCTION

"Frank McKenna had the Liberal leadership almost
for the asking. Except that he didn't ask."
GLOBE AND MAIL COLUMNIST JEFFREY SIMPSON,
JANUARY 31, 2006

EVERYONE THOUGHT THAT they had Frank McKenna pegged, that
they knew what it was he wanted—including the media, his friends
and allies, his (few) foes, and Canadians making small talk at Tim
Hortons and office water coolers from St. John's to Victoria. The media
had been priming the citizenry with speculation that McKenna was a
sure thing to run for and win the leadership of the Liberal Party of
Canada. Having been elected premier of New Brunswick three times,
he understood the art of the campaign. Having been appointed as
Canada's ambassador to the United States, he understood the art of
modern diplomacy. Having been named deputy chair of TD Bank and
as a director on a myriad of boards, he understood the art of corporate power. Having established relationships with some of the world's

most influential figures, he understood the art of celebrity. And having shared his vision for the future of Canada in public forums and in writing, he understood the art of communication and political leadership. In speeches he gave from coast to coast, it was as though he were the head cheerleader at a perpetual Canada pep rally. With all of these credentials in play, the pathway to 24 Sussex Drive seemed scripted and plotted out. He was perfectly dressed for the part. The moving van was parked right out front.

But it turns out that everyone was wrong. He would astonish one and all by turning his back on the highest political office in the land—not just once, but twice between January of 2006 and November of 2008.

"Frank McKenna had the Liberal leadership almost for the asking," *Globe and Mail* columnist Jeffrey Simpson wrote on January 31, 2006, declaring McKenna to be the only "gold standard" candidate in the Liberal party stable. "Except that he didn't ask." Just what was Frank McKenna thinking?

They say that once you're a politician you're always a politician: that politics races through your veins like heroin, that when it takes hold it never lets go. "No matter what you do, you never get rid of your brand as a politician," says David Peterson, McKenna's friend and former premier of Ontario. "I can walk down the street and nobody is going to say, 'There's a lawyer,' and nobody is going to say, 'There's a chancellor.' They are going to say, 'The guy's a politician.'" But as we examine McKenna up close and personal, there are clear signs that he is proactively shedding the political brand with which he is most associated. Clues emerge to what he was thinking when he gave an unequivocal no to the very real possibility of becoming prime minister.

So much has changed in McKenna's life since 1997, when he completed his ten-year run as premier. Although this book will examine some key moments in his formative past and his political life, the primary focus is more recent events—particularly during this last very eventful decade—and how those events have perhaps reshaped his life. While he loves his home province and his country, he has discovered that there are no borders or boundaries to realizing his personal fulfillment. He has become engrossed in global humanitarian matters and he associates more and more with people who can truly make things happen for the better, wherever in the world they choose to engage. McKenna is as keen to unload bags of relief supplies from a truck in storm-ravaged Haiti as he is to help solve broader economic development challenges with the political leadership in Rwanda. He has learned how to use his political skill and down-to-earth personality to bring attention to the issues that matter to him, whether they are global or local, humanitarian or political.

Consider the remarkable event he orchestrated in May of 2009. Before a packed house at the Metro Toronto Convention Centre, McKenna played host to former presidents Bill Clinton and George W. Bush. The first and last baby-boomer Chief Executives, whose ideologies and terms in office could not have been more different, had an amicable and meaningful "conversation," as it was billed. McKenna's role was to introduce the two before they made prepared speeches, then to moderate an armchair question-and-answer session on a wide range of topics. Given the long-standing animosity of the two former presidents, which had been heightened during the pitched presidential battle of 2008, such a dialogue was, to say the least, remarkable. The following day, a photograph of the three men in conversation ran on the front page of the *New York Times* and in media around the world.

Having led similar events in cities like Calgary, Atlanta, Halifax, Moncton and Montreal, separately featuring Clinton, Bush and former British prime minister Tony Blair, McKenna has become a global statesman in Walter Cronkite clothing, a bipartisan interlocutor who rises above traditional politics in mass forums that do not intimidate him. He would not have been able to create and stand front and centre at such an event but for the unanticipated, life-altering circumstance of serving as Canada's ambassador to the U.S. and, to a lesser but still important degree, as deputy chair at TD Bank. In that brief but seminal period in Washington, we can find both evidence and affirmation that McKenna realized—perhaps to his own surprise—that there exist more stimulating opportunities in life than simply being Canada's prime minister.

At TD, he found the platform from which to speak freely and the tools and resources to make things happen. Surely there are things he would love to see fixed in Canada, but there is far more to fix in the rest of the world, much of it grave.

In his post-ambassadorial and post-political life, it has become clear that the fix McKenna craves is in the form of helping people in need in more direct, powerful and satisfying ways than being prime minister would ever have allowed. He has avoided the layered, smothering Canadian civil service bureaucracy which, more than politicians, really runs the country, and the distasteful partisan quagmire that federal politics has come to represent in the minds of so many citizens. He has traded all that for a harmonic collaboration with TD Bank President and CEO Ed Clark. When Frank McKenna goes to work in the morning, it is in a more collegial environment where he is in even greater charge and control than during his days as premier of New Brunswick.

His recent brand may seem to be more banker than politician, but that isn't quite accurate either. He is more like a man who has set out on a quest. His experience in politics and banking is merely a series of checkpoints along his own lengthy and inquisitive life search.

FRANK McKENNA ·

Perhaps no one has understood, until now, that McKenna is undergoing such thought-filled transformation; everyone simply saw him as a politician and assumed everything he would do would stem from that brand.

When I first met him, it was during his time as premier, when he was a politician through and through. I was working as New Brunswick's executive director of tourism in the Department of Economic Development and Tourism. As premier, McKenna was certainly regarded as important; but his importance seemed at the time couched in a Maritime kind of context—he was just one of a number of colourful regional premiers of the same era, such as Prince Edward Island's late premier Joe Ghiz, Nova Scotia's John Buchanan or Newfoundland's Brian Tobin. It was the same when he was first touted early on in Atlantic Canada as being prime prime-minister material; it was wishful local-boy-does-good fantasizing.

But there was something acutely different about McKenna relative to his counterparts. He made himself seem familiar. I learned first-hand that he was aware of nearly everything going on inside his government. When he stopped me in a corridor of the Fredericton Centennial Building, he wouldn't simply ask, "How are things in tourism?"—which exceeds what other premiers would ever bother to ask. Rather, he would inquire specifically about how the Day Adventures program was going, or the province's Quebec advertising campaign, or the redevelopment of Parlee Beach Provincial Park. Years later, when we were both living different lives, whenever I ran into him at an airport he was still keen and curious and specific about such things.

After more than a decade of very sporadic contact, I approached McKenna in the winter of 2008, suggesting that it was timely to consider a book focusing on his life in business and diplomacy. He agreed to cooperate thanks in part to intervention on the part of two long-time McKenna confidantes: his former aide, our mutual friend and my former deputy minister, Francis McGuire, and McKenna's assistant, Ruth McCrea.

At that point, there was conjecture about his potential candidacy to lead a Liberal party in trauma; the McKenna question popped up everywhere I went. During the earliest research phases of the project, there was the ever-present possibility that the storyline could be radically altered at any moment. At certain intervals in the interview and research process, I believed he just might go for it. If he had gone for the "cheese," as he once put it, this book would have taken an entirely different slant and would have had a different subtitle. When in the fall of 2008 he declared for the second time that he would not seek the candidacy, it was absolutely clear that the book would never be about a McKenna leadership campaign. I became determined to find out why.

We began to talk in August of 2008 at McKenna's home, overlooking the Northumberland Strait in southeastern New Brunswick. He met me in nothing but shorts, sandals and an even tan. Playing with a long sprig of straw between his teeth, like the New Brunswick farmboy that he once was, he led me to the edge of the cape overlooking Friel's Beach, named after the family of his wife, Julie. In stark contrast to the TD Bank office tower where he works in downtown Toronto, this secluded, cherished respite is undoubtedly one of the most inviting crescents of sand in all the Maritimes. Although he said or exhibited nothing to this effect, I felt that with every second I took of his limited time there, I was robbing him of his brief, therapeutic appointment with the ocean before he returned to the Moncton airport to board yet another plane.

I learned in that first meeting that although he used to keep a diary when working as premier, it's no longer part of his daily routine.

Instead, if something noteworthy or important happens, he'll scribble it down or save a clipping, then throw it in a box, as he used to do during his time in Washington. Some of the research for this book came from that random collection of his personal hen scratches, copies of old speeches, photographs, research he had done and related ambassadorial paraphernalia that he loaned to me as part of his agreement to cooperate.

Sifting through his trove turned out to be nearly as revealing as interviewing the man at his seaside home or in the suite of executive offices at the TD Bank building on Wellington Street in downtown Toronto. It is not for the sake of posterity or for the authorship of a future memoir that McKenna saves these objects. He does it because the materials might have tangible use as reference for some future speech or policy consideration. As for a memoir, so far McKenna has decided that one is unnecessary. By being in the public eye, he has learned that someone else always happens along who is intent on chronicling what he's been up to and where he's going.

During our interviews, there were no rules. If I wanted to test his emotions over his role in the Meech Lake Accord, no problem. When I pointed out that he has at times acted melancholy over what he sees as his own shortcomings, he remarked that this was an interesting observation—and did not hesitate to talk about it. As the dialogue progressed in face-to-face discussions, through emails and on the telephone, I never crossed the line with McKenna, for one simple reason: there was no line to cross. Everything was on the table.

I · A Public Life

ONE

100%

"Let's talk about this 99."

FRANK MCKENNA'S PATERNAL GRANDMOTHER, MARY ITA,

QUESTIONING HIS PERFORMANCE ON A SCHOOL EXAM

THERE IS SIMPLY no debating that Frank McKenna is a perfection-
ist and a workaholic. Countless witnesses have given testimony to
this, and first-hand evidence arrives when he moves from our
interview table in his TD Bank office toward his desk and a stack of
documents; he is obviously intent on checking a fact or finding
something he wants to show me. There's a habitual tic, almost a
sense of impatience, to the way he ferrets through the files. One
can imagine him doing this even more emphatically if there was
no one there to watch.

McKenna has a few such habits. For example, he has long had
the practice of writing short notes and tucking them in his pockets.
In a feature article for *Diplomat & International Canada,* writer David

Stonehouse wonderfully described these notes as "small declarations of discipline, reminders of principles that ground him." *Be optimistic,* he would write for his later self-reference and consumption. *Call home. Be decisive. Eat right. Exercise.* I remember this as I watch him rifle through his files.

Julie McKenna is more to the point about her husband. She calls him "totally anal." It's a trait that she and Ruth McCrea, McKenna's personal assistant, have long had to contend with. To know Frank McKenna's basic family history is to know that he came by such habits honestly.

It was his paternal grandmother, Mary Ita, who instilled in young Francis his work and lifestyle disciplines, accompanied by a relentlessly high set of expectations. "I've just always had this sense I haven't done enough. I think in my case it's probably the result of my grandmother pounding it into me," McKenna says.

"Look," she would say if he were to come home from school with five 100s and then, on one exam, a 99 per cent. "Let's talk about this 99."

Mary Ita's tough motivational approach reflected the Old World values of her and her husband Durward's generation. Those values had arrived in the New World decades before there was even a place known as Canada. The names and specific origins of McKenna's great-great-grandparents have not been successfully traced, but it is a virtual certainty that they originated in County Monaghan, Ulster, Ireland. Next to McMahon, McKenna is the second most common name there, with North American descendants who can be traced to arrival points such as Charlottetown, PEI and Chatham (now part of Miramichi), New Brunswick, in the early 1800s. It *is* recorded, however, that McKenna's great-grandfather, Hugh Osmond McKenna, was born in New Brunswick in 1841, and that he married Ellen

Elizabeth McManus in 1872, and that they had ten children, the sixth of which was McKenna's paternal grandfather, Durward.

The family's connections to Ireland were made vivid when Frank, Julie and their children Jamie and Christine visited that country in 1997, soon after the City of Miramichi, home of McKenna's riding as a New Brunswick MLA, was twinned with County Monaghan. It was an emotional time for McKenna. He walked the soil of his ancestors and studied the fading inscriptions on their headstones in the Catholic cemeteries of small communities with names such as Emyvale and Carrickmacross.

As a direct result of Mary Ita's influences, McKenna has carried the pressure of high expectations throughout his life. Philip Lee's 2001 McKenna biography, *Frank,* cites passages from daily diaries in which McKenna seems never to be satisfied, even sounding melancholy, over things he feels he has failed to accomplish. McKenna doesn't deny that this is the case. "I'm not Freudian enough to figure it out," he says. It is a side of the outgoing, gregarious, often ebullient politician and speechmaker that one rarely if ever sees. That's probably because, in the way of perfectionists, he never slows down enough to experience satisfaction or dissatisfaction. As a result, he rarely if ever feels he has truly achieved what he wants, exactly how he wants. It was that way while he was premier in New Brunswick; it was that way during what I call the "eight-year bubble" he spent between his premiership and his appointment as Canada's ambassador to the U.S.; it was that way while he was in Washington, and it remains that way today. Friend and former Ontario premier David Peterson agrees that McKenna measures himself by harsh standards. "He's not easy on himself."

No matter the magnitude of power brokers and celebrities McKenna has rubbed shoulders with, Mary Ita remains, more than four decades after her death, the most pivotal person in his life. The relationship between grandmother and grandson was hardly typical: Francis Joseph McKenna was only five years old in 1953 when he began to live with Mary Ita and Durward, his "Grammie" and "Papa."

It is not entirely clear in McKenna's memory how he came to live, not with his own parents and seven siblings, but rather with his grandparents. Mary Ita and Durward had been sharing their Route 121 farm home with McKenna's parents, Joseph and Olive, and brothers and sisters, (in order from oldest to youngest) Anne, Loretta, Cynthia, Rosemary, Doris, Larry and Kevin. "I'm told that my grandmother had a nervous breakdown," McKenna explains. "I was born shortly thereafter and apparently had a very positive effect on my grandmother's health. More or less by accident, I became the 'fair-haired boy.'" It was decided McKenna would live primarily with Papa and Grammie when his parents managed to purchase a nearby farm and moved out on their own. "Somehow or other, it was agreed that I would be designated to be the continuity between the two households." The fair-haired-boy status carried with it a number of wonderful perks which McKenna would not have enjoyed in his immediate family's household: an indoor toilet, a house that was not cold and drafty, and school lunches consisting of perfectly cut sandwiches which Mary Ita made and packed in distinctive chocolate-bar boxes and which were the envy of his classmates.

When Papa Durward died in 1960, it became even more important for twelve-year-old McKenna to stay with his grandmother on the farm. It was a matter of having somebody around the house to look after things and also provide some level of security. "We also kept a lot of our cattle at my grandparents' and I was responsible for finding the cows and helping my father milk them."

With Papa gone, McKenna and his Grammie grew more and more kindred. Day by day as their closeness progressed, she shaped his ambition, insisting that he was destined to be either a Roman Catholic priest or the prime minister of Canada. Nothing less would do. Much of the time they spent together was at the kitchen table, where he read books aloud to her and she drilled him on the memorization of lengthy and sophisticated poems. His older sister Loretta says that while everyone else was reading the juvenile-targeted Nancy Drew and Hardy Boys mysteries, her brother was being introduced to much more complex subject matter.

Loretta recalls everyone's astonishment as McKenna, at just seven or eight years of age, performed before his schoolmates and their parents at the annual Christmas festivities, reciting syllable for syllable the entirety of "Casey at the Bat" by Ernest Lawrence Thayer. It wasn't just that he knew the poem's entire thirteen verses; the entertainment value was in his arm movements and the emphasis he placed on certain words and phrases as the succession of strikes were called on Mudville's famed Casey. In addition to his performances on stage at school, Mary Ita would also trot him out as a parlour trick whenever company came.

McKenna can still recite all of the expansive verses to Robert Service's "Clancy of the Mounted Police," although he has a bit more trouble whenever he tries to remember every line of "The Wreck of the Hesperus" by Henry Wadsworth Longfellow. And he didn't just recite such tomes; he was schooled on their meanings. In Service's "Clancy of the Mounted Police," for example, the lesson is clearly about personal honour, determination and commitment.

While there's no doubting Mary Ita's encouragement of his literary performances, she was probably less aware of his ability to be naughty or humorous when the notion struck him. Boyhood friend Joe Monahan, who retired in June of 2009 after thirty-four years in teaching and administrative roles at their alma mater, Sussex Regional High School, recalls their schoolhouse teacher Oscar Boyde motivating his students to create a yearbook cover design commemorating their time at the small but beloved Apohaqui Superior School. McKenna raised his hand at a school assembly to suggest they should just use the school's initials.

During the winters, Mary Ita would often spend several months visiting with various members of her family elsewhere, allowing McKenna to spend more time at the home of his parents and siblings. "With my parents and brothers and sisters so close and people moving back and forth so readily between the two properties, the situation did not seem unusual to me, although my brothers and sisters would probably have a clear impression that I was far less attached to our family unit as a result of the separation."

This episode of McKenna's life must have created a streak of independence in the young man. As he has said, he is not Freudian enough to try and analyze such things, but being moved out of the traditional familial structure may also have created within him the need to be close to his own three children and increasing brood of grandchildren, and to work hard on keeping them close to one another. The importance of family informs the personal and professional decisions he has made, especially in recent years.

Loretta gives him a lot of credit for having come through the period spent with Mary Ita, explaining that although she was a nice woman, she could also be very temperamental. What Julie calls Frank's "anal" nature Loretta calls his need for "control"—not of others, but of his own emotions. He was always extremely focused.

She also observes, "I didn't realize it at the time, but he had such a high degree of respect for people no matter what." She sees the self-control and the respect for others as being inextricably linked. She says, for example, that he never lost his cool the way young boys do when they're playing or competing at sports. "I've never seen him angry."

Mrs. Marion Otis lived near the original McKenna farmstead for more than half a century. Sometimes, driving to work in Sussex, she would spot the teenaged Francis on his way to school and pick him up. These were the days before yellow school buses were deployed throughout New Brunswick under the regime of former premier Louis J. Robichaud. Kids took whatever rides they could get from family and neighbours, or else they walked. Mrs. Otis says Francis was unusually polite and respectful for a boy his age. She knows full well it was the adults in McKenna's life that shaped his manners. "The McKennas came from hard work and brought their children up the same way." As well, it would be not unusual for an only child—which in some ways he was—to be observably more "mature" than his peers, especially a boy living with an elderly relative.

Former McKenna aide Francis McGuire says there are two things that drive his old boss's outlook on life, both of which seem to be a result of the large amount of time spent with his grandmother: "First, he is existentialist in the way of leading French philosophers and writers Sartre or Camus and, second, he is profoundly Catholic."

On the existentialist side, McGuire says McKenna finds meaning through active involvement. "Contemplation and hedonism give him very little satisfaction, thus his need for the extravagant pleasures of life are minimal. Pleasure that often fulfills other people adds little to the meaning of life for him." This is not to say McKenna does not know how to enjoy his latter-day success and the material things that come with it. He loves to golf, he has an incredible home overlooking the Northumberland Strait and there is now a family compound in the Turks and Caicos. Oh, and he likes to dance and loves the music of ABBA, and he'll have a beer. But McGuire insists these are not the things which drive and motivate him. Rather, he derives his pleasure by going full out, totally committed to everything he takes on.

Joe Monahan concurs that McKenna has always been a very driven individual. "He is a determined, tenacious person with a large desire to succeed," he says. Monahan recalls the time they spent together as army cadets at the former military training installation, Camp Sussex, where McKenna was recognized for being the best cadet.

On the religious side, it should not be overlooked that Mary Ita cherished the dream of her grandson becoming a Roman Catholic priest. Accordingly, McKenna was well schooled in the Catholic way. Joe Monahan vividly remembers McKenna blessing himself with the sign of the cross before eating his lunch at school, much in the way that Latin American major league baseball players do when they arrive at bat. However, McKenna's actual attendance at church as an adult is less regular than that of his wife, Julie. Rather than a need to be in church, McGuire says McKenna carries with him a "profound Catholic sense" that one is put on the earth to help one's fellow man, that through giving one can redeem oneself from Original Sin—not a term you hear used much anymore.

"Frank is very aware of his shortcomings as a human being," says McGuire, "and believes that it is only through service that one can compensate for these human flaws. As a Catholic, he believes in commitment, in duty and in discipline; discipline for himself and for others." McGuire sees McKenna as non-judgmental in his approach to others' failings. "He believes that through discipline and caring they can be redeemed as he can be redeemed, and that duty and compassion obligate him to assist them. Compassion gives his life meaning."

Perhaps equally influential as the Catholic church and its holy catechism were the Horatio Alger Jr. books that McKenna read aloud as a boy to his grandmother at her kitchen table. One of North America's most prolific writers, Alger was a nineteenth-century figure who knew ahead of his time that a formulaic style would sell juvenile novels like hotcakes. He wrote dozens of books that traced the lives of the downtrodden—bootblacks, newsboys, peddlers, buskers, beggars and other impoverished children who rose from poverty to respectability. The stories froth with expressions of moral values. Their simplistic rags-to-riches plotlines show down-and-out boys realizing the American Dream by dedicating themselves to hard work, courage, determination and concern for others.

"Those books became my favourites," McKenna says, "and probably ended up representing a major influence on my life." The one Alger book that lingers foremost in his mind is *Phil the Fiddler*. It's the story of Filippo, anglicized as "Phil," a young Italian-born street musician. He is one of a stable of boys sold by their parents in Italy to a tyrant padrone who brings them to work and beg for him on the treacherous streets of mid-nineteenth-century Manhattan. Published in 1872, the tale depicts the escapades of Phil, his encounters with good and evil and his eventual escape from the wretched padrone and his equally wicked nephew, both of whom get their comeuppance in the end.

But here is the key to the story and why it is so relevant to McKenna: like each of Alger's protagonists, Phil cannot make it on his own. In his case, street merchant Paul Hoffman—a key figure who appears in other Alger books, including *Slow and Sure* and *Paul the Peddler*—uses his ingenuity and street smarts to help win the day for Phil. McKenna does not identify himself with the one needing help, the underdog Phil the Fiddler. He identifies himself with Paul Hoffman, the one who helps.

McKenna's life shifted when Mary Ita died of a stroke in February 1965. He was only in grade eleven at the time, two years away from attending university—a very vulnerable, impressionable time for teenagers. Her sudden absence took a great toll on him, but her influence did not wane. It was she who had decided that Frank would attend St. Francis Xavier University, the pride of Antigonish, Nova Scotia, the only post-secondary institution which had had a place in the lives of the entire McKenna family. McKenna's Uncle Jack was Mary Ita's favourite son. Described as natty, handsome and charismatic, Uncle Jack distinguished himself serving in World War II, then returned to Canada to attend St. FX. McKenna recalls sitting with Mary Ita at the kitchen table, poring over Jack's university yearbooks and listening to her stories about his hockey and academic achievements. It was St. FX time all the time for Mary Ita, and so, unavoidably, for McKenna himself.

He characterized his university experience, years later, in the second annual Allan J. MacEachen Lecture, delivered at his alma mater. "Probably the biggest influence in my entire life, St. FX has defined me, created the context as to who I am. It was where I met my friends who remain my friends today. It was where I met my wife, Julie." And it is where his children received their post-secondary educations.

McKenna professes that St. FX is more than just a university or an institution. "It is really a state of mind. It's a concept. It's a culture." St. FX has a heavy historical relationship to Roman Catholicism, it is set in the relatively remote Nova Scotia community of Antigonish, and it's a compact, intimate campus that fosters closeness among its alumni well beyond one's years there. The university has an impressive list of alumni which includes such public figures as former prime minister Brian Mulroney and Allan J. MacEachen, the Pierre Trudeau loyalist and cabinet minister.

McKenna's high expectations and drive went well beyond academic achievement, becoming the norm of every part of McKenna's everyday life. Francis McGuire says McKenna finds meaning in life through exertion, whether it's the hard farm work he did during his youth or keeping exhaustingly long hours or playing as hard as he can in any sport. McKenna thrives "by sweating, feeling pain, feeling the thrill of victory or the agony of defeat, which drives his competitiveness." McGuire says McKenna throws himself headlong into a cause, whether it's a court case, a political campaign, a policy discussion, a bank transaction or just reading a good book. "Without total commitment, Frank feels an existential void."

According to David Peterson, McKenna is first and foremost a hard worker. "There isn't a lazy bone in his body," says Peterson, adding that McKenna was hands-on enough as premier to often answer his own phone and develop a detailed knowledge of dozens of files. Even today, he picks up the phone in his TD Bank office with the greeting, "McKenna."

"You can phone Frank anywhere in the world," says Peterson, "and he will be back to you in two hours and he is one of the most important guys. The worst people I know are the people who aren't important and you go through three levels of secretaries." Peterson adds that the hard-work ethic is backed by substance. "He's well-read and he's intellectually curious. He is not a patsy. He is tough-minded. He's got lots of points of view and he can do all of that in a very charming way. He can tell you that you're stupid in a charming way. What a blessed skill to have."

One recurring theme is that McKenna relates to simple stories, fables and anecdotes, which he regularly refers to in speeches. As well-known author John Kotter says, "fables can be powerful because they take serious, confusing and threatening subjects and make them clear and approachable."

One of McKenna's favourites helps to illustrate his philosophy about the meaning of dedication and hard work. "Every morning in Africa, a gazelle wakes up," he recounts. "It knows that it must run faster than the fastest lion or it will be killed. Every morning a lion wakes up. It knows that it must outrun the slowest gazelle or it is going to starve to death. So it doesn't matter whether you are the lion or the gazelle. When the sun comes up, you better start running."

Francis McGuire is right about McKenna's constant need to exert himself. He has the instinctive need to keep moving forward, to get running every morning like both the gazelle and the lion. Exertion is a recurring theme of his life. In high school, McKenna played six varsity sports—soccer, volleyball, badminton, track and field, cross-country and hockey, which is clearly his favourite. He managed once to score five goals in a single game as a midget all-star hockey player. It would have been one of those games when McKenna imagined, the way boys do, that he was Bernie "Boom Boom" Geoffrion or some other star from his beloved Montreal Canadiens. "I worked hard, had lots of enthusiasm," he says, "but I was the proverbial jack of all trades and master of none."

Hockey certainly was the first love of boys of his ilk and upbringing. Although he was small, McKenna took hockey very seriously and gave the game everything he had. His sister Loretta is adamant that if not for his size, he could have been professional hockey material. McKenna and Joe Monahan spent countless hours shooting pucks up against a sheet of plywood in anticipation of playing pond hockey on the Kennebecasis River as soon as it had formed a crust of ice, in locations known locally as "the First Chance" and "the Half Moon." The latter was unique for its shape, while "the First Chance," distinctively marked by a large tree, was so-named as the easiest spot on the river to access. Monahan says that the ice was often so thin and clear you could see a muskrat swimming silently beneath the surface.

When they weren't playing hockey at the First Chance, McKenna, Monahan and their friends would light tires to form a bonfire there for nighttime skating parties, warming their hands and feet on the way home by ducking into the Jones family's cow barn. In the off-season they'd take turns casting themselves as Los Angeles Dodgers pitcher Sandy Koufax and other baseball heroes of the day.

Apart from his antics on rural ponds turned into imaginary Montreal Forums and rough fields turned into Dodgers Stadiums, McKenna held a number of regional records for pole-vaulting—mainly because he was one of the only athletes in the pole-vaulting competition. It should not be lost on readers that McKenna might also hold the record as the shortest pole-vaulter in the history of the region.

McKenna remembers what was probably his most personally rewarding sports achievement, coming sixth out of seventy-four entrants at a provincial cross-country championship in Rothesay, New Brunswick. "The reason that this result was so memorable was that I ran the entire race on a sprained ankle. I tried to wimp out but my coach convinced me that it was not a serious sprain and, properly strapped, I should not use it as an excuse. It became a classic case of mind over matter. I felt an enormous sense of satisfaction in finishing the race and meeting the coach's expectation, even though I distinctly remember barfing my guts out after I crossed the finish line."

When they weren't playing sports, McKenna and Monahan were busy checking their traplines for muskrat and the odd mink. "We were quite hardy in those days," says Monahan. "We often got our feet wet as the traps were set along the edge of the water." With the spring freshet, their traps were sometimes immersed under four or five feet of water. Avoiding ice cakes floating with the current, the boys would remove their shoes and hook a toe onto the traps to lift them to the surface. Monahan jokes that it never occurred to them they could have had their toes or feet caught in their own traps.

IN ADULTHOOD, MCKENNA's principal outlet for exertion is not pole-vaulting, not running cross-country until he barfs his guts out and not checking traplines for furry creatures. It is simply the release of walking, a lifelong habit which began in his days as a young boy in the family's rural New Brunswick. "Walking was an everyday part of our life on the farm," he says. "We had a dairy herd that had to be collected twice a day for milking. They would often roam miles away in some of the deepest forest on the farm to get away from the flies or get fresh grass. It was my job at sunrise every morning to go out and find the cows. I have many memorable recollections of tracking cows through the dew, following the distant tinkle of the cowbell, cavorting with the dog and coming face to face with wild animals ranging from skunks to squirrels to deer. Although it didn't seem like much fun at the time, I continue to have vivid memories of the smells and sounds of the forest."

Walking has been seamlessly integrated with McKenna's overall work ethic. He walked to work as premier whenever he could—in fact, he was noted for being seen on his early morning walks to Fredericton's Centennial Building—and he walked to work whenever possible from the official ambassadorial residence to the Canadian

Embassy in Washington. Apart from the obvious health benefit, walking affords him time to think things through. But there's another angle to being out there on the street, whether it's in Fredericton, in Toronto, in Washington or on a beach in Jamaica. Being out there makes him feel connected to all levels of society. "It's like taking the subway. I just feel more connected that way than driving back and forth to work in the bank car. Walking or on the subway, you just talk to people, you see people, you just get a better sense of what the hell is going on."

It's true that McKenna's penchant for walking and exertion has its origins in his youth, but it also connotes a restlessness of body, and perhaps of spirit, in his adulthood. He is more likely to fixate on what he perceives as his inadequacy than to bask in the glow of success. McKenna has never once taken the time to look at film or video footage of the Liberal leadership convention he won in 1985, or speeches he's made, or debates he participated in, or other highlights of the three elections he ran and won as provincial Liberal leader. "When it's over, it's over," he swears, "and I forget about it as soon as it's gone, and just move on." And it's the same with accomplishments and recognitions he's received.

It drives McKenna's family crazy that he never stops to smell the roses long enough to see what it is he's achieved. "There's just never been a moment of 'Man, that's great.' My family rags me about that all the time. I've just never felt that [reflecting on the past] was helpful to me in getting where I wanted to move the province," or in other endeavours since, he says. "I can't explain it."

A telling example is the handsome parchment record of his credentials, signed by then Governor General Adrienne Clarkson, signifying his appointment as ambassador—a once-in-a-lifetime document which most people would have hanging for bragging rights on their office or den wall. More unique and more suitable for framing than any PhD, the document was folded in half and tucked into McKenna's box of records from his time in Washington. He had no recollection that it was even in his possession.

TWO

A Shooting Star

"He probably didn't get more than four to five hours sleep a night."
FORMER AIDE NAT RICHARD
ON FRANK MCKENNA'S WORK ETHIC

When McKenna was elected premier of New Brunswick on October 13, 1987, he made Canadian history. With that election, his favourite number became fifty-eight, the final tally of legislative seats he swept—a complete annihilation of the Progressive Conservative Party led by seventeen-year veteran premier Richard Hatfield. McKenna would spend the next ten years attempting to raise New Brunswickers' self-confidence, adopting social reforms and acting as salesman-in-chief, attempting to bring new and more contemporary business to his home province. Part of his populist image came from the pitch to corporate executives that he would answer his own toll-free provincial promotion line: 1-800-MCKENNA.

The training to be an effective premier had taken place over several years across several fronts. As a student at St. FX, McKenna became increasingly involved in campus politics, including events associated with Students for a Democratic Society, an organization formed in 1960 that espoused views well to the left of the Liberal party. Before joining the Liberals, he was briefly exposed to the inner workings of the Progressive Conservatives by working in a junior security job and running errands at the 1967 PC convention at Toronto's Maple Leaf Gardens, where Nova Scotia's Robert Stanfield upset westerner John Diefenbaker. This reinforced his interest in the drama and intrigue of the field.

McKenna's political appetite was further whetted in his final year at university when he was elected St. FX's student union president and president of the Nova Scotia Union of Students. After graduating, he went on to study for his master's degree in political science at Queen's University in Kingston. After only one year in the program, though, he realized that law was the field he should be studying if he wanted to become seriously involved in politics. This took him to the University of New Brunswick (UNB) Law School in Fredericton in the fall of 1971. It was during the summer between Queens and UNB that his first true Liberal party association occurred, in the form of St. FX University figurehead Allan J. MacEachen.

Under MacEachen's tutelage, McKenna gained his appreciation and understanding of what really drives politics. "I learned my lessons well," he says of his time working in "the big leagues" of MacEachen's Ottawa office. It was there that he learned about politics at the highest and lowest levels. At the highest level, he was responsible for research on the empowerment of Members of Parliament, the better functioning of the committee system and, later, an analysis on proposals for amending the Canadian constitution. At the lowest level, he was responsible for ensuring that members of the local RCMP detachment fuelled their squad cars at only certain Liberal-owned gas stations between Judique and Goshen, Nova Scotia. "I also became part of a very exclusive club in Canada: Allan MacEachen proteges," every one of whom became political activists, in a fraternity McKenna calls "the brothers and sisters." Delivering the MacEachen Lecture at St. FX University in November of 1998, he acknowledged it: "I owe an enormous debt of gratitude to Allan J. MacEachen, who was my employer, my mentor and my protector." But, McKenna says, working with MacEachen taught him more than just politics from the Liberal point of view. He was also instilled with "a passion for the country that I've never lost to this day."

After finishing law school, McKenna made the unusual choice in 1974 of moving to the town of Chatham, a New Brunswick community comparable in size to Sussex, where he'd grown up. Chatham would later be amalgamated into the City of Miramichi, together with the Town of Newcastle and a variety of surrounding small communities, but when McKenna lived in Chatham it was a proud community unto itself. There, he joined a law firm which had at its core two important Liberal party figures—brothers Denis and Paul Lordon. In hindsight, McKenna had made two wise choices: he'd chosen a small-town firm where he could garner more attention than at a larger city firm, and he'd connected with a pair of Liberals who could help cement him in the party politic.

As a young trial lawyer, McKenna's tenaciousness and local visibility—he was a big fish in a small pond—positioned him to get the call that engulfed him in a 1977 criminal case sensational enough to make national headlines. It was as if McKenna had been scripted into a Hollywood movie as the small-town underdog lawyer who saves the life of a small-town underdog accused of murder.

The accused was Baie-Sainte-Anne, New Brunswick, native Yvon Durelle, known to boxing fans as "the Fighting Fisherman." Durelle was a four-to-one underdog when he challenged and almost defeated world light heavyweight champion Archie Moore in a 1958 match at the Montreal Forum, at the apex of a boxing career that would leave him permanently worn and punch-drunk. But he was the underdog of underdogs when McKenna took on his case in the shooting death of local troublemaker Albin Poirier.

There was no disputing that Durelle had shot and killed Poirer in the parking lot of Durelle's Baie-Sainte-Anne bar, but the circumstances of the shooting were at issue. The defence was that an intoxicated and unruly Poirier had posed a serious threat to Durelle's life by trying repeatedly to run him over with his car after being physically removed from the bar. At only twenty-nine years of age, McKenna—along with his trial partner Denis Lordon—and thereby Durelle emerged victorious from a stressful episode that had carried on for nearly four months.

By the time the trial was over, Durelle was acquitted by a New Brunswick jury after less than an hour of deliberation. The acquittal came in the aftermath of an emotional, thirty-minute closing statement in which McKenna successfully convinced jurors of the plausibility of the self-defence plea.

It was a momentous occasion in McKenna's life and career, one that would earn attention from the media and within the legal ranks right across Canada. The Durelle trial became a heroic calling card for McKenna, vaulting him to Perry Mason status just four years out of law school.

Riding on that wave of publicity, and having since then helped clients on a long list of criminal and other legal matters in the Miramichi area, McKenna was elected Chatham's MLA in the 1982 provincial general election.

In one of the most important political lessons of his life, McKenna went on in just three short years to win the Liberal leadership. It was a contest that he initially believed he had no hope of winning. He had imagined himself climbing the New Brunswick political ladder slowly and systematically. His competitor for the leadership, veteran politician Raymond Frenette, had enormous name recognition, respect and affection among many constituents. Even McKenna liked him. McKenna, on the other hand, was the newest MLA in the province and therefore the lowest on the totem pole. He had been encouraged to seek the leadership, but when a group of party insiders called him to a Fredericton hotel to tell him he wouldn't stand a chance against Frenette, McKenna pretty much decided to get behind the man who had the aura of an incumbent.

But two things persuaded him to reconsider his chances. When he returned to his Miramichi riding, people told him he would be guaranteed to lose his seat if Frenette led the Liberals into the next provincial election. Frenette was talked about as being a great guy with name recognition all right, but also as a guy who was almost certain not to defeat veteran premier Richard Hatfield. "And I said, 'Shit, well I don't want to lose my seat,'" says McKenna. With that message in mind, he decided to run for the leadership just to save his own seat. But he still did not believe the leadership was within his grasp.

The second thing to influence him was the polls. It was pointed out by his party backers that in reviewing Frenette's poll numbers, McKenna had failed to adequately interpret their meaning. Instead of reading just the positive side, which indicated 52 per cent knew and liked Frenette, McKenna should have paid attention to the fact that nearly 40 per cent held a negative view of his opponent. McKenna may have had only 4 per cent recognition, but that meant almost nobody could possibly have a negative view of him. From that point in his political career, McKenna knew how to read polling results from many angles. He campaigned hard, won the nomination and took on Richard Hatfield to win the premiership of New Brunswick.

Once elected and settled into the premier's office, McKenna spent the next ten years leading a frenetic, workaholic life. Of course, when you operate on a schedule as intense as McKenna's, everyone else has to be on his or her best game to keep pace. In the Winter 2009 edition of *Atlantic Business Magazine*, McKenna described the intensity of those years, recounting far too many mornings when he couldn't walk to work because he had to be in the government car by six in the morning on his way to some far-flung corner of New Brunswick to deliver a speech or to meet with groups until nine or ten at night. He drove himself and his people hard. In keeping with his tendency not to stop and reflect on his success, if he and his economic development team managed to attract five hundred jobs to the province on a Tuesday, on Wednesday morning he'd be completely focused on the next five hundred jobs. Perhaps because of his relentless schedule, McKenna has a low tolerance for lack of efficiency and lack of attention to detail.

Like everyone else who has worked in McKenna's inner circle, Nat Richard knows these things all too well. He worked in McKenna's office during his final eighteen months as premier, filling a slot left vacant by Prince Edward Island native Steve MacKinnon. Before working in New Brunswick, Richard studied political science, served as president of the Young Liberals Association of New Brunswick, worked at the junior level in Ottawa political circles and picked up the nuances of political life around the family dinner table; his father, Bernard, was a McKenna cabinet colleague who became a one-time provincial Liberal leadership aspirant and went on to become New Brunswick's ombudsman. Although he was not one of the main power players in the premier's office, Richard is the only person from the New Brunswick days who would later be recruited to join his old boss at the Canadian Embassy in Washington.

Richard's role in the premier's office was to liaise with the Liberal caucus and the party office. He burned a lot of energy trying to keep up with McKenna's travels within the province, while more senior aides like Maurice Robichaud and Charles Harling accompanied the boss on business-pitching forays across Canada and around the world. "They didn't tend to do the trips to Minto and Caraquet," says Richard, only half jokingly. "They left those trips to the new guy."

No matter where they travelled with him, McKenna's intensity and work ethic no doubt shortened the lifespans of aides like Richard. Working in the premier's office took over Richard's life. He was in by eight in the morning and remained until eight in the evening, in addition to relentless weekend work and the legendary in-province travel. As others have attested, it was all he could do at twenty-four to keep up with a man who was double his age. "He is just a dynamo and he set very high expectations on himself first and expected everyone around him to do the same, says Richard. It was a pressure cooker of an environment." Richard admits that it was tough sledding and a very intimidating place to be at first. If you were going to work for McKenna you had to be on your game all the time. He recalls being admonished in the early going for pulling together a briefing book that was not up to snuff. "Frankly, I did a pretty sloppy job and he called me on it. Fair enough. He could be tough at times, but sometimes it was well-deserved."

He recalls the night the two were driving to Fredericton following a speaking engagement McKenna had delivered in Saint John. "I don't know how I did it, but I missed an exit to Fredericton and I was on my way to Saint Andrews." The turn Richard is referring to is very subtle and easily missed in daylight, let alone at night. McKenna was sitting alongside Richard catching up on some sleep.

McKenna suddenly woke up and immediately realized the terrain was all wrong. He was not too impressed with the fact that Richard had gone a full half-hour in the wrong direction, meaning they'd lost an hour. "Where the hell do you think you're going?" McKenna exclaimed.

"He probably didn't get more than four to five hours sleep a night, if that," says Richard, who was loath to impede such limited shut-eye. The premier settled back into his attempt at catching forty winks, leaving Richard alone in the silence of the night drive to stew over his mistake. Although the two would go on to drive all over hell's half acre in New Brunswick, Richard felt bad enough about the incident that he never made the same mistake again. It wasn't a question of retribution. It was simply that no one wanted to let McKenna down.

With that kind of schedule and lifestyle, something or someone has to keep things grounded. No one other than Julie McKenna has gone through more walls for Frank than his long-time assistant Ruth McCrea, who is nearly as obsessive about work as he is. They are a highly effective team, even though she operates either from her house near Sussex or her family's long-standing farm home in Shannon, New Brunswick, hundreds of kilometres away from McKenna's TD Bank base of operation.

McCrea was already in the New Brunswick Liberal party official opposition office in Fredericton when McKenna and Conrad Landry were the only two new members of the legislature elected in 1982. "He didn't hire me," she insists. "I hired him!" She has been in the middle of his life ever since, organizing his work life and acting as his official gatekeeper.

McKenna says that he and McCrea have a "love-hate relationship" and are playfully contemptuous of one another virtually every day. She is as apt to answer the telephone with an abrupt, "What the hell do you want?" as opposed to a simple, "Good morning." "I called her this morning at nine o'clock," says McKenna, "and I said, 'So, you're up, are you?' 'Of course I'm up,' she quipped back. 'What do you want? Get to it!'" In truth, of course, McKenna is a huge admirer of McCrea. "We've got twenty-two years together and I'm totally loyal to her; she's been loyal to me." McCrea can stand her ground more than adequately. "He has a bit of an ego, but what man doesn't," she jokes.

Everybody inside McKenna's circle knows McCrea is the go-to person if you want to get in touch with him, and those who aren't in the circle soon find out. She is the quintessential backroom organizer. McCrea can be very forceful, or as McKenna politely puts it, she is "disarming. It's the most amazing thing," he explains. "I'd go to Toronto as premier and at my hotel room the president of Royal Bank would show up and I'd say, 'What are you doing here? I thought I was going over to see you.' He said, 'No. somebody named Ruth told me I was supposed to be here at your hotel room.'"

Similarly, when McKenna visited British Columbia several years ago, Premier Gordon Campbell was waiting in the airport baggage claim area. "I said, 'Gordon, geez, you're too busy for this.' He said, 'Look, just call Ruth and tell her I did what I was supposed to do.'"

McKenna, it should be noted, is too polite to be Ruth McCrea himself, so he has always needed her to get certain things done. One gets the sense that without McCrea, McKenna's perpetual 100 per cent momentum could be seriously diminished.

McKenna's landslide winner-take-all election made national news. In spite of its status as a have-not province situated far from the central Canadian focus of most major domestic news organizations, New Brunswick had garnered national attention over the years. Former broadcast journalist and current PEI senator Mike Duffy says that New Brunswick had been a go-to place for news on all sorts of fronts, including federal-provincial relations, innovation, the adoption of the harmonized sales tax and Richard Hatfield's ability to create both legitimate and off-colour news. Newsmen like Duffy paid attention to New Brunswick during the Hatfield era, and the interest carried on through McKenna.

"As much as Richard was a shooting star, Frank was a shooting star as well, but was grounded and not at all eccentric," according to Duffy. One of the things he remembers most about McKenna is his willingness to think outside the traditional political and public policy box—he was "not a prisoner of the past and not afraid to try something different that might or might not work."

Like Duffy, recently retired CBC reporter Don Newman spent years covering McKenna in one manner or another. He clearly recalls the first time they met at the Ottawa Press Club. Someone asked Newman if he wanted to meet the new leader of the Liberal opposition from New Brunswick. McKenna was on no one's radar screen at the time. So Newman went over and introduced himself, and the two engaged in a discussion about McKenna's chances in the forthcoming provincial election.

Newman recalls warning McKenna he was in for a long, hard slog trying to unseat long-time premier Richard Hatfield. 'Oh, I think I can beat him,' was McKenna's response. Laughing, Newman recalls that he cautioned McKenna again not to get his hopes up. The result, of course, was one of the biggest electoral turnarounds in Canadian history. "Not only had my prediction that it would be difficult turned out to be wrong," says Newman, but the electoral map "was all revised by the time the election came. It was madness." McKenna, he says, has never thrown the prediction back in Newman's face. "No, he's too kind to do that."

During his time as Ontario premier, David Peterson had many dealings with both Hatfield and McKenna and noticed a stark difference in how each of them handled New Brunswick's affairs. Peterson has a less positive memory of Hatfield than does Duffy. He says that McKenna inherited what in 1987 was still a relatively "unsophisticated, old-school, rooted-in-the-past political culture where patronage was the order of the day."

When they first met, McKenna was "an obscure little leader of the [New Brunswick] opposition." McKenna went to Toronto to meet Peterson. "Frank was always curious about what's happening, in what other people are doing and to see if he could steal any tricks from us." This was in preparation for the forthcoming 1987 election, which saw McKenna's debut as New Brunswick premier with nothing but Liberals filling the seats of the legislature. "There's a certain camaraderie among thieves, as you know, and they were looking for help. We were happy to do it."

The more Peterson and McKenna saw each other and the more they worked together, the more their friendship deepened, eventually extending to include their wives and families. The friendship circle also included Joe Ghiz and his family, and mostly involved ski trips and visits to the Peterson family farm, where all three families hung out. "All the kids were little and raising hell and playing with each other," Peterson says.

Ghiz was a marginal participant in the athletic things they did. "Joe wasn't much of an athlete. There are pictures of us sitting on the ski lift and there's Frank looking totally comfortable. Joe looked absolutely scared out of his mind, so he would take one run and head back to the lodge." Peterson loved Ghiz. "He was so passionate [when they discussed politics]. He would always get so wound up."

Peterson believes that McKenna totally transformed New Brunswick, largely on his own merits. "I don't want to be unkind to the departed," he adds, referring to the deceased Hatfield and some of his political team, "but I saw those guys and they just whined and bitched and accomplished nothing...Frank changed all that. Frank was the beginning of a whole new generation of Maritime leadership." Peterson believes that some of the finest leadership in this country today originates in the Maritimes, and it began with a political sea change in the late 1980s, when McKenna lunged forward to the front of the pack.

THREE

Underdogs

*"McKenna got people to endorse the theory
of a chicken in every pot by embracing
the idea of doing some difficult things."*
RETIRED JOURNALIST MIKE DUFFY
ON FRANK McKENNA'S WORKFARE PROGRAM

CERTAIN ASPECTS OF McKenna's leadership momentum came from paying attention to lessons he had learned or sought out; originally from the Horatio Alger books, and later from then governor Bill Clinton's social development efforts in Arkansas. Each spurred McKenna's social conscience, his championing of the underdog in society. "I believe [former premier Louis J.] Robichaud was an underdog in New Brunswick, a little guy. I thought Yvon Durelle [the retired boxer McKenna defended successfully against a murder conviction] was an underdog. I always liked the stories of underdogs"—and how they eventually achieve great success by never giving up, so long as they're linked to a figure like the Horatio Alger character Paul Hoffman.

As premier of New Brunswick, McKenna certainly didn't have to look too far to find a population of underdogs. All he needed to do was look at the long list of names on the province's welfare rolls. The province was in bad shape economically, socially and emotionally. You could see it and feel it when you drove through New Brunswick, which is what most people visiting the region tended to do; it was ridiculed as "Canada's Drive-Through Province."

McKenna's response—one of a few key social initiatives undertaken by his administration—was NB Works, one of the first workfare programs of its kind in Canada. It was considered by many to be a resounding success, helping change the lives of thousands of New Brunswickers. According to McKenna, his inspiration for spearheading the program came from Arkansas and the work of Bill Clinton. "As a premier, I was looking all over the world for ideas, and you find them everywhere," says McKenna. "Every state had different ideas and every country did, but at one stage I found Arkansas to be quite an interesting place because the governor there was really innovative."

What attracted McKenna's attention was the way Clinton introduced a combination of incentives and tough love, or "carrots and sticks," as McKenna calls it, for people to make their own move: "all the things you need to do when people are in the grips of dependency." He says Clinton's initiatives were especially remarkable because they emerged at a time when it was out of fashion for Liberals in Canada or Democrats in the U.S. to challenge the traditional welfare system. "I could never understand why the left wing would claim the poverty agenda," says McKenna. "It never made sense to me. And I became even more angered about that when I saw them making the case that the poverty agenda simply involved more money all the time. Because that never made sense to me either. And what I really saw was that attitude creating a welfare trap that people couldn't get out of."

FRANK McKENNA ·

This system gave welfare recipients financial support but not the means or the tools to exit the traditional system. McKenna says that one of the keys of NB Works was that people were not forced or threatened into the work option, but rather, those with the motivation took the option, and the left-wing hue and cry over forced workfare was beaten down.

The success of NB Works was thoroughly documented over several months on the CTV news program *Sunday Edition*, hosted by Mike Duffy. The government program was portrayed through one woman's personal story which proved to Duffy, a long-in-the-tooth, somewhat cynical journalist, that "it is possible for a political leader to change an individual person's life."

That woman was Karen Knox, who "had been on welfare all her life, since she was fourteen or fifteen." Duffy remembers how she took her kids to the shopping mall and felt awful because she couldn't afford to buy them anything they wanted. "Finally, she'd had enough. She basically would rip your heart out," he recalls. Completely captivated, he and his show's producers decided to follow Knox's personal story.

Through NB Works, Knox was coached in how to dress and present herself better. With wage subsidies from NB Works, she interned at NB Power. The program was also a motivational pathway for her to return to school and obtain her high school equivalency. Knox talked about doing homework at the kitchen table with her kids, taking care of her household and taking courses in providing seniors' care, how she held down two jobs in nursing homes across the street from each other, working from seven in the morning until three in the afternoon and then from four until midnight. She eventually managed to buy a modest house and a used car. "If I can do it, you can do it" became the theme of her episodic appearance on *Sunday Edition*.

NB Works was "designed to give people an opportunity to help themselves," Duffy says. In the jargon of the day, "Frank's for workfare" not welfare. Duffy recalls McKenna speaking about NB Works and skills development at the Atlantic Supper Club in Ottawa. "McKenna is a social experimenter and innovator but he is still of the old Liberal values. McKenna got people to endorse the theory of a chicken in every pot by embracing the idea of doing some difficult things."

Whatever effect NB Works had on the individuals it enrolled, it also had a profound and lingering effect on McKenna himself. He says that of all the nice things that people say to him around the province of New Brunswick, it is the comments from those who participated in NB Works that resonate the loudest. "The ones who move me the most are people who just stop me on the street and say, 'You saved my life. I was a welfare mother and you saved my life.'" The ability to help create positive change for individuals, especially the underdogs within society, was and remains a marker in McKenna's life.

FOUR

Lesson in Leadership

"What a mistake I made."

FRANK McKENNA SPEAKING TO MILA MULRONEY
ABOUT HIS INITIAL ACTIONS CONCERNING
THE MEECH LAKE ACCORD

McKENNA'S FUNDAMENTAL LEADERSHIP persona had been formed over a lifetime by his grandmother, his university life, his work with Allan J. MacEachen, his decade as a criminal lawyer and his campaigns for political office. But nothing in his career would challenge and test his leadership acumen as dramatically and as completely as the Meech Lake Accord, the now infamous set of amendments to the Constitution of Canada negotiated in 1987 between Brian Mulroney and the provincial premiers, aimed at bringing the Province of Quebec into the Canadian fold.

Meech Lake was the political hornet's nest that gripped the entire nation concurrent with McKenna's election as New Brunswick premier. It involved the most costly political mistakes of his life, and led to deep personal reflection. Even twenty years later, perhaps no other single professional, political or personal topic can trigger a visible emotional response from him the way Meech Lake can; it haunts him enough to have given him serious doubts about the prospect of pursuing the leadership of the Liberal Party of Canada.

Long-time political aide and friend Steve MacKinnon says McKenna was thrust onto the national scene via Meech Lake almost before he knew what was happening to him. "He had an early indoctrination, not only as a young premier," says MacKinnon, "but a young premier who had to assume a pivotal role on critical issues of the last twenty-five years: free trade, unity and Canada-U.S. relations. He got his PhD experientially and earlier than any of his other peers. He had those things burned into him so early."

McKenna and Mulroney seemed almost destined to meet up at some point in their lives. Both came from meagre Roman Catholic upbringings in rural Canada (Mulroney hails from Baie-Comeau, Quebec), both are alumni of St. FX and both have a unique combination of political and business experience. Both also have ties to Miramichi in New Brunswick; Mulroney attended St. Thomas High School in Chatham, where McKenna later won his seat as a member of the New Brunswick legislature.

They first met when McKenna was elected in 1987. Meech had been deliberated over by the Canadian first ministers at a meeting in the Gatineau Hills of Quebec on April 30, 1987, with Premier Hatfield still sitting in the New Brunswick chair. In the weeks following that meeting, it became clear that several of the provinces were beginning to rethink their positions on key features of the agreement, particularly the distinct society clause and limitations on federal spending power. These concerns were raised at a subsequent meeting of the first ministers at the Prime Minister's Office (PMO) on June 2 and 3, 1987.

Ultimately, several amendments to the original agreement were required before they could agree upon the final legal text.

By October, of course, Hatfield was gone, and McKenna was a virgin premier in the midst of a national constitutional debate that had just reached its apex. He walked through the election and into that debate under pressure from the powerful francophone Acadian community of New Brunswick to amend the accord. Sticking to his election promises, McKenna's first act as a national player was his refusal to ratify the accord without certain changes that favoured the Acadians as a constituency.

He may have been a virgin premier, but it turns out he was no tenderfoot on the nature and history of the Canadian constitution and how politicians had wrangled over constitutional affairs since early in the twentieth century. In 1970, for one of the final assignments of his senior year at St. FX, McKenna submitted a fifty-page essay—essentially a thesis—to his political science professor, John Stewart. A former Columbia University public law and government academic, Stewart had gone on to serve as a thrice-elected Liberal Member of Parliament for the old riding of Antigonish-Guysborough and spent a year revising the rules of the House of Commons at the behest of former prime minister Pierre Trudeau before taking a position at St. FX (he also later served as a Canadian senator). Titled "Changing Canada's Federal Constitution: The Background," McKenna's essay provided an intricate examination of the federal nature of the constitution and the methods attempted over the decades to amend the British North America Act, as well as a history of how prime ministers and provincial premiers had, at various intervals, confronted the need for constitutional change.

As a result of his in-depth research years earlier, McKenna—although new to the premier's office—must have understood the significance of what lay before him. In a sense, Meech Lake was presaged as early as 1906, when British Columbia opposed an amendment proposed by Prime Minister Wilfrid Laurier, thereby marking the first real example of provincial participation in the constitutional amendment process. McKenna's paper set out to chart "the reefs and shoals" upon which past constitutional amendment efforts "have foundered," including the endless string of federal-provincial conferences that followed Laurier's set-to with B.C. in 1906. Many of those reefs and shoals, of course, involved Quebec and the matter of two nations within a nation.

McKenna himself gives the example of 1965, when Quebec premier Daniel Johnson demanded recognition by delegates to the Confederation of Tomorrow federal-provincial conference of Canada as a "*deux nations*" society. Johnson continued to press Ottawa three years later for an entirely new Canadian constitution that would "associate in equality, two linguistic and cultural communities, two founding peoples, two societies, two nations in the sociological sense of the word." The situation became a political stalemate between Quebec and Ottawa, forming a scenario that would ring all too familiar for McKenna a full generation later.

It was very unusual for a senior-year student to take Canadian political science—typically it was delivered to first- and second-year candidates—but Professor Stewart says McKenna was intent on doing so. Stewart recalls the McKenna paper with extraordinary clarity, partly because of who McKenna became and partly because Stewart dug the paper out of the St. FX library many years later, after running into the then former premier at an Ottawa social function. McKenna "approached it with a legalistic mind," Stewart says of the essay. "He was looking at it with the kind of precision that a lawyer would have used," in spite of the fact that McKenna was still a year or two away from the realization that he wanted to move into the law program at the University of New Brunswick. "He must have had some early inclination to law or he wouldn't have picked the subject of the federal aspect of the constitution." As for the paper itself: "It is not a romantic document which is trying to arouse your zeal or your emotions. It is trying to be a precise statement of the legal situation. I may have impressed that on my class. He apparently got it."

Of course, some believed McKenna did not "get it" when it came to Meech Lake. In his expansive *Memoirs* and in subsequent discussions concerning Quebec and the Canadian Constitution, Mulroney had lots to say about McKenna and his involvement in Meech. In an interview he claimed that McKenna "shilly-shallied" on ratifying the accord, giving Newfoundland premier Clyde Wells the opportunity to "come in and sabotage it. I hold responsible Wells, [Pierre Elliot] Trudeau and [Jean] Chrétien for sabotaging it," leading to the 1995 referendum during which "we came close to losing the country." That, Mulroney claims, is when "Chrétien panicked" and tried to implement the pillar provisions of the accord one by one.

Mulroney says he considers it all water under the bridge by now. "In Frank's case, I always tended to take a less harsh view of his view in this. He was brand new [as New Brunswick premier] and didn't really understand the national implications of what was going on around him. He didn't have a full appreciation of what he was about to do" when the accord did not pass through the New Brunswick legislature. "He was misled about the implications of it." In his book, Mulroney recognizes that in New Brunswick it wasn't just McKenna who had shied away from ratifying the accord. "During the summer of 1987," Mulroney wrote, "I had urged Richard Hatfield to move forward with the ratification of Meech Lake, but to no avail."

In his book, Mulroney differentiated firmly between McKenna and Wells on their handling of the matter, making clear his disdain for the latter. "Not for [Wells] the admission of an error of a Frank McKenna," he wrote, "or 'the country must come first' attitude of a David Peterson." The book reveals extensive passages from Mulroney's personal journals on Meech and other matters. On April 17, 1989, just before another round of first ministers' conferences—this one on the economy and Meech Lake—he wrote that McKenna was "agile enough" to find a way to support Meech Lake in the end, which of course he did the following year. Wells and Manitoba premier Gary Filmon, however, were, in Mulroney's words, "beyond the pale."

"In all of the many debates and interviews that I had about Meech Lake, I can never recall saying that I would not ultimately vote for it," recalls McKenna. This is because ultimately McKenna is very much on the side of Quebec. But he is not on its side to the point of ignoring the wider realm of everyone's responsibilities in maintaining nationhood. McKenna is not afraid to examine what he views as Quebec's responsibilities face-on. He says that Quebec is unique in how it's been almost "mollycoddled" by Canada, that Quebeckers need to do more to accept some of the responsibilities of citizenship in the country. "I think we do them a disservice when we do that. Quebec governments have been allowed to continue a hue and cry about how the rest of Canada is consistently screwing them while in fact they receive transfer payments of between eight and ten billion dollars a year. It's almost a reverse psychological thing. I don't blame the people of Quebec for feeling they are being let down by Canada. [But] it's the duty of our country to let Quebeckers know that they are the huge beneficiaries of the largesse of other provinces." Right now, as a province that is deeply in debt and experiencing high levels of unemployment, Quebec is not acting like a self-sufficient society, says McKenna. He says the Canadian flag has got to be flown higher in Quebec, and Canada needs to do a better job of explaining the benefits of Canadian citizenship.

No matter how supportive he thought he could be of Quebec, McKenna also had a strong obligation to represent the interests of various constituents he was serving—in particular the Acadians, who wanted to see greater protection for minorities, including of course themselves. "However, if the issue had been forced by Hatfield, there is no question in my mind that our party would have supported the accord. In spite of reservations that I had and continue to have about some of the details, it would have been unconscionable for the Liberal party not to support it." New Brunswick, McKenna says, has always been on the side of a strong national government and has at important intervals promoted national compromises "because we have a sense in our province of how difficult they are to achieve."

But Hatfield never brought the accord to the legislature for ratification before the 1987 election, something McKenna says he "will never understand." Thus, consciously or unconsciously, Hatfield allowed enough time to lapse that the accord became vulnerable to whatever faults lay within the proposal, and whatever doubts people had about it. The longer it sat there, in other words, the less certain an agreement became. Looking back, McKenna says, he felt his predecessor saddled him with the problem.

With Hatfield seemingly in no rush and others dilly-dallying, McKenna admits to misreading what Clyde Wells and Gary Filmon would end up doing to the agreement. "The Clyde Wells thing particularly stunned me. None of us knew that Wells was going to turn out to be such a dogmatic opponent of Meech." Near the point of no return in the negotiations, both Wells and McKenna called in as invited guests to the CBC's Sunday talk radio program, *Cross Country Checkup*, the subject of the week being Meech Lake. During that broadcast, Wells said things of an extreme nature about the accord that McKenna and others had not heard him say before.

With the passage of time—maturing into the premier's office, talking to his contemporaries, analyzing what had happened in 1987— McKenna was able to re-evaluate his and New Brunswick's association with the accord. He had developed a new passion for settling the agreement. In Mulroney's journal entry of August 16, 1992, recounting a first ministers' conference at Harrington a few days prior, he wrote that McKenna "exploded" in response to a laissez-faire remark by Filmon that Quebec would never separate. "For Christ's sake, Gary, read the Quebec papers," said McKenna. "It's staring you in the goddamn face every day."

In our interview, Mulroney spoke warmly about McKenna on the matter. "The fact is that he came around in such an elegant manner to make sure he escaped the problem of history. And by doing what he did in 1990, he placed himself on the right side of history. Frank got himself in under the wire."

Academics have their own viewpoints on the unfolding of Meech and McKenna's place in the saga. Peter Hogg is a retired professor from the Osgoode Hall Law School and currently scholar in residence at the Toronto law firm of Blake, Cassels and Graydon. A specialist in constitutional law, he authored *Constitution Law of Canada*, a two-volume text which has been published through four revised editions, the last in 2007. It was challenge enough writing the original edition, but the revisions have also been gruelling because constitutional law is such an active field—mainly because of the activity within Canadian courts, as well as unique occurrences such as Meech Lake and the constitutional dilemma of late 2008 between Prime Minister

Stephen Harper and the coalition opposition, brought to conclusion by proroguing of Parliament by Governor General Michaëlle Jean.

Being so completely immersed in constitutional matters day to day, Hogg was very concerned that the Constitution Act of 1982, which included the Charter of Rights and amending procedures, had never been agreed to by Quebec. At the time of the Meech Lake discussions in 1987, he did not know any of the main political players of the day except Clyde Wells, whom he'd met while the two were co-counsel for an offshore conference years earlier. A supporter of the accord, Hogg knew that Wells was opposed. He arranged a meeting with Wells while attending an Osgoode alumni meeting in St. John's. "I had hoped to persuade him," says Hogg, "but I got the clear impression in talking to him that his position on Meech Lake was firm."

Hogg's argument focused on the accord's potential to settle long-standing grievances with Quebec, while Wells's counter-argument focused primarily—as did that of most Meech opponents—on the distinct society clause. Hogg's support for the accord was predicated on his belief that Meech had the potential of making the Charter of Rights more legitimate in Quebec and dampening the separatist threat. Wells said he believed the clause was in direct conflict with classic concepts of federalism and was not a desirable inclusion in the constitution.

McKenna later came to the conclusion that Meech Lake, for all its flaws, was a great achievement. "Unless you've been in that circle, you cannot appreciate how difficult it is to get consensus on anything. So I started to appreciate the magnitude of the achievement and became increasingly a collaborator in trying to get it through."

After the initial accord's failure and into the 1990 second round of Meech, when Mulroney held new first ministers' talks aimed at introducing amendments to the document, Professor Hogg worked as constitutional advisor to Ontario premier David Peterson, whose government had supported the original accord three years earlier. Hogg was in the building in Ottawa, although not in the room, when the "companion agreement" was drafted.

Never having met McKenna, Hogg is careful to say he does not know why the former New Brunswick premier chose the path he did in 1987, although he suspects he may have been partially influenced by other leaders of the day. When Pierre Trudeau came out strongly against Meech, the effect was to bolster the resistance being levelled by Opposition Leader Jean Chrétien. Hogg believes those voices swayed public opinion against Meech and had an impact on some politicians. "That was probably why McKenna as a Liberal felt that he could be opposed to it as well," says Hogg, admitting that this is pure conjecture. "I thought that was very unfortunate, but I felt it was quite understandable."

Although Hogg supported Meech, he admits that he was in the minority on the Osgoode Hall campus and that most lawyers involved in the considerable discussion and debate at the time were lukewarm or completely against the accord. That the majority of legal academia was voicing opposition to the accord says something about Trudeau's, Chrétien's and McKenna's decisions at the time. In a sense, what took place within the well-informed Osgoode faculty mirrored what took place within the country.

Hogg says that at the core of the failure of Meech, followed by the companion accord and the successful Charlottetown Accord, is what he calls "the doctrine of linkages" as a primary characteristic of the Canadian constitutional dialogue. "I think they were wrong in that you should do one thing at a time," rather than attempt multiple constitutional changes all at once, such as Quebec, women's rights, aboriginal matters, and fixing the Senate. Hogg said this Canadian characteristic is completely unusual in comparison with successful democracies. "The Americans and Australians do it one thing at a time." Canada, he says, has a bad political attitude about constitutional matters. He referred to the lingering questions over the constitution as Canada's "third rail," as in the rail in a subway system you dare not touch because it will electrocute you.

Mulroney says he and McKenna never exchanged harsh words about the turn of events. The late Quebec premier Robert Bourassa, he claims, was harder on McKenna. When Mulroney told him it was Wells, not McKenna, who sabotaged the accord, "Bourassa said, 'Yes, but Frank made it possible for him to do what he did.'"

McKenna believes Bourassa did not hold anything against him on account of Meech. This is the only point about Meech on which McKenna and Mulroney disagree. McKenna accepts his share of responsibility for all of his actions surrounding Meech, but stands firm that he and Bourassa had a "great relationship." He recalls being at his cottage and telephoning Bourassa a week after the collapse of Meech to say how terribly concerned he was about the country and the risk of things falling apart. But Bourassa went out of his way to put McKenna at ease. "Frank, don't worry about it," McKenna recalls Bourassa saying. "The Latin blood is boiling right now. As soon as it cools down, we'll go back and we'll get this thing fixed." From then on, says McKenna, "we had a wonderful relationship." In fact, in the middle of the Meech mess, the two premiers helped complete negotiations to move the Montreal Canadiens' farm team to Fredericton.

Meech stirs emotional memories for both McKenna and Mulroney. During the hours of interviews conducted for this book, Meech was the only subject that visibly altered both McKenna's physical posture and his facial expression as he retreated into his chair and looked down. And that was by no means the first time the subject had drawn an unusually strong response. "One night at the [1991] Summit Francophonie in Paris he was extremely emotional about it," Mulroney recalls. He was speaking to Mulroney's wife, Mila. "What a mistake I made," Mulroney's *Memoirs* quotes him as saying. As McKenna spoke, his eyes welled up with tears. "I thought I was doing the right thing, but it turned out I made a great mistake by acting the way I did."

Publicly, he bared his soul over the matter during a June 1990 first ministers' conference in Ottawa. "I was against Meech Lake when it was popular to be in favour of it," he said, according to the account in Mulroney's book. "Now I have become increasingly in favour of it as it has become popular to oppose it. I have matured as the country has over a three-year period. I understand the country better. Canadians are hurting. Our love for the country has to be unconditional. I could not have lived with the failure to reintegrate Quebec. I would have carried the scar to my grave."

David Peterson says he and McKenna have talked about Meech a lot over the years. "It's the one thing he may think, in retrospect, he may wish he had done differently." Peterson had supported the proposal, thinking it was a winner and the right thing to do for the country, "and I think history has proven that in spades. But at the time, it was a very, very difficult issue. The death of Meech Lake was one of the seminal events in the history of this country, not unlike the death of Louis Riel." Unlike Riel's, Peterson says, the death of Meech was predictable. He has a hard time with those who were sideline critics of the Meech outcome versus those politicians who had actual responsibilities to bear on the matter. Peterson likens those who were directly involved to a parent throwing himself or herself in front of a moving car in an effort to save their child. The parent is prepared to abandon his or her own interests for the sake of the child, the child in this case being the country. "We almost lost the country over that."

FRANK McKENNA ·

Peterson says that McKenna, as one of the custodians of the health of the nation, rose to the occasion of Meech like few others did and that his actions were born of conscience. Through the Meech experience, McKenna came to understand Canada better than he ever had before. "He learned with an intellectual humility that I think has served him very well." Meech was, according to Peterson, the stage upon which McKenna was transformed from a local Maritime figure into a national figure.

II · In Public Hiding

FIVE

Lougheed of the East

"Some people have described it as a narcotic."
FORMER CANADIAN PRIME MINISTER PAUL MARTIN
ON THE ADDICTIVE NATURE OF POLITICS

WHEN, AS PROMISED, McKenna resigned as premier of New Brunswick after ten years in office, he had to face the hard, stone-cold reality that he was going to be left with a serious case of the political DT's. His rise as a national figure would be, in a sense, put on hold. He would no longer have a team of aides to call upon from the various government departments, nor could he use the resources of the Liberal party office in New Brunswick any longer.

And McKenna didn't just view those people he'd worked with as "resources." He was very sentimental about them and what they had all achieved together. On October 7, 1997, he gathered those loyalists in his office and took the stairs one flight down to the news conference room on the Centennial Building's main floor. "I tried to make only promises that I could keep during my public life," he said to those friends, political colleagues, civil servants and media gathered, "and I'm proud I've been able to deliver programs such as kindergarten and better highways; things we said we would do and have done. I'm here to keep my final promise to the people of the Province of New Brunswick." And with those words, he began the process of vacating the premier's office within a mere week.

Before he left the room, however, he waxed sentimental and humble. "I've had a public much more faithful and supportive than I deserve." He spoke about the sadness of leaving, but also the relief for both himself and his wife, Julie, relief from the high expectations of himself that he had taken to the office every day. "We've carried a huge burden these last ten years. I don't know what it's like for other premiers or leaders. But for me this has been an intense, emotionally filled exercise. I felt every pain in New Brunswick, every joy. It affected me if a river was flooding or if a forest was on fire. I checked the weather every day to see how our potatoes were doing. If someone wrote to me looking for a job, I'd look after it personally. Every issue became my issue, and it's such an emotional relationship that it's almost too much to bear indefinitely. I just feel now that I've the weight of the world off my shoulders, and I feel quite good about it."

Before he left the premier's office, he distributed one of his favourite little stories to his team, and included it in the hundreds of replies he wrote to those who had written him when he announced his retirement. It was his way of saying that the people remaining behind had much to accomplish as he pursued the next leg of his life and his career. It is called *Even Eagles Need a Push: Learning to Soar in a Changing World* (Dell Publishing), written by David McNally:

The eagle gently coaxed her offspring toward the edge of the nest. Her heart quivered with conflicting emotions as she felt their resistance to her persistent nudging. "Why does the thrill of soaring have to begin with the fear of falling?" she thought. This ageless question was still unanswered for her.

As in the tradition of the species, her nest was located high on the shelf of a sheer rock face. Below there was nothing but air to support the wings of each child. "Is it possible that this time it will not work?" she thought. Despite her fears, the eagle knew it was time. Her parental mission was all but complete. There remained one final task—the push.

The eagle drew courage from an innate wisdom. Until her children discovered their wings, there was no purpose for their lives. Until they learned how to soar, they would fail to understand the privilege it was to have been born an eagle. The push was the greatest gift she had to offer. It was her supreme act of love. And so one by one she pushed them, and they flew!

McKenna's departure had a domino effect among his loyalists. In no time, key individuals in McKenna's New Brunswick success story—people like Francis McGuire, Maurice Robichaud and Charles Harling—followed their old boss's cue and headed for the private sector. No one could blame them for leaving when McKenna did. They had done their jobs, exhausting yet gratifying themselves in the process. And who, to pose an analogy, would want to be a member of the National Football League's Green Bay Packers after illustrious coach Vince Lombardi was gone? Not the players on the McKenna team.

As he entered the private sector, McKenna needed to adjust to no longer being surrounded by people who could implement his ideas and generate new ones. The only source of workplace continuity he retained was assistant Ruth McCrea, who spent most of her working days in the downtown Moncton law offices of McInnes Cooper, which McKenna used as a base for his exploding range of corporate commitments.

McKenna admits that as he faced this transitional period, he struggled to figure out just where he belonged, and whether he could successfully leave the nest. He was busy, but not nearly as fulfilled as during his time as premier. As David Peterson described it, politics can shape an individual's lifelong brand if they've had any degree of success at the profession at all. So what does a person do when they wake up and their primary identity is gone? Who do they become?

"When I left public life, what kind of bothered me was the finality of it all," says McKenna. "I'd devoted a lot of my life to building up networks and constituencies and, arguably, some credibility, and I wanted to continue to use it for good purposes." It didn't seem right that he should just walk away from public office and cease doing things to help move the public agenda. He felt bare. He felt as though he had suddenly stopped giving of himself.

In an interview, Don Newman guessed that McKenna may have looked to former Alberta premier Peter Lougheed in modelling his career transitions. It so happens he was right. Lougheed is widely regarded as a Canadian statesman, and McKenna has been dubbed the "Peter Lougheed of the East." At one point after McKenna left office, Julie suggested that he talk to Lougheed about his remarkable transition from public to private life.

Like McKenna, Lougheed experienced an unprecedented unbeaten run as premier and left while at the top of his game, of his own volition and with impeccable timing. Lougheed became an extremely active businessman, serving on a wide range of corporate boards. And he was pressured to seek the leadership of the Progressive Conservative Party of Canada during the lead-up to the convention at which Brian Mulroney defeated Joe Clark. Like McKenna, Lougheed decided he had had a good run in provincial politics and declined the opportunity. "I knew and understood the complexities of the federal scene," says Lougheed. "I was not afraid of the challenge, but you make your choices."

Newman says Lougheed still outclasses all or most of his contemporaries, with the possible exception of McKenna. Lougheed "is the standard against which other premiers, both in Alberta and around the country, are measured."

"It's their capacity to elevate the spirit," says Peterson of the two former premiers. He defies anyone to name a political figure who, more than a decade after leaving office, still has the following McKenna has across the country. "There's something Obama-esque about these guys. It's not just narrow provincialism. It's not just immediate self-interest. It's a willingness to take people beyond their own local concerns. I mean, Obama would say that it's about appealing to their better angels." Peterson says that life and politics represent a constant struggle between an individual's good and bad instincts. "Sometimes, your jealousy takes over, your greed, your avarice, your mean-spiritedness and then sometimes it's your generosity of spirit, your love, your capacity to include others and their general welfare." For Peterson, Lougheed and McKenna represent the latter.

Lougheed had left his role as premier by the time McKenna was elected in 1987, and most of Lougheed's political exposure to New Brunswick had been through first ministers' conferences and Richard Hatfield. His relationship with McKenna began when he phoned and wrote to congratulate McKenna on sweeping every one of the fifty-eight seats in the New Brunswick legislature, topping Lougheed's record of taking seventy-five of seventy-nine seats in the 1982 Alberta general election. "I wanted him to know that I was jokingly distressed," says Lougheed. From there, Lougheed began watching McKenna as he grew in stature as a politician and, eventually, as ambassador to the United States. He believes that on the national scene McKenna had a significant influence on the deliberations of his peers and that as premier he understood the role of the premier in federal-provincial relations. "He excelled at it."

Where McKenna and Lougheed may differ is in their approach to the ranks of business. Lougheed decided he had already run the biggest company in Alberta—its government—and therefore declined offers to lead various companies. He chose rather to accept directorships. "I learned that your background as premier gives you an overview of so many areas, and as a director you need to have a broad perspective." As premier, he feels, he was able to bring a broader perspective than some of his corporate peers—not a better perspective necessarily, but broader—whereas others would have specializations, such as finance or other technical areas. Lougheed says McKenna also brought this broader perspective to his own directorship roles.

McKenna feels flattered to be compared with Lougheed, whom he considers a friend and for whom he holds a great deal of respect. He felt that Lougheed's transition from public to private life was one of the best. "He was a national leader," says McKenna. "He did not allow his provincialism to overcome his respect for Canada and his love for Canada. He had national networks and a national leadership role and I thought that was very commendable. Not every Alberta leader has been successful in achieving that balance. And since that time he has conducted himself with a great deal of grace and honour."

In spite of his vaunted view of his colleague, McKenna didn't do a very good job of following Lougheed's advice to take his time in transitioning from politics to private life. Lougheed cautioned him not to jump at opportunities as they arose, which they inevitably would and did. McKenna's credibility and reputation, Lougheed warned, should not be frittered away by associating with the wrong people or corporations or causes. As it turned out, McKenna generally made good choices in his corporate and business pursuits—but he became involved with far too many of them.

Former prime minister Paul Martin also understands the stimulus of working in public life and the vacuum that can follow leaving politics. "There is almost nothing as exciting in life as public policy and certainly nothing as exciting as public policy when you're on the front lines," says Martin. "In [McKenna's] roles, he was on the front lines." Martin says that while the experience of being post-political might feel almost like flatlining, it would for most individuals feel like hyperactivity.

Frank and Julie McKenna agree that the "flatlining" analogy is a pretty accurate description of those eight years he spent in the bubble between premier and ambassador, even though he was actually doing anything but lying flat on his back. Instead, he was working feverishly, actively searching for meaning in his daily activities and encounters. At the heart of his search was his love for Canada.

SIX

My Canada I

*"...a race to the bottom and one that we could
never hope to win."*
FRANK McKENNA ON CANADA'S CHALLENGE
OF CONTINUING TO COMPETE GLOBALLY
ON A COMMODITY BASIS

PERHAPS AS A way to keep giving of himself and satisfy the call to public life, McKenna began speaking so often around the country that you'd have thought he was campaigning federally. One engagement in particular provided him with a prestigious public platform from which to speak about his vision for public policy in Canada. He was no longer premier and he was no longer a political player on the national scene, but his speech on "My Canada," the topic he'd chosen for the second annual Allan J. MacEachen Lecture at St. FX, allowed him to feel reconnected to the national political agenda. The lecture took place in November 1998, just a year after he'd left the premier's office.

Consider for a moment the full circle his association with the university had taken. His much-talked-about uncle Jack had made his mark there. McKenna was weaned at his grandmother's kitchen table with stories about Jack, and together they spent time poring through Jack's yearbooks. Frank attended the school and became a key member of its student body. When he returned to deliver that lecture, his political mentor and St. FX star alumnus Allan MacEachen sat absorbing his every word. "The qualities that I think are important in Mr. McKenna are his energy and his drive," says MacEachen today. "When he gave the MacEachen Lecture he bristled with energy and impact. He made a connection with the audience."

Even then, and as he would again eight years later, when he first declined the leadership, McKenna addressed some people's expectations about his further political ambitions. He knew that accepting the invitation to speak would inescapably lead to talking about the nation, the federal government and national politics. "Being a recently retired premier, I can tell you, puts one in an enormously delicate position. If one talks about the national government, the federal government, you are accused of having an ambition. I have none." Not a soul in the room could have believed him. It would take more than a decade for him to prove he was telling the truth, even if he wasn't certain of it himself at the time. But just because he wasn't running for office didn't mean he wasn't passionately overflowing with ideas and beliefs about his Canada. Nevertheless, he made it clear that he was delivering the MacEachen lecture as "citizen Frank," not as a former premier, not as a Liberal and not as a political aspirant.

He began by talking about Canada in sweeping and positive terms, praising the country's achievements and bragging about the place it has achieved in the world, including the United Nations' recognition of Canada as the best country in the world in which to live.

"On our worst day, we're still better than any other country in the world," he said.

Then the speech peered into the darker side of the nation's psyche, claiming that the achievements strangely "camouflage a lassitude, a weariness or a boredom with our continuing star status, a sense of listlessness." He said Canada suffered from "a sense of drift which, at the level of the media, is manifested in a palpable cynicism in the form of a deep sense of mistrust of institutions and leaders. At the citizen level, it assumes the nature of a national angst, almost a sense of foreboding that all is not completely well in the Garden of Eden. In many ways, as Canadians we are victims of our own success. We live in a country where it has been just too easy. We live in a country with an abundance of natural resources. It has been easy, almost too easy, to make a passable living from our seas teeming with fish, our millions of acres of arable land, our limitless forests. Ours is a history of prosperity and peace bordering on docility. Our patriotism is muted. Our country is taken for granted. We have no natural enemy, and without a natural enemy we have very little energy in our country to mobilize." Referring no doubt to the two world wars, he said that Canada has always been at its best when challenged by some type of enemy.

With the contents and the context still fresh in his mind eleven years later, McKenna says that his "My Canada" script is even more relevant today than it was then. Surveys and polls would clearly demonstrate late in the first decade of the new millennium that people had become more jaundiced about politics and politicians than at any other time in the past.

McKenna might have said at the outset of the lecture that he had no national ambitions, but the more he spoke, the less believable on that point he seemed. He began to focus on his desire to create a rallying cry for Canadians. "We need a cause so important that it will fixate the attention of all Canadians, make them feel good again and give them a sense of purpose. I believe that that national agenda, that national rallying cry of political will, must be the pursuit of knowledge."

He posed the knowledge challenge as a necessary response to irreversible and disruptive globalization of the world economy, a factor which is definitely more present and devastating today than it was even at the turn of the millennium. "It's like the Niagara River cascading over the Falls; it's a force too vast to be stopped. The globalization of trade is really the second phase of a trend that commenced over a decade ago [in the 1980s]. The first was even more profound: it was the globalization of information. It's the megaforce of information moving at warp speed that has so dramatically changed the world landscape." McKenna said that a knowledge impetus would give Canada a national resolve; it would be the rallying cry.

He talked about how, in the absence of a dramatic shift toward a knowledge strategy, Canada would be in "a race to the bottom," competing globally on a commodity basis, rather than employing a dynamic new strategy for a knowledge-rich and innovative society that could bring "additional values to our goods and services." He proclaimed that the richness of Canada's future knowledge base would be the principal ingredient for success. In an analogy to the growth and emergence of the great cities of the world—the New Yorks, the Londons and the Tokyos, which became great because of their strategic position within transportation networks of the ocean, rivers or railroads—he forecast that the great centres of growth in the world will be based around knowledge generated through universities, community colleges and research and development facilities. Rather than on the banks of rivers, the future could be built virtually—and virtually anywhere.

McKenna is both an idealist and a realist. When he became premier of New Brunswick, there was a stark obviousness to what needed to be done. The province was suffering from a permeating economic, social and emotional cancer. Its image as Canada's "Drive-Through Province" was terribly ironic for a place dubbed "The Picture Province" in tribute to its rivers, its Appalachian Mountains and the Bay of Fundy. Instead, an image prevailed of corduroy roads and the proverbial tarpaper shacks. New Brunswick almost needed chemotherapy to bring it around to the point of pride and prosperity. The citizenry understood the challenges because they were so visible.

Canada, in contrast, is not suffering from anything so grave. There is no pressing crisis compelling the nation to embark on its own rescue. Attaining a greater Canada based on a knowledge economy strategy does not make for a compelling campaign platform, given the normal stresses, strains and preoccupations in most people's daily lives. McKenna says that to campaign on such a notion would be "effectively fashioning a solution to a problem that people don't know exists." Even though he was and remains confident that the knowledge economy strategy is what Canada needs most to advance in the world, McKenna is acutely aware that it is a proposition that is essentially unsaleable to the average citizen.

With his "My Canada" lecture delivered, McKenna boarded a plane and returned to his increasingly frenetic legal and corporate life and the promise of more speeches to come. He was in no position to see his challenge through to fruition. He had become Joe Q. Public. He could only sit on the sidelines and watch alternative public policies unfold as Jean Chrétien ran the country, doing constant battle with separatists, trying to explain away the retention of the federal goods and services tax and fending off the leadership aspirations of Paul Martin.

SEVEN

The Eight-Year Bubble

"Any role for Frank that does not include
contributions to public policy and particularly
economic policy is a waste."
FORMER AIDE STEVEN MacKINNON ON
FRANK McKENNA'S ABSENCE FROM PUBLIC LIFE

ALTHOUGH McKENNA UNDOUBTEDLY benefitted both financially and in networking terms from his long record of corporate directorships over those eight years between his premiership and his ambassador-ship, he knows he paid a physical and to some degree emotional price. Financial rewards are greater in the private sector, says colleague and former U.S. ambassador to Canada Gordon Giffin, but the ability to influence public policy is its own reward. "We get paid more as an offsetting reward," he says of his private sector work, "but it's not enough to replace the satisfaction."

McKenna immersed himself in a wide range of commitments, leaving him both breathless and rudderless. He had a hard time saying no to anyone during the eight-year bubble. He was involved in about twenty separate board interests, a simply frenetic baptism into the corporate world, with interests ranging from Air Canada to General Motors Canada to United Parcel Service. (For a complete list of his corporate interests from 1998–2005, see the Appendix.)

He was half in Toronto, half in Cap Pelé, half at the McInnes Cooper law offices in Moncton and half in airports. That's two halves too many, and sometimes he wasn't sure what he was doing from one minute to the next. Where were the halves or the quarters or the eighths which, for example, could have allowed adequate time for family or his love of recreational exertion? This situation took a toll on McKenna for two reasons: he was physically weary because he was darting in so many directions, and he was frustrated emotionally because he held no platform or clear role by which he could realize his aspirations for Canada.

There were, however, some commitments that would pay long-term dividends. One of the most interesting and valuable was to the Carlyle Group Canadian Advisory Panel, under the direction of former Carlyle chairman (and later chairman emeritus) Frank Carlucci. The Carlyle Group marked a shift in McKenna's playing field, allowing him to be an advocate for his ongoing preoccupations with the state of the nation. The firm is a Washington-based global private equity investment interest with advisory panels in jurisdictions where it does business, including Canada, Hong Kong, Japan and Europe. The company today employs more than a thousand people, with committed funds approximating $90 billion and revenues over $100 billion.

Though now in his late seventies, Carlucci is still active and independent enough to spend time in his downtown Washington office each day. His office walls are a virtual rogue's gallery of Republican America, exemplifying his reach into the White House, where he served no fewer than three U.S. presidents, including Richard Nixon, Ronald Reagan and George H.W. Bush. For Nixon in the 1970s, Carlucci served as undersecretary of health, education and welfare, showing the ropes to protege and former Princeton roommate Donald Rumsfeld. For Reagan during the 1980s, he succeeded Caspar Weinberger as U.S. secretary of defence. Among other roles he played in Republican administrations, he was deputy director of the CIA under Stansfield Turner.

Carlucci met McKenna when "some of our people who were dealing with Canada came up with his name." Those "people" turn out to have included former Canadian ambassador to the U.S. Allan Gotlieb, who also spent time on the Carlyle panel. Carlucci took a liking to McKenna, and McKenna spent three or four years on the Canadian panel, even hosting the group at his seaside home in Cap Pelé.

McKenna's involvement with Carlucci and the Carlyle Group offered him access to an unprecedented network of some of the most powerful people in the U.S., including the first President Bush. For someone who was almost lost in a swirl of boardrooms, airplanes and conference podiums, this reconnection to such high-level political power brokers had to be thirst-quenching. Other boards were sprinkled with former politicians, but there was something particularly stimulating about hanging out with the Carlyle crowd.

Another satisfying thirst-quencher was McKenna's idea of using the relationships he had developed to try and bring Maritimers together, to put them into contact with interesting new personalities they might not otherwise ever become connected to. To that end, he created an annual summer networking event which to this day helps nourish his need for public life. It was inaugurated quite modestly at McKenna's beachside home in 2001, with Paul Martin as the keynote speaker.

Feeling good over the success of that first effort and stunned at the number of senior business leaders who didn't know one another within Atlantic Canada, McKenna decided to grow the event. The second one was held at Royal Oaks golf course near Moncton, and featured President George H.W. Bush. By 2003, interest in what McKenna was doing was booming, hence the decision to find a venue which could accommodate larger numbers of invitees and which could be used on a recurring basis. Former British prime minister John Major was the first celebrity speaker to appear at McKenna's choice of location, Fox Harb'r Resort near Tatamagouche, Nova Scotia. Continuing to this day, the makeup of McKenna's Fox Harb'r delegates varies from Maritime business leaders to premiers, federal ministers, academic leaders, private equity experts and star speakers, including Bill Clinton in both 2004 and 2006, former U.S. ambassador to Canada David Wilkins in 2005, hockey great Wayne Gretzky in 2007 and a split agenda with actor and senator Fred Thompson and former U.S. Democratic presidential contender and senator John Edwards in 2008. The 2009 event showcased former U.S. president George W. Bush.

Clinton "loved" McKenna's Fox Harb'r program, according to Maryscott "Scotty" Greenwood, executive director of the Canadian American Business Council, based in Washington. Greenwood is so vibrant and talkative that she could easily fill any vacant slot on the cast of ABC TV's *The View*. Because of her up attitude and the jobs she has held, she can get through on the phone to virtually anyone of influence within U.S. Democratic ranks, including the likes of U.S. secretary of state Hillary Clinton.

Greenwood remembers McKenna's style in running the Fox Harb'r event. With one hundred and fifty people assembled at fifteen tables packed tightly into the function room, McKenna preceded his introduction of Clinton by touring the room talking about a couple of individuals at every table. "It felt like he talked about everybody in the room," says Greenwood. "I mean, he talked about me. Like, I'm nobody, and he's like, 'Scotty Greenwood. You know, when Canada needs somebody to take on Lou Dobbs on CNN, she's our girl.' And he went through each person, doing a little tidbit completely off the top of his head, and obviously he'd been thinking about what it is he is going to say and how he is going to do this."

After McKenna finally introduced Clinton, the ex-president went on about the news from the previous winter that McKenna would not enter the fray to become prime minister. Greenwood recalls Clinton saying something to the effect of "Does anybody here actually believe him?"—to the delight of the audience.

In a larger sense, the satisfaction McKenna draws from this networking event speaks to a perspective he has developed for looking at life through a global lens. Somewhere between his Carlyle Group experience and the development of Fox Harb'r, his sense of world citizenry began to compete with his sense of Canadian citizenry— not that he would ever abandon the latter. "Part of it is to bring sunshine into our region," he says about Fox Harb'r. "I want people here to think bigger than their own parish, and that means understanding the way the big world works and why Pakistan's important and why what's going on in Afghanistan is important."

U.S. Ambassador David Wilkins received a McKenna popularity baptism by fire when he was invited to speak at Fox Harb'r in 2005. Having barely arrived in Ottawa, the new ambassador could readily discern how McKenna was seen by his peers. "It was obvious to me that that crowd had the greatest respect for Frank McKenna and that he was really revered." Wilkins says he knows why. There are those, he says, who have great people skills but aren't exceptionally smart or savvy; there are those who are exceptionally smart and savvy but don't necessarily have great people skills. McKenna, he believes, has both.

When it came to donating his time, McKenna was just as over-stretched as in his corporate and legal responsibilities, lending his name and time to a host of non-profit and public organizations ranging from the C.D. Howe Institute to the Capital Campaigns of the University of New Brunswick and the Université de Moncton. Even though he tried to be careful with the weight of these types of commitments, there are always instances when, in the words of David Peterson, you really feel compelled to say yes. "If the Cardinal asks you to run a dinner," says Peterson, speaking figuratively to underscore the obligatory nature of some requests, "it's something you're probably predisposed to do." Funnily, McKenna's extensive list of volunteer commitments includes the time he *was* actually asked to run the Cardinal's dinner in Toronto.

Prince Edward Island native Steve MacKinnon has known Frank McKenna ever since being plucked fresh out of the Université de Moncton by the newly minted premier in 1987 to be his executive assistant. After several years in the premier's office and a stint as executive director of the New Brunswick Liberal Party, MacKinnon has gone on to become the director of the Liberal Party of Canada. His latest political role has been as a key aide to federal Liberal leader Michael Ignatieff. "Any role for Frank that does not include contributions to public policy and particularly economic policy is a waste," he says. "The most invigorating half an hour you can spend is talking with Frank McKenna. He has a very active mind when it comes to public policy. He sees everything. He misses nothing."

MacKinnon is not alone in his perspective on McKenna's time in the eight-year bubble, nor in his nostalgia and his fervent wish that his former boss return to some high elected office. A lineup of people from Fredericton to Kingdom Come, or at least to Vancouver, feel the same way. And the closer you get to McKenna's former inner circle—the Steve MacKinnons, the Maurice Robichauds, the Francis McGuires, the Charles Harlings and the Nat Richards, to name just a few—the more intense the nostalgia was and is.

Unlike his loyalists, however, McKenna had managed to fend off the nostalgia for public life as he'd known it. One might have thought he'd completely kicked the habit after those eight years in the private sector. But, as with that one offer of a cigarette or that one little nip of vodka, it doesn't take much to unravel one's ability to fend off a serious addiction. In McKenna's case, being drawn back into public life took just a single telephone call.

III · Public Diplomacy

EIGHT

The Call

> "*Something was broken, so there was this*
> *feeling that we had to try to fix it.*"
> FRANK MCKENNA ON THE STATE OF
> CANADA-U.S. RELATIONS WHEN HE WAS
> OFFERED THE AMBASSADORSHIP

IN NOVEMBER 2004, John Webster, then an advisor to Prime Minister Paul Martin and today the president and CEO of the Maple Financial Group, called McKenna to ask if he would be interested in becoming Canada's ambassador to the U.S.

Martin's choice of McKenna, with his unique combination of political, business, networking and communication skills, was part of a larger strategy intended to set Canada-U.S. relations on a healthier and more productive path than had prevailed for years under Jean Chrétien. Martin and his team had formed a special unit in the PMO to oversee the relationship; they had set up a cabinet committee on Canada-U.S. relations, of which the new ambassador would be a member; they had agreed to the establishment of a new advocacy secretariat in the Canadian Embassy, and a process was in the works to significantly increase the number of consulates in U.S. cities. The plan had all the ingredients of an effective formula.

When Webster asked him if he would be interested in taking the post, McKenna's initial response was that he thought the position was the most important one the government had to offer, but that he wasn't sure if he would be interested in it. For one thing, he wanted more details. "I asked him if this meant that I was part of a list of potential names or if I was the only name," McKenna wrote in a lengthy set of notes during the winter of 2005 summarizing what had happened during the ambassadorial appointment process. He hadn't kept a diary since his days as premier, but the matter of becoming ambassador and the associated interaction with the PMO obviously made him think things were suddenly more worth keeping track of. Webster told him his was the only name under consideration. "I explained to him that I was very flattered to be asked, but thought that David Peterson would be a much better choice." Webster told him that Peterson was not the person being recommended for the job; only McKenna was. He requested that McKenna get back to him with some indication as to whether or not he was interested, in which case the prime minister would call him directly.

McKenna admits that the offer simply took his breath away. "Wow," he said to himself at the time. "I'd never in my life thought about doing this." But was he interested? Yes, indeed. "I realized that this was qualitatively different from all the other things I'd ever been offered. And when a prime minister asks you to do something, you take it seriously."

In fact, at the time, McKenna had little respect for ambassadors generally. On trade missions around the world in the role of New Brunswick's premier, embassy staff were known to corral him and his accompanying delegations into events where they felt boxed in by diplomats and foreign service people. "I didn't want to waste time with these guys," he says, explaining that he preferred to be out doing business with real clients. "I realize now I was wrong on that; [the foreign service] had a better opportunity to help organize the visit than we could on our own. And, used properly, these posts can be very powerful tools. So I never really took the time, I guess, to be as respectful as I should towards these people who do this work." McKenna says he understands now that, especially in a place as complex as Washington, it is essential to have the embassy corralling politicians and business people so they don't end up propagating a dozen or more versions of what Canada wants.

At the time he took Webster's call, McKenna was sitting on some eighteen boards, working at two law firms with any number of legal files in progress, and involved with numerous non-profit organizations, plus he was taking on consulting contracts and overseeing the family business, Glenwood Kitchen, which is based at home in New Brunswick. "I was making a lot of money, but was feeling increasingly as if I had very little time for myself. By dividing myself into so many different areas, it was impossible to spend much serious time on any particular issue." He had reached the stage where there were just too many balls in the air, with more balls tossed at him every week or two. He just couldn't find any real amount of meaning in his work.

"This sounds a little pretentious, but I'll give it to you straight," says McKenna. "I'd been asked to do a lot of things over those eight years. I'm asked all the time. It's fairly hard to flatter me." He had been asked to do everything from university presidencies to taking on a lofty executive role at a Canadian chartered bank. In addition to being less stimulated by the work than he had been in public life, McKenna was worried about lifestyle issues. Although to some extent he was exercising and watching his diet, there was no doubt he was not living healthily. Every board meeting he attended put before him unhealthy food choices, exacerbated by at least one commercial dining experience a day.

Over the next few days, he talked it over with Julie. "We discussed the possibility of starting fresh in Washington with a healthier lifestyle and taking advantage of the better weather," says McKenna. "This was a chance to just totally un-clutter my life, get rid of everything and start back with one singular focus." Most importantly, he felt it was an opportunity to serve his country at the very highest level.

Any hesitation McKenna did experience was tempered by Julie's positive view of the offer. "Well, I think you should think about this," she told him. "You get one call to do this. You know what, don't dismiss it. Let's think about this for a while." Julie knew that the ambassadorship would be a chance for her husband to recapture some of the excitement and sense of fulfillment he had enjoyed while premier of New Brunswick.

While the two thought about it, their three children, Toby in Calgary, Christine in Ottawa and James in Moncton, reportedly thought their parents would be crazy to step out of their flourishing business and social life in Toronto to gamble on a stint in the U.S. "But I'd always wanted to live someplace different," Julie says, meaning not just someplace else in Canada, but in another country. Besides, with their children all married with children and shaping their own lives, the McKennas clearly had to continue to shape their own. Several days later, McKenna called Webster to say that while he was still far from committed, he was prepared to discuss the matter with Prime Minister Martin.

When the prime minister called, they discussed a number of things, particularly the commitment formula that had been designed to right the Canada-U.S. relationship. Martin emphasized that by having a seat at the special cabinet committee mandated to work on the relationship, McKenna was to be more than just another ambassador; he would be, for all intents and purposes, a junior member of the federal cabinet who would spend much of his time scooting back and forth between Washington and Ottawa to play an important role in that committee's deliberations. As far as McKenna was concerned, that was vital. Being on the cabinet committee, close enough to the main cabinet where so many issues are deliberated and decided upon, would put him closer to genuine political action than he'd been in years. As well, although his primary role was to focus on the United States, in large measure he wanted to concentrate on the Canadian part of the Canada-U.S. relationship. "Because unless we could cool the rhetoric down in Canada or shape public opinion in Canada towards a solution on certain issues, we weren't going to be able to get the job done."

The Canada-U.S. relationship was as bad as it had been "for a long, long time" partly thanks to the inflammatory and frosty rhetoric that had formed primarily between Prime Minister Chrétien and the administration of President George W. Bush. Canadians knew it and Americans knew it. Things had gone particularly sour in the aftermath of Canada's perceived weak emotional response to 9/11 and Chrétien's refusal to send Canadian soldiers into the Iraq War. Canada was increasingly seen by many influential Americans as non-cooperative. "Something was broken, so there was this feeling that we had to try to fix it," says McKenna. The glory days of Canadian ambassador Ken Taylor's heroic aiding of six Americans during the 1980 Iran hostage crisis were ancient history. And there were many outstanding important economic issues gnawing away at the relationship, including mad cow disease, the Devils Lake environmental dispute and the never-ending softwood lumber negotiations.

McKenna felt instinctively that he could do a lot to improve the Canadian attitude toward the U.S. by travelling widely and frequently throughout Canada, speaking on the importance of the relationship. He'd been doing this for eight years without any vested authority, so he knew how to perform on the Canadian stage and how to handle the Canadian media. "There's no other ambassador posting in the world who would be coming back to home base as often as I would be and speaking or trying to influence public opinion." McKenna was and remains convinced that the more positive the attitude of Canadians—especially those influential Canadians involved in U.S. government and cross-border business affairs—toward their neighbours, the healthier the relationship and the easier his job in the long run.

"I find that the relationship is so poignant to Canadians," says McKenna. "I mean, they [Canadians] just live and breathe the U.S. relationship all the time and take offence very quickly and have a lot of needs." McKenna is talking especially about the overwhelming influences of American culture here, from television to film to books to the broader entertainment scene, which together tend to make Canadians think like—and at times subliminally become like— Americans. This does not happen in reverse, of course, because Americans have never really been absorbed in anything Canadian except for the odd breakthrough cultural export such as Lorne Greene, Anne Murray, Michael J. Fox or Dan Aykroyd, none of whom Americans would recognize as being Canadian anyway.

McKenna believes that although Canadians are vastly more preoccupied with Americans than vice versa, there is still something engrained in both populations as they continue to share the continent together. He thinks there exists a dormant nostalgia—whether due to shared experiences or family connections or intertwined popular culture—which can affect both Canadians and Americans when the right emotional triggers are pulled.

The Canadian business community was less nostalgic than hungry for somebody to help defrost the Canada-U.S. relationship. McKenna is aware that going into the appointment, he had a uniquely high level of national recognition and support within business circles—not only as a former entrepreneurial premier, but also now as one of their own kind. The time invested inside the eight-year bubble suddenly looked like it had all been worthwhile. "The business community seemed very, very ecstatic about the appointment because they wanted this thing fixed," he says.

What they wanted fixed included the lengthy list of unresolved economic development files, especially those which impacted U.S. border states where the level of economic interdependence is highest. "I think they were very supportive of the appointment."

The third audience to be addressed, the media, consisted of some who would be naturally supportive of efforts to fix the relationship and some who would be naturally critical and adversarial, depending upon how far to the right or left their leanings went.

McKenna believed then and continues to believe today that the unconventionality of his appointment—with his mixed background of law, politics and business—had the potential of taking Canada's target audiences in Washington by surprise and of drawing an unusual amount of attention to Martin's choice. "The traditional public service appointment, unless the characteristics of the appointee are particularly outstanding, really don't allow you to do the job that you have to do down there."

McKenna believes that a couple of former ambassadors, Derek Burney and Raymond Chrétien, came close to breaking through the stereotype of the traditional career appointees. Their respective qualifications came not only from prior foreign service but also from their connections in Ottawa: Burney was former chief of staff to Brian Mulroney, while Chrétien had the ear of his uncle Jean. People in Washington were made aware of these connections. The closer to the political heart of Canadian affairs the appointee comes, the better, McKenna says. "Because in actual fact, the United States is a totally different jurisdiction from any place in the world. Access to government is different." A communicator-cum-salesman, rather than a pure diplomat, is what McKenna believes applies best in the U.S.

Given that McKenna had set a unique standard in Canadian public life for strong communication and entrepreneurial skills, it appeared that Prime Minister Martin had made a brilliant choice.

NINE

Almost Ballistic

"I did not solicit this position and did not expect
to be offered it, and quite frankly am extraordinarily
surprised that I ever accepted it."
AMBASSADOR DESIGNATE FRANK McKENNA
BEFORE THE CANADIAN PARLIAMENTARY
STANDING COMMITTEE ON FOREIGN AFFAIRS
AND INTERNATIONAL TRADE

PRIME MINISTER MARTIN's choice for Canadian ambassador to the
U.S. may have been brilliant, but McKenna would be reminded very
quickly of an inescapable fact about politics, public life and indeed
business: it's not just what you do that makes the world turn; it's how
well you do it.

For McKenna, problems in execution began almost immediately
after he and Martin had come to terms about the posting. McKenna
had asked Martin that the announcement be held off for about a month,
giving him time to provide orderly notification to the corporations on

whose boards he sat, not to mention the principals of the two law firms where he served. Martin said that keeping something of that magnitude under wraps might be difficult—and his prediction turned out to be right. McKenna nevertheless left the conversation feeling that every effort would be made to avoid premature disclosure of the appointment.

Instead, the story broke while the McKennas were in San Diego on Christmas vacation, before he'd had time to manage the proper protocol of communications. Recalling that leak, McKenna pulls no punches: he feels the matter was intentionally mishandled by someone in the PMO.

"It is my feeling," he wrote in his notes at the time, "based on the evidence available, that it wasn't simply an accident that the story got out. The prime minister made it clear to me that the quicker he announced it the better, because he was getting a reputation for being indecisive. It is now clear to me that the PMO leaked the story to the press so that they could have the benefit of the story without the specificity of an announcement. It was all designed to try and deal with the Mr. Dithers label." Martin had been branded "Mr. Dithers" during his term as prime minister because of perceived or real inaction on a number of important files.

McKenna is certain the PMO leaked his appointment, but he is equally firm in his conviction that Martin supported him on many fronts, especially when it came to allowing him to manage his own media agenda in the U.S. A series of confusions as he warmed into the job prepared him for almost any predicament, but he says he had the unequivocal and unconditional support of the prime minister even though it was considered unorthodox for ambassadors to be as visible and vocal as he would become. He jokes that even when he pushed the agenda a bit too far or hard, Martin took on the attitude, "Yeah, look, this guy might be an asshole, but he's my asshole."

"He was totally supportive all the time," says McKenna. "He never sold me out on anything and there were times when I was pushing it." McKenna takes this stand to defend Martin specifically, in spite of the Martin administration's mishandling of matters surrounding the start of his ambassadorship. This is typical McKenna: he refrains from public criticism of anyone if it can at all be avoided, even when someone's mistakes or shortcomings are obvious. On the subject of how he really felt about the Martin team's handling of things, it's possible that McKenna would fail a fib detector test.

Next, McKenna appeared before the parliamentary Standing Committee on Foreign Affairs and International Trade, then under the chairmanship of Liberal MP for Pierrefonds, Bernard Patry. He was led to believe his appearance before the committee would be a run-of-the-mill drill on matters involving the U.S. and Canada, but the questions he faced went beyond run-of-the-mill.

On Tuesday, February 22, 2005, Ambassador-Designate McKenna made an opening statement and then took a string of questions from representatives of all sides of the House of Commons. In the heat of those moments, several questions levelled at him seemed far more invasive and challenging than those normally directed at ambassadorial appointees. In doing so, the MPs were testing his political acumen, but they seemed to be criticizing his appointment and almost questioning his motives in agreeing to become the new ambassador. He stood his ground and showed his mettle, however, reminding the media present that he was more than capable of adapting to public issues and situations as they would confront him in the hours, days, weeks and months to come.

In response to Bloc Québécois criticisms over his selection as ambassador, McKenna took the time and opportunity to explain how he came to be sitting before the committee. "I think only time will tell whether the prime minister has made a mistake or not. I can tell you this. I did not solicit this position and did not expect to be offered it, and quite frankly, am extraordinarily surprised that I ever accepted it, because I was very comfortable with the life that I had, the privacy of it and the challenge of it. But I thought this was a high calling, and I wanted to do it because my period of public service before was the most fulfilling period of my life and perhaps in some small way I wanted to regain some of that." His surprise and humility over the job had a tempering effect, effectively dousing any fires that might have erupted at the committee table had he not managed his demeanour and his answers so well.

The Honourable Denis Coderre asked McKenna how he intended to handle himself in Washington, whether he planned to "get involved in everything" and whether or not he thought that he had a privileged position to be effective for Canada, or that he might be just a mouthpiece for the Government of Canada. "In terms of personal style," McKenna responded, "I think leaders govern best who choose a small number of issues and concentrate on those. I don't fall into that category. I've never been able to restrict myself in that fashion and so I don't qualify as one of those great leaders." With those remarks, McKenna further reinforced his humility, sounding prescient of his explanation a year later, when he decided to not seek the federal Liberal leadership: "I love my country and would do anything for it, but I am not vain enough to believe that I alone can provide the leadership that our great country and party need at this time."

As to his own "style," McKenna went on to tell the committee: "I want to get things done very quickly and tend to want to become involved in a wide array of issues and try to bring closure to them as quickly as possible." He said he anticipated his style of working would prove difficult in the role of ambassador, an admission that must have left some committee members puzzled. "On the other hand," he added, "I have a political background and I'm hoping that will allow me to talk to like-minded people who are short on time and achieve a little bit quicker resolution to issues. That's what we're going to find out."

Parking his humility momentarily, McKenna explained to the committee why he thought his blend of professional backgrounds made him well-suited for the job. "I do know from having been a lawyer, politician and businessman that people talk differently. I talk differently when I'm talking to other lawyers. As a politician it's almost like members of all parties have certain understandings and certain ways of communicating. And I'm hoping that I'll be able to speak with other people, like-minded people, in a way in which I can communicate." Of course, his political background would prove more than just useful in the Washington scene; it would prove to be his calling card.

McKenna was successfully navigating his way through the hearing—until he answered a question about Canada's position on protecting the North American continent through military partnership with the United States. McKenna responded that the North American Aerospace Defense Command (NORAD) amendment had given the Americans much of what they wanted in terms of Canadian cooperation. Until that point, the government line had been that as a partner in NORAD, Canada was a de facto participant in the ballistic missile defence (BMD) shield, even though an explicit policy announcement about becoming more directly involved in BMD had not been made by the government. McKenna went out of his way to say that any final decisions concerning BMD had to come from Parliament after a thorough hearing process, but the media pounced all over it, forming a sizable scrum outside the hearing room. They treated McKenna's comments as a declaration that Canada was already part of a BMD agreement with the U.S.

When the story broke, PMO communications man Scott Reid asked McKenna to appear on CTV's political and public affairs program *Question Period* to set the record straight. "I flatly refused," wrote McKenna in his personal account of events. "I said this is my first day on the job and I'm not going to be taken out to the woodshed in front of a national audience on something that I do not think I made a mistake on." What further pissed McKenna off was that, in the same manner, his pre-committee briefing had failed to anticipate the hard line of questioning he ending up facing; there had been no warning of, nor preparation for, such a vigorous media scrum. He had been left standing on his own without bureaucratic or communications support to speak about the details of a job he had yet to start. Where were the Scott Reids when this stuff was hitting the fan? McKenna had begun to wonder then and there just what it was he was in for.

No sooner was McKenna out of the committee hearing than he was caught between a rock and hard place because of the shifting policy machinations of Prime Minister Paul Martin's government. Martin and others severely changed course on the direction of Canada's BMD policy, cutting a new and deep divide between the Government of Canada and the Bush administration. More than the other bungling associated with his appointment, it was this that would most negatively affect McKenna's start in Washington.

The government had gone ahead and informed the Americans, without informing McKenna, that Canada would not go along with their BMD propositions, bypassing a promised debate on the matter in the House of Commons and looking scattered and inept all at the same time. It was like a Keystone Cops serial episode set on Parliament Hill, featuring cameo appearances by Paul Martin and Foreign Affairs Minister Pierre Pettigrew. This abrupt and highly significant shift left McKenna upstream in the U.S. without a paddle.

The government's mistake was all the more grievous from McKenna's perspective because he had done his homework. "I specifically asked him [Martin] about the ballistic missile defence issue," McKenna wrote later, "knowing that was the major issue on the horizon between the two countries and that it would cause us significant damage if it did not go in a positive way. The prime minister said that issue wasn't all that hard to resolve. There would simply be an exchange of letters and Americans would be happy. I said, 'Prime Minister, don't screw me on a big issue like that or I'll start from a big hole.' The prime minister said, 'No problem, you won't have any difficulty with us on that.'"

MCKENNA CHRONICLED HIS discussions with several ministers in Ottawa over the weeks before his arrival in Washington. The ministers seemed very confused. He got the impression that his own minister, Pierre Pettigrew, was in favour of Canada's cooperation on BMD, but that later turned out not to be the case. When McKenna heard the news that Martin had spoken to President Bush and Secretary of State Condoleezza Rice about Canada's non-participation in BMD, he was furious. He told Pettigrew that he wished it conveyed to the prime minister just how disappointed he was that he had not been consulted on the matter and also that he had not been told in advance.

On a point of fairness, McKenna believes Pettigrew had tried to phone him as he entered the Parliamentary committee hearing room but that they were cut off due to poor cellphone transmission. "Presumably," wrote McKenna, "he was trying to provide me with a heads-up as quickly as it came to his attention. In fact, he said he was calling me as soon as he realized a decision had been made." But there was no subsequent action to get to the new ambassador on the issue until after it became a public airing of the government's laundry.

Martin's BMD decision marked the second time in two years that Canada had run headlong into one of President Bush's largest aspirations involving Canada, the first occasion being when Jean Chrétien refused to participate in the Iraq War. Even the *New York Times* picked up on the debacle, noting McKenna's obvious sense of embarrassment and the uproar that ensued after it became clear just how far out of step he was with the government he had just begun to represent.

The *Times* quoted then opposition leader Stephen Harper as saying, "How could this prime minister secretly make this decision, clearly breaking every commitment he's made to this House and to Canadians?" It might have been one of the only times McKenna would have agreed with the man to whom he would tender his resignation within a year.

At home in Canada, *Globe and Mail* columnist Don Martin called the affair "a three-day convergence of extreme political ineptitude by a prime minister who had decided to follow the polls and flip-flop." He referred to the situation as a result of "a year of indecision" influenced at least in part by Prime Minister Martin's predicament of trying to survive in a minority government. Don Martin wasn't just tracking the government's decision; he was also tracking McKenna's anger over being caught supporting a policy platform that had collapsed without warning. His sources described McKenna as being "seriously pissed." McKenna had been hung out to dry at the very time when his credibility would be his calling card in the one international capital which, perhaps more than any other, is highly discriminating—and tends not to forget.

Don Martin was not alone in his attack on the Martin government. In an op-ed for the *Montreal Gazette*, L. Ian MacDonald also went after the prime minister for leaving McKenna publicly in the lurch. "Frank McKenna needn't have bothered to show up for work as our ambassador in Washington," wrote MacDonald, "not after he said Canada was part of ballistic missile defence, only to have the prime minister announce two days later we aren't." The BMD story ran very hard for the ensuing twenty-four hours in media far beyond just the *Globe and Mail* and the *Montreal Gazette*. Every time McKenna heard a news clip or read another inch of copy covering the story, he had a "sinking stomach." The story pounded away at him and the government over the days that followed.

The next time McKenna saw Martin was at 24 Sussex Drive for U.S. Ambassador Paul Cellucci's going-away party. "Everybody at the dinner was aghast at the prime minister's decision," wrote McKenna later. "Jimmy Pattison ripped him on it, as did Frank Stronach. Nobody could understand the rationale. The prime minister joked several times during the night that Sheila had to be put between Paul Martin and me to keep us apart." When the evening began, Paul Cellucci, Paul Martin and McKenna spent some time in the foyer, discussing the mess that had ensued. "[*Globe and Mail* editor-in-chief] Ed Greenspon entered and took one look at us and said that he would love to be able to listen in on what we were saying. Before I left that evening, I told the prime minister that he and I had to have a chat to clear some things up. He said, 'Any time.'"

When the two finally met some weeks later to discuss what had happened, McKenna's impression was that Martin had not been in tune with his own cabinet's lack of clarity on BMD. In spite of the slamming he took in the media and the embarrassment it caused, McKenna was prepared to move on.

The new ambassador had imagined himself spending time in Washington proactively, delivering an old-fashioned stump-style sales pitch to the American media, to the U.S. government leadership, U.S. power brokers and the average American on the street: "'Look, in all this world of turmoil and insecurity, you've got a long-time, safe, secure friend and neighbour on your northern border. We've got your back covered.' You know," says McKenna, "I don't think anybody else can say that to America. So that's what I wanted to tell them: 'We've got your back.'"

But McKenna wasn't even off the plane in Washington when it became clear that no one had *his* back. "I guess when I went to Washington, I didn't know what I was getting into," says McKenna today, "but it became obvious to me very quickly that this was not going to be a normal posting and I wasn't going to be a normal ambassador and my relationship with the United States and Canada was not going to be normal."

McKenna's Canadian Embassy foreign service chief Claude Carrière, who later joined the Privy Council Office in Ottawa as foreign and defence policy advisor to Prime Minister Stephen Harper and to serve as deputy secretary to cabinet, was one of the bureaucrats who, while awaiting the arrival of their new ambassador, had to be rolling their eyes over the BMD mess. Carrière agrees with McKenna that there was significant confusion among the ministers involved, and in particular between Minister Pettigrew and Prime Minister Martin. "From our point of view it was sort of a negative," says Carrière, "because he [McKenna] had just arrived and he hadn't been told" about the government's decision. Carrière characterizes this as an extremely challenging period. "There was concern on the part of the U.S. administration at the way this was communicated and there was an attempt at the time to improve the relationship with the Martin government. This was the beginning of the non-improvement, if I can put it that way." It was all the worse, Carrière adds, because there were such high expectations with McKenna as the ambassadorial choice. As far as Carrière knows, a situation that ridiculous had never occurred before.

Former U.S. assistant secretary of state for western hemisphere affairs Roger Noriega, now the visiting fellow at the American Enterprise Institute for Public Policy Research and managing director of his own firm, Visión Américas, LLC, remembers thinking at the time that Martin had "changed calls" on McKenna, leaving the ambassador standing out in the cold and thinking, "Where'd everybody go? I thought I was supposed to be making things work here." Noriega is an avid Canada-watcher who was well aware of McKenna when he took the job in Washington. In fact, several people in Noriega's circle knew that McKenna had served as a Canadian premier, and in their eyes he was close to having the stature of a former U.S. state governor.

To Noriega, the BMD debacle was all the more unfortunate after Martin's effort to send someone of McKenna's stature to improve relations between Canada and the U.S. In a meeting with his boss, Secretary of State Condoleezza Rice, it was clear to Noriega that she was very upset with McKenna over the BMD mess. Noriega suggested that Rice raise the matter when McKenna presented his official credentials to President Bush, but she did not bother to hide the fact that she was prepared to penalize or embarrass the new Canadian ambassador. "Well he just earned himself having his credentials accepted by the deputy secretary of state," Noriega quotes her as saying, which was her way of sending the message that McKenna's stature in Washington was diminished before he'd even started the job. The deputy was Bob Zoellick, who later became head of the

World Bank and who was sitting right there when she made the remark. Zoellick looked up over his glasses and told Rice he couldn't do it because he was going to be out of town. That left the task to Nick Burns, who was undersecretary for political affairs, but who was not at the meeting to say whether or not he would be in town. "So then Nick can do it," she chirped. "This was one of the early times," says Noriega, "that I saw Rice kind of overreact and take things personally."

After the meeting with Rice, it became Noriega's "unappetizing responsibility" to introduce himself to McKenna over the phone and tell him that he was being shunted by the secretary of state in favour of a junior person, not exactly a great start for a ceremony that was intended to be the start of a key relationship. Noriega was told not to sugar-coat the explanation. He was under explicit instructions to explain the exact reasoning why. "You can't do something like that and then just pretend it's something else, and McKenna picked up on that right away. He was very nice about it," Noriega says. "That was the thing about the guy. He is a remarkably even-keeled, kind fellow."

From that point on, Noriega made a point of developing a strong relationship with McKenna. He later told him how unconscionable it had been for Rice to deal with McKenna the way she did at that time, expressing that he was just plain embarrassed over the whole thing.

As for McKenna's subsequent relationship with Rice, Noriega says that in spite of the way she treated him at first, Rice did not write McKenna off. He refers to the incident as "totally episodic. It was not something that she held a grudge about, as far as I could tell." He and Rice patched things up and developed a working relationship. There really wasn't much choice, as the two had so much common work to deal with that it behooved them to get along. "I worked at it," says McKenna. "I was the ambassador from Canada. She had to deal with me."

But Rice did not work at it to the same extent. McKenna said to her on one occasion that he found it difficult to get on the radar screen with the U.S. "You don't want to be on our radar screen," she told him. Given the chilliness he felt from her, McKenna got things done mostly by going around her and getting results from other quarters.

It's difficult to imagine that the BMD episode and the premature disclosure of McKenna's appointment did not have a serious impact on any ambitions he might have had for a future in federal politics. He was not oblivious, after all, to the goings-on in the national political theatre. He had had countless dealings with Ottawa when he was premier, including everything from negotiating transfer payments to attendance at first ministers' conferences. And there were the machinations involving the Meech Lake Accord. Why would he subject himself to the less palatable side of federal politics when he could function day-to-day in a relatively more collegial and loyal private sector environment?

In spite of the early speed bumps and the potential friction it could have caused between the two, Martin looks back with satisfaction over his choice of McKenna as ambassador. "On the one hand he is smart as hell and on the other hand very, very articulate—and that's what we need in Washington," says Martin. "We needed someone who could drive to the heart in Washington and deal with the administration, but under the American congressional system."

TEN

Getting to Know
the Neighbours

"We have to get it through the bureaucracy.
I hate that, when they can't get things accomplished."
PRESIDENT GEORGE W. BUSH TO FRANK McKENNA,
ON THE LONG-STANDING SOFTWOOD LUMBER DISPUTE
BETWEEN CANADA AND THE UNITED STATES

WITH THE TRANSITIONAL hiccups seemingly cured, it was time for
Frank and Julie McKenna to get on with settling into the Washington scene. Before he could begin his official work and enter the social
fray, protocol called upon McKenna to present his official credentials
to President George W. Bush. Ordinarily, of course, the ambassador's
counterpart, the secretary of state, would be a participant in the proceedings. As it turned out, Secretary of State Rice's huffing and puffing
over the BMD affair, together with her pronounced absence at the ceremony, had absolutely no negative impact on how it all went.

While the McKennas say they were not easily swayed by the celebrity, pomp and ceremony of Washington, the same cannot necessarily be said for their extended family members who were invited to attend. Things started off with a touch of awkwardness and humour. Little did McKenna know that because of his family's protocol-controlled trip to the White House that day, he would be in for a tongue-lashing from some folks back at home. Canadian television media had covered their departure for the ceremony, showing the new ambassador ushered by handlers into the embassy sedan while Julie was ushered around to the other side of the vehicle. That night at home McKenna received call after call from friends in New Brunswick wondering when he had stopped opening the car door for his wife.

The family members in attendance had been instructed that there was to be no videotaping the proceedings, no stopping to ogle on their way into the White House, no nothing. "Christ almighty," says McKenna. "You know, with my family, they're totally undisciplined. Jesus, we're driving up to the White House and I see a couple of my in-laws, the daughters-in-law, and they've got video recorders going and they're on the phone to back home saying, 'Mom, I'm right here at the door. I'm just getting in now. Can you see it?'

"And just as we get to the front steps of the White House, a Cheney motorcade goes by, you know with all the motorcycle riders and the whole thing. So we're stopped, waiting to get out. One of the motorcycles flips around, comes flying back and pulls up to my window." The cop said that he had seen the Canadian flag and wondered whether McKenna was the Canadian ambassador. "'Look,' he says, 'I'm trying to get into Canada. I want to go live in Canada. Can you help me out?' Turns out the cop was in love with a girl from Windsor, Ontario, and was having trouble getting through the immigration red tape to enter the country and be with her." McKenna actually did follow up on it for the cop, although he never learned how it resolved.

It was at the Oval Office credentials ceremony that McKenna had his first opportunity to meet and take the measure of President Bush, a man he characterizes as "a really good guy to be with"—jocular, friendly, plain-spoken and direct. For people like the McKennas, who believe that everyone puts their pants on one leg at a time, there was something about this president—who had retained his Texan groundedness in spite of everything he'd been subjected to as a member of a wealthy family, as the son of a previous president and as a former Texas governor—that really spoke to them. He joked, for example, with McKenna's eldest son Toby that he presumed as the eldest he was the smartest, which was the same as in his own family (referring to his father, the former president, who was an eldest son). "My daughter Christine interceded that she might not be the eldest," McKenna says, "but that she was the smartest in the family." "That's exactly what my sister says," joked the president, according to McKenna.

As they made small talk, President Bush made several references to the softwood lumber problem. It was obviously at the top of his mind at the time, so it's not like he was out of touch with what was topical in Canadian-U.S. affairs. He either had a good memory or had been well briefed. "We should be able to get that resolved somehow or other," McKenna recalls him saying. "We have to get it through the bureaucracy. I hate that, when they can't get things accomplished." Given the seemingly endless bureaucratic and partisan-driven gridlock in Washington, if Bush was that frustrated over the softwood lumber issue, then he must have lived in dread of his job during most of his time in office.

Aside from the mention of that one issue, McKenna felt he and his family were genuinely and warmly received by a president who felt the relationship between Canada and the U.S. was positive. McKenna recalls Bush saying that in spite of the perception of stresses and strains between the two countries, he liked Prime Minister Martin. McKenna believed him. "I know he's got to throw rocks now and then at me," he quotes Bush as saying, "but that's all right."

Paul Martin was scheduled to make an official visit to the Bush ranch in Crawford, Texas, shortly after the credentials ceremony. McKenna was also to attend. Bush remarked on how much easier it was to get business done in the surroundings of the ranch rather than the crush of Washington. In reference to the Washington press corps, Bush told McKenna, "All we have in Crawford are cows, and they don't talk back to you, at least since I stopped drinking." Their discussion involved mostly rambling small talk, but fascinating small talk nonetheless. The two men chatted about how tough the press could be both in Washington and in Canada. Bush wondered aloud why then president of Russia Vladimir Putin didn't seem to have the same kinds of problems with the media. "You seemed to have had a very productive visit with him last week," McKenna recalls saying. Bush's reply: "Sometimes things aren't as good as they seem to be or as bad as they seem to be. I'm not sure about him. My job is to smoke him out."

From Putin the small talk turned to neckties, with Bush saying how much he hated black-tie events such as that week's forthcoming White House ambassadorial reception. "In fact," said the president, "I hate wearing any ties at all." Also upcoming that Saturday night was the annual Gridiron Dinner, a black-tie-and-tails event hosted by the Gridiron Club, which comprises the elite Washington media and performs charitable work. The ultra-formal annual dinner always includes remarks by the sitting U.S. president. When McKenna mentioned that he and Julie would be attending the event, Bush showed just how much he disdained formality and some aspects of his obligations. He grimaced and said he absolutely hated attending the Gridiron Dinner. "A lot of people think they're funny," he told the ambassador, "but it's sheer pain for me. I have to speak at 11:30 and it's awful. I can guarantee you that my remarks will be very brief."

McKenna characterizes the Bush presidency as one of contradiction: between a president who, on a one-to-one basis, is "a really good guy to be with," and the dangerously destructive decision-makers with whom he surrounded himself. McKenna's harshest judgment of the Bush era is not of Bush himself, but of the "wrong influences" that Bush permitted to shape his outlook and his multitude of ill-fated choices. McKenna describes those less to be admired, including the likes of Dick Cheney, Donald Rumsfeld and others in the Bush administration, as the president's "dark forces," men who shaped much of Bush's negative international image. In particular, McKenna was not enamoured of Rumsfeld. "I think he's just a sour guy anyway. He's a dark person," says McKenna. It was clear from the start that Rumsfeld and those close to him were not happy with Canada on practically any front, especially Iraq and ballistic missile defence. "And he would often make snide comments to me," says McKenna— so from the get-go there was a strained relationship on that front.

However, McKenna did enjoy good relationships with two consecutive Joint Chiefs of Staff, generals Rick Myers and Peter Pace, and a few others inside the White House who stood out as good people, including Energy Secretary Samuel Bodman and former director of Homeland Security Frances Townsend, as well as White House officials James Connaughton, chairman of the White House Council on Environmental Quality, and Al Hubbard, former assistant to the president for economic policy and director of the National Economic Council.

McKenna believes Bush is smarter than most people give him credit for. Saying there are smarter people than himself who will psychoanalyze the former president over his performance in office, McKenna adds, "I think he is a good guy who has enjoyed a pretty carefree life. You know, he grew up having a very privileged life. And he was never really an operator, but he ended up winning in Texas and proved to be a pragmatic and good governor. And I think he felt like he could govern the United States of America without being intellectually curious. If he had a fault, I would say it would be that."

McKenna suspects Bush was not a good student of history, did not spend a lot of time trying to understand the complexities of issues around the world and was probably not much of a world traveller before his time as president. McKenna says that if you spend all your time inside the United States of America, you tend to become isolated from a lot of stimulation that exists globally, "and Americans, more than most people in the world, don't let that stimulation in. So, if you're a governor from Texas and you're [suddenly] in Washington, the Middle East looks like just a sandbox." Unarmed with knowledge of history, Bush was unaware of thousands of years of inter-tribal warfare in the Middle East; it was easy for him to believe that with a huge army he could crush the opposing forces and that everyone would be tickled with democracy and the U.S. could just leave. McKenna thinks being uncurious as a political leader is dangerous: leaders who lack intellectual curiosity suffer from a "constipation of inaction."

McKenna believes Bush's information vacuum was filled by the darker forces on his team. He recalls being in Israel following the U.S. invasion of Iraq and being told by political leaders Benjamin Netanyahu and Shimon Peres that they were fans of Bush and supported what was going on in Iraq. But when McKenna pressed them further on what they actually thought about U.S. actions (thereby exhibiting his own insatiable curiosity), they confided that the

Americans did not understand the complicated history of the Middle East and that they were carrying on a continuum of naïveté undertaken by successive U.S. administrations. What the Americans didn't get is that every square inch of thousands of square miles of Middle Eastern territories is riddled with the bones of combatants of tribal warfare. So long as the Americans were fighting Arabs, the Israelis were supportive, even though they knew that it was futile. In this vein, McKenna says, the Bush doctrine of never talking to your enemies— reiterated by defeated Republican candidate John McCain—was ill-fated. "You can't do that," McKenna says, echoing the emerging foreign affairs policy stance of current U.S. president Barack Obama.

Beyond Bush's lack of intellectual curiosity, McKenna believes, was also his continual demonstration of "dogmatic and dogged conviction that one is right against all the evidence," which McKenna regards as the result of a lack of self-confidence. "Really confident people are prepared to say, 'Hmmm, I think we've got to tweak this or move off this. I think we're wrong on this.' But the president, because I think he has a reputation for being a lightweight, I think he's fought against that by cloaking himself in this aura of dogmatic firmness." In plain terms, this is often referred to as "short-man syndrome," even though Bush is nearly six feet tall.

ELEVEN

No BS

*"We weren't trying to be socialites, we weren't trying
to be anything that we weren't, but we are just
two straight-talking, ordinary Canadians...they knew
when they were with us that it was no bullshit."*

FRANK MCKENNA ON HOW HE AND JULIE
APPROACHED THE WASHINGTON SOCIAL SCENE

FRANK AND JULIE MCKENNA were not a couple of hicks just up from "Upper Hooterville," as McKenna likes to put it, referring to the fictional hayseed town from the 1960s hit television sitcoms *Petticoat Junction* and *Green Acres*. For years they had been active in political and social circles that exposed them to all kinds of personalities and situations. Nevertheless, Washington is in a different league—it can challenge the unwary.

Comparing his wife to himself, McKenna says it is not Julie's inclination to pretend to be something she is not. "It's just not her style." Not easily impressed by titles or someone's station in life, Julie "likes who she likes. She flies with her flock, but she was also a premier's wife for ten years, so she knows the role that's expected. What she is, is a no-bullshit hostess who people really get to like." McKenna says that's pretty much the way it is for both of them. "We weren't trying to be socialites, we weren't trying to be anything that we weren't, but we are just two straight-talking, ordinary Canadians, who looked and felt like Americans, except that we had different views on things. I think people kind of liked it. They knew when they were with us that it was no bullshit. We weren't trying to blow smoke up their ass."

There was one aspect of being outside the familiar surroundings of Canada, however, that came as a bit of a pleasant surprise to Julie in particular. It was the sense of anonymity she felt in the U.S. capital. She found it fascinating to be in a community where they initially knew no one. "This means there are no preconceived ideas," she says. "There's nobody looking like, 'You should be doing this or wearing this,' or 'Why is she doing this?' or 'What's wrong with her?' or 'Isn't she great!'" Anyone watching from the sidelines might have thought the opposite, that the scrutiny of the Washington elite—those who were already connected and had their established circles—might be very daunting and judgmental, but Julie says it was not so.

She found the ability to walk into a room and know not a single soul to be a form of release. For newcomers, as opposed to members of the establishment, there is a greater sense of anonymity in big-city social circles, unless one goes looking for competition or tries to put on airs. In elite urban social circles like Washington's, it's possible to fly beneath the radar of urban gossip. In the Maritimes, where everybody knows everybody, being talked about by neighbours is almost unavoidable. Gossiping is considered a regular pastime.

If projecting a "no bullshit" style was important for the McKennas' forays into the social side of Washington, it was seen by McKenna as doubly important for the work he was hired to do. Roger Noriega says McKenna was a straight shooter in Washington. "I thought he was very serious and sincere and very candid—I think just a tad more candid than I might have been comfortable being." McKenna's candour was infectious—when he was in McKenna's presence, Noriega found himself talking with the same degree of directness. He says McKenna did not play the stereotypical diplomatic role of having his "game face on at all times," playing it like "My government is always doing the right things for the right reasons." "He was not the devious kind of personality that you see here a lot."

Noriega points out a section from author David McCullough's book *John Adams* to draw a comparison to McKenna's arrival in Washington. The passage concerns Adams's appointment as America's commissioner of France in 1777, an appointment which preceded his election as the second president of the United States. It is part of a letter from Adams's friend Benjamin Rush:

"I am aware that your abilities and firmness are much wanted at the Court of France and after all that has been said of the advantages of dressing, powdering and bowing well as necessary accomplishments for an ambassador, I maintained that your knowledge and integrity, with a common share of prudence, will outweigh them all . . . I am willing to risk the safety of country upon this single proposition; that you will effectively baffle and deceive them all by being perfectly honest."

Friends who knew McKenna best might well have given him the same advice when he was officially appointed Canadian ambassador. When you talk to people in Washington who encountered McKenna, they all agree that he took everyone off-guard by telling it exactly as it was. Carlyle Group chairman emeritus Frank Carlucci, for example, attended a welcoming reception for the new ambassador and recalls the atmosphere surrounding McKenna's arrival. "There was the feeling, which certainly I had and I suspect others had, that Canadians had sent us a real comer," says Carlucci, "somebody who had access and knew the world and could do something for U.S.-Canadian relations."

There are a surprising number of people playing key roles in Washington who share McKenna's freewheeling, no-BS style. "Scotty" Greenwood had first encountered him in New Brunswick just after he'd stepped down as premier in the fall of 1997. She felt that if anyone in public office acted like himself instead of putting on an act, it was McKenna.

Living in Ottawa and working as President Clinton's Chief of Staff to then U.S. ambassador to Canada Gordon Giffin, Greenwood had organized and led an inaugural tour of Canada to familiarize Giffin with the power players in each region of the country. The U.S. consul general for New Brunswick said if they were going to pay a visit, they had to see members of the prominent Irving and McCain families and Frank McKenna. Part of the story the delegation had heard about McKenna was that he'd left office after ten years, on cue, as promised. "I thought that was fascinating," she says, "because I hadn't met a politician who didn't stick around forever."

So after the requisite visits to the Irvings and the McCains and a few others of note, they visited McKenna at his McInnes Cooper law office in Moncton. "He was telling some story and he got up and acted it out, so he was jumping around his office, and I was like, 'Oh my God, this is the best thing,' because [normally] I couldn't get through the day it was so boring." Greenwood left with an impression that McKenna was a bundle of talent. In the years since she first met him, Greenwood has never reconciled for herself why on earth he left the premiership.

With the memory of that introduction to McKenna still fresh in Greenwood's mind, when she first heard of his appointment as ambassador, her spontaneous reaction was, "Va-voom!" Greenwood talks about the magnificence of the Canadian Embassy on Pennsylvania Avenue, architecturally impressive and strategically positioned along the presidential inaugural parade route, near the National Gallery, the Capitol, the White House and the National Mall. The embassy already stands out from the traditional ones on Embassy Row, fifteen to twenty minutes away by car, where the old Canadian Embassy used to be situated. "And then you have this enormous talent come in," says Greenwood, "that kind of breathes light into the place."

And right there in the ranks with McKenna was the team of individuals who Greenwood says were a refreshing departure from the Canadian career diplomatic community, guys like Minister of Advocacy Colin Robertson and public affairs man Bernie Etzinger. "So instead of having the traditional, 'We are the Department of Foreign Affairs and International Trade and this is how we handle diplomacy,' it was like, 'Okay, we're going to do politics the way you do politics in the States and we're going to represent Canada's interests.'" With McKenna willing to lead that charge and be the front man for the team, Greenwood explains, all of the pieces were in place for a fresh and dynamic era for Canada in Washington.

The fact that McKenna was a politician-ambassador meant that he was destined to be effective in the U.S. because his outlook would be understood by American politicians. The elected leadership there would be less preoccupied with whether McKenna was Conservative or Liberal than with the simple fact that he was a politician. This is partly owing to the fact that the practice of party discipline is not as rigid in the U.S. as it is in Canada. Sure, there are Republicans and there are Democrats, and people are known to be fiercely loyal to their party, but the American sense of individuality overrides this tendency. In order to do business, therefore, you have to influence each congressional and senatorial leader on the basis of the personal relationship you can create with each of them.

Whether he was tuning in to politicians or business leaders, McKenna uses one analogy to explain just how easily some of those relationships got locked into place. It has to do with common connections and backgrounds more than one's party DNA, and is especially felt among politicians. He calls it "the secret handshake." Within minutes of meeting, McKenna and people like him understand one another—it's like an offbeat form of love at first sight.

Nobody knows better how to deliver the "secret handshake" than three former U.S. ambassadors to Canada with whom McKenna formed close relationships. These men have strong views about McKenna's performance as Canadian ambassador and as an individual, and they believe he is as down-to-earth as they are. They are Jim Blanchard, David Wilkins and Gordon Giffin.

Grounded and friendly in McKenna's plain, "no bullshit" style, former U.S. ambassador and former Michigan governor Jim Blanchard took the trouble when our interview concluded to personally escort me to the street front of his well-appointed 8th Avenue Washington office building. He met McKenna in 1993 on a cross-Canada familiarization tour aboard a private VIA Rail car. Travelling with his wife and aides, Blanchard paid visits to mayors, Lieutenant-Governors, premiers and leaders of the official opposition.

"I had traced the Great Lakes shoreline by boat when I was governor," he says, "and I thought, 'I'm going to go to Canada and I need to see the whole thing before I get situated in Ottawa. I know that it's a confederation of regions and provinces, and so let's do the train.'" Blanchard is aware that only a smattering of Canadians have had the experience of travelling the breadth of their country by train. In that sense, he's more aware than most Canadians of what Canada looks and feels like on the ground. Since his time as ambassador, Blanchard keeps tuned in to Canada through his business dealings and personal relationships. "I talk to somebody from Canada almost every day. I'm up there a lot. I'll read the *Globe and Mail* and if I don't, my wife does."

When Blanchard's train arrived in Fredericton, he paid his respects to then premier McKenna. He felt a stronger connection with McKenna than with other premiers he'd met on the tour, even though he'd paid visits to such dynamic personalities as Alberta's Ralph Klein, B.C.'s Mike Harcourt, Ontario's Bob Rae, Quebec's Robert Bourassa, Saskatchewan's Roy Romanow and Manitoba's Gary Filmon. "They were all a talented group. I liked them all. But, you know, Frank was just a real fireplug. We hit it off immediately," he says, confirming McKenna's "secret handshake" theory.

Of course, they were of a similar political ilk, Blanchard describing himself as a moderate Democrat and McKenna as a moderate Liberal, but they shared something deeper than just their politics. "We just hit it off really well. Well, I think probably Frank hits it off with almost anybody really well." Blanchard was so taken with McKenna that he became a fan, following his premiership and energetic promotion of New Brunswick. Both Blanchard and McKenna worked hard to promote their jurisdictions, and both have a keen interest in national and international politics.

Blanchard always expected McKenna to enter federal politics, even though he was aware that premiers never become prime minister, while U.S. governors often segue to the presidency—four of the last six presidents were previously governors. Blanchard notes that if a guy like Obama had existed in the Canadian political system, he would have spent time as a backbencher in the House of Commons and would have had to await his turn to climb through his party hierarchy and perhaps eventually run for leader. "By that time he might be too old and not care. If you had our system, [Michael] Ignatieff would have gone in there and knocked down all the primaries in Canada to become the Liberal leader and then he might be the prime minister." But Canada is Canada, and its system is entirely different from the U.S. system.

Blanchard sees McKenna as the one premier who could have broken the trend. When he first heard about McKenna's appointment as ambassador, he was thrilled, believing full well that McKenna would energize the embassy and everyone he came into contact with in Washington. The fact that he was a politician did not hurt matters. The fact that he was only there a year certainly did.

Personalizing the relationship between the two nations and reinforcing the ways in which Canadians and Americans are not really much different, McKenna tells a story about another U.S. ambassador to Canada, David Wilkins, and how they discovered that they were going to be simpatico after Wilkins took his post in June 2005, about four months after McKenna's arrival in the U.S. capital.

Just after Wilkins had gone through a training and familiarization session at the outset of his appointment, which apparently the U.S. government provides for all of its ambassadors (McKenna's own training, of course, consisted of getting thrown in the deep end at the parliamentary Standing Committee on Foreign Affairs and International Trade, then side-swiped on the BMD issue on his first day in office), he paid McKenna a visit at the Canadian Embassy, providing the opportunity to shoot the breeze about their respective backgrounds and interests.

Wilkins asked McKenna how he would describe himself. "I guess I'm a northern liberal," McKenna responded, which prompted him to ask in return, "What about you?" "I'm a southern conservative,"

Wilkins said. "I guess that's what I am." McKenna asked Wilkins what he liked to do. Wilkins responded: "My idea of a good time is to sit on my verandah with a good cigar and a bottle of Moosehead beer." McKenna looked at Wilkins and responded wryly, "Then I think I'm a southern conservative too."

If not for the natural chemistry between the two men, the relationship could easily have gone south after an Empire Club speech McKenna delivered in Toronto in September 2005. He had been on a whirlwind speaking tour that week, which is what he had said he would do as ambassador to influence Canadian public opinion about the importance of the relationship with Americans.

McKenna took the Empire Club occasion to deliver some humorous anecdotes about diplomacy—including one gleaned from *Uncle John's Bathroom Reader* that got the audience laughing. Calling the *Reader* a "great bible of information for me," McKenna referenced a quote from iconic American humorist Will Rogers: "The art of diplomacy is saying, 'There, there, nice doggy,' until you can get your hand on a big rock." He then spoke about the U.S. Constitution as being a wonderful thing, expressing his understanding that it serves as a check-and-balance system on the exercise of power. "And I can tell you categorically that what has been institutionalized instead is total gridlock. The government of the United States is in large measure dysfunctional. The United States is a great country," he added. "That's a different issue. But in my humble view, it's a great country in spite of its government structure rather than because of it."

He went further, saying that the congressional community in Washington is like a bunch of freelancers going off in different directions. "It would be like having 535 Carolyn Parishes in one place," he said. (The unpredictable and uncontrollable Ontario Liberal MP Carolyn Parrish embarrassed the hell out of the federal Liberal party by slamming George W. Bush and the American people, and was eventually booted out of the Liberal caucus. "Damn Americans, I hate those bastards," became her most oft-quoted outburst.)

McKenna talked about the complexity of dealing with a legislative environment which in its 107th Congress introduced 9,000 pieces of legislation, 377 of which got passed. He said there was such a lack of structure that it made it difficult to develop a coherent policy and implement it. "One senator has seventy-five staff members working for him—*seventy-five*—just to navigate through the myriad of layers of government and try to figure out who's doing what." He said Washington has something on the order of 35,000 lobbyists and more lawyers per capita than any other place in the world. "That's why they say it's not safe to walk on the streets at night," he quipped.

Those were the verbal triggers which caused a strong enough media reaction that he ultimately felt compelled to apologize to Ambassador Wilkins.

THE U.S. SYSTEM of government was a theme he had commented on several times since being appointed ambassador, but never with Wilkins sitting right there in the audience, no doubt disbelieving what it was he was hearing from the lips of his Canadian colleague. Surrounded by media hungrily seeking a volatile reaction as the event wound up, Wilkins decided right there and then that he was not about to start a public feud with his friend. He didn't feel warm and fuzzy about the level to which McKenna had taken the discourse by using the word "dysfunctional," but he couldn't really disagree with his colleague's description of how the American system of government works, nor that sometimes it doesn't seem to work at all. He decided to take the stance that McKenna was entitled to his opinion.

When McKenna called him after the media blew the story up in Canada, Wilkins put McKenna at ease by saying he was okay with the outcome of events and that they should just move on.

McKenna was really using the at-home platform to tell Canadians they don't give themselves enough recognition for what they have and who they are—everything from their political system to their health care system to how the nation has historically been viewed as one of the greatest places in the world in which to live—and that if Canadians fail to appreciate what they have, they will never be as effective as the U.S. is in promoting itself (Americans, of course, being known as relentless self-promoters). McKenna was trying to condition the Canadian attitude to elevate itself. Looking back on his days as premier, this is exactly what he did with New Brunswickers; he crafted "no bullshit" messages for the electorate while at the same time finding ways to build up their spirits. Echoing his 1998 "My Canada" speech at St. FX, he was doing what he could as ambassador to encourage Canadians to yank themselves out of what he had called their "weariness or a boredom with our continuing star status, a sense of listlessness." He wanted to see Canadians save themselves from their sense of what he had referred to as "drift."

Former Canadian Embassy staffer and long-time McKenna political aide Nat Richard recalls that the Toronto speech was basically a case of McKenna "winging it" even though there was a prepared text at hand. Working without a prepared text always poses the threat of controversy, even for an experienced winger like McKenna. It's the kind of thing that gives even the most seasoned PR people heart attacks. Four months earlier, McKenna had jokingly revealed his strategy for diplomatic practice when he spoke to a luncheon gathering of the Canadian Association of New York in Manhattan. "I used to go off the cuff and say outrageous things," he had said, going off text again. "Now I'm a diplomat. So if I say anything outrageous, it's a mistake—I misread my notes."

There had already been a couple of instances since his appointment as ambassador when McKenna had "misread his notes," and there would be more to come during his short tenure. Former embassy press secretary Bernie Etzinger, who left that post in 2007 after a five-year stint to become director general of communications and information services for the Afghanistan Task Force back in Ottawa and whom Richard reported to in Washington, describes what it was like putting speeches together "with" rather than simply "for" McKenna. A first draft would be written and presented for his consideration. The public affairs team wouldn't recognize it by the time it came back. McKenna had the habit of spending a lot of time personally working and reworking the text with reams of handwritten notes. "He's a workhorse," says Etzinger.

Once the public affairs team and McKenna got to know one another, a pattern developed. "He essentially wanted the equivalent of a diplomatic stump speech; a mantra," explains Etzinger. "He would have a particular message that he always wanted to drive home—the energy message, or the border message." Etzinger knew that the speeches they would submit to him were predictable and dry. "What you got at the end of it was the McKenna-fication of the speech. And it worked well with his cadence and it worked well with his rhythm."

McKenna speeches, as Etzinger accurately describes, typically start out very slow and "then they just build and build to this kind of crescendo at the end that would take the message and elevate it to a level of passion. Etzinger says McKenna always finds a "rhetorical flourish" at the end which leaves the audience experiencing a buzz.

David Peterson loves the way McKenna addresses a room. "He would get all wound up and hooting and hollering and yelling and it was all very intransient. He was good." This could describe McKenna speaking anywhere, especially if the subject had to do with Canada. "He'd start yelling about Canada and you'd think he was going to blow the doors off the barn."

The Empire Club speech did not go unnoticed by David Jones, former political counsellor for the U.S. Embassy in Canada. In the October 17, 2005, edition of the *Hill Times*, Canada's politics and government weekly newspaper, he scolded McKenna for failing to understand the role of a diplomat. Acknowledging that McKenna had arrived in Washington with a reputation for speaking frankly, which he described as a "Canadian euphemism for throwing barnyard products at a banquet," Jones went on to say: "A diplomat informs one of his country's positions, seeks to clarify ambiguous points and suggests balanced solutions to problems." In this prescription, Jones makes diplomats sound like vanilla, preprogrammed robots. He accused McKenna of confusing frankness with insult. "It is increasingly tiresome," he wrote, "to encounter Canadians who believe that North America is a zero-sum continent; that any U.S. success diminishes the Canadian reality. They find it impossible to be proud of their country's accomplishments without denigrating ours." Ironically, McKenna was trying to focus Canadians on their accomplishments and encourage them to be better self-promoters, like the Americans.

Jones was insightful, though, in his look back at McKenna's own political history. He took the former premier to task for railing against all the frustrating checks and balances of the U.S. political system when McKenna's first electoral win as leader in New Brunswick wiped out all political checks and balances except the media—the

Liberals took all fifty-eight seats. "Now that's the way to govern," Jones wrote sarcastically. "Democracy (U.S. style) is so irritating." In fact, in spite of the glee they shared on election night in 1987, McKenna and his political colleagues went on to share concerns over their absolute legislative domination and the lack of a credible opposition.

Richard still thinks the reaction McKenna got for the speech was a bit unfair. He felt his boss was just trying to compare the U.S. system's lobbyists and complicated layers with Canada's relative simplicity. "There was nothing unusual or particularly original about what he said." Richard cites the book *The Broken Branch: How Congress Is Failing America and How to Get It Back on Track* by Thomas E. Mann and Norman J. Ornstein, which chronicles the malfunctioning state of the U.S. Congress and how it has grown worse over the past forty years.

The lack of collateral damage to the relationship between McKenna and Ambassador Wilkins was exemplified by the fact that they cooperated with several event organizers who sought to have them share the same podium to talk about Canada-U.S. affairs and the state of bilateral relations. Richard recalls one such event in St. John's, Newfoundland: the annual meeting of eastern Canadian premiers and New England governors, where he watched Wilkins and McKenna cement their bond. Hurricane Katrina hit while they were attending the meeting. As they all sat together in a hotel room, watching the disaster unfold on CNN, McKenna was already thinking about Canada's role in providing relief and assistance to the people of New Orleans, and about how to mobilize help. He was deeply moved by the turn of events there, reminding himself as well about the cultural and genealogical ties that exist between New Brunswick Acadians and Louisiana Cajuns. With Katrina as a very tangible, urgent and visible background to the dialogue, Richard says the two ambassadors seemed to be acknowledging that this was but one of many tough files ahead. "But it was obvious that these guys really got along and that there was a lot of respect there."

Former U.S. ambassador and Bill Clinton confidante Gordon Giffin, who had developed a relationship with McKenna just after his resignation as premier, stepped uninvited into the Empire Club speech aftermath to gently admonish his long-time friend by telephone. After meeting years earlier in Moncton, the two had served together on boards over the years, and had social contacts in common. Giffin decided that based on the nature of their relationship, he could freely give some advice to McKenna whenever it seemed appropriate.

"I think Frank more than many Canadian ambassadors intuitively understood about dealing with Congress," says Giffin, "which is a different animal than the Canadian federal government in that it is not a parliamentary democracy." But he thought McKenna went too far in describing those differences in the Empire Club speech. "I called him up and said, 'Frank, do not confuse dysfunction with democracy,'" then elaborated on why it's important for 435 elected members to each have true influence, versus the Canadian system, where MPs can languish in backbench obscurity for ages.

Giffin says McKenna was uncharacteristically "sheepish" during the call. "I sort of caught him." Giffin suggested that McKenna would never have shown up in Atlanta, for example, and delivered such a speech. McKenna acknowledged that Giffin had a point, and took the lesson in stride.

From that episode on, Giffin watched as McKenna worked Washington and travelled the U.S., giving speeches in places like St. Louis, Atlanta and Chicago. He says McKenna was making the most of it. "You can tell when someone's enjoying themselves. I was enjoying myself every day [as U.S. ambassador to Canada] and it made it easy to do the job." He says one of McKenna's most noteworthy skills as a leader is his ability to listen. "His tongue isn't always engaged. A lot of people in politics don't get an opportunity to listen much because they're too busy talking. And for a lot of people in public life, there is not much particularly distinguishing about them. Frank would be one who is in his own mould."

Although both Wilkins and Giffin had taken exception to what McKenna had said before the Empire Club, McKenna got a different reaction when he arrived back in the States. There, rather than hearing more chiding, he found that everyone back in the U.S. agreed with his portrayal of the American system of government. They tended to use the word "gridlock" rather than "dysfunctional," but that was just semantics. Either way, Americans pride themselves on the way the system works, saying that it has contributed greatly to the shaping of American culture and character as a people of resilience and independence rather than a people desiring big government to control their lives.

Further convincing him he wasn't so far off the mark, shortly after the speech McKenna had lunch with veteran syndicated newspaper columnist and former CNN public affairs commentator Robert Novak, who was effusive in his praise over McKenna's remarks and said that McKenna had gotten it right. The American system had been designed to be that way, Novak told McKenna.

Meanwhile, some back in Canada were also happy about McKenna's having been so honest and frank. "God bless him," says David Peterson. "It's a good way to get a little attention, right? But, you know, he's a great communicator. It's another one of his skills. So some people thought he went over the line. I thought, 'Good for you, Frank.'"

Weeks later, in an interview with the *Globe and Mail*, McKenna more or less admitted that he was wrong to have made the remarks, particularly because Wilkins had been seated in the audience. "Look,

I gave an off-the-cuff speech, which is more difficult to control, and as soon as I had used that word I regretted it and told Ambassador Wilkins so. I apologized to him personally. It was not my intention to go that far. But that's that."

It wouldn't be long before Prime Minister Martin would inadvertently step in to replace McKenna as the one angering the U.S. administration. The controversy erupted during the federal election campaign in December 2005, when Martin criticized the United States. Wilkins delivered a clear warning to the prime minister to stop. "I understand political expediency," he said in a speech to the Canadian Club at Ottawa's Château Laurier hotel, "but the last time I looked, the United States was not on the ballot for the January 23 election."

McKenna was originally to share the bill with Wilkins, but had to back out because of the election campaign, throughout which he lay low. It was just as well, given the brusqueness of Wilkins's speech. "It may be smart election-year politics to thump your chest and constantly criticize your friend and your number-one trading partner," said Wilkins, "but it is a slippery slope."

The New York Times reported that it was perhaps the strongest message delivered by the U.S. to Canada since the Cold War. Just before his departure as ambassador in December 2008, Wilkins would tell Sun Media writer Greg Weston why he stepped out of his characteristic disposition of southern charm to criticize Martin so heavily. "I did not intend to be condescending, not belligerent," Wilkins told Weston, "but I simply thought it was time to make a marker there."

The situations that disrupted McKenna's ambassadorial game plan are the type of time-wasting things that drive him crazy. Whereas he wants to hunker down and get the job done—whether as a premier, ambassador or businessman—unnecessary incidents like these aggravated and worried him. Right after the Wilkins admonition speech, Nat Richard spoke to McKenna, who was visiting his daughter Christine in Ottawa. McKenna was clearly worried about how Martin's anti-American election rhetoric and Wilkins's response might affect their relationship. But the two ambassadors had already secured their friendship, and the electioneering was not about to put it off track. Within a month, with the election lost, Martin was gone anyway, followed within a heartbeat by McKenna.

On one of the final days of his posting after the election of Barack Obama, Wilkins reflected in his Ottawa office on the value of closeness between the two nations, underscoring a shortcoming shared by both. "Canadians sometimes think they know everything about the United States, and they don't. And sometimes Americans think they know enough about Canada, and they don't. So we can both benefit from continuing dialogue and education."

McKenna, meanwhile, still sees the U.S. very much as he described it that day at the Empire Club. But in the same way that he believes Canadians can be rallied and changed, he believes that the election of Barack Obama as president is one of those things about the American people that was a surprise in contrast to their political quirks on so many other fronts. "You know, the country, at times it just drives you crazy with its disappointments and its short-sightedness and its dysfunctionality, and then at other times it just rises above all of that and you just see this magnificent face of America."

McKenna says that Obama is an extraordinary testament to the best things about America. "I think this is a superbly talented human being who has got a pragmatic and a tough side to him that doesn't show as much perhaps as the intellectual self. But he has got to have a veneer of hardness that allows him to get where he is. He's dogged, determined, ambitious, visionary, highly articulate, capable. He's got the one gift that we haven't seen since Clinton, and that is the ability to communicate large and lofty ideas." McKenna says that if Obama can get the policy and the substance right, that—combined with his oratorical and communication skills—should make him the right man for the times. McKenna believes Obama was able to reconcile black and white without ever having to show a side of himself that might have exhibited disenfranchisement or a sense of anger or pain for what happened with black America. "As a result, we have a stain of the Original Sin erased and a new frontier. Because this is like a Catholic being elected (as was the case with John F. Kennedy), this is a frontier we will never have to recross again." Embedded somewhere in McKenna's language and admiration for the rise of Obama is a hint that he still longs for the day when Canada too can experience a similar kind of rising up and renewal of the type he evoked whenever he spoke as ambassador—and as early as 1998 in his "My Canada" St. FX lecture.

TWELVE

Mr. Ambassador, You Don't Understand

*"The people at the embassy just started telling me
constantly, 'You don't understand. You're the man.
You're the guy that can get a meeting with anybody.'"*
FRANK McKENNA ON HIS INDOCTRINATION
INTO THE WASHINGTON DIPLOMATIC SCENE

WHEN McKENNA FIRST arrived at the embassy, staffers presented him with a comprehensive series of briefing books which were well beyond the standard fare he'd been used to from New Brunswick's government departments and corporations he had worked with as a board member. The depth and weight of the Washington stack was a whole different monster.

As he began reading the contents, it surprised him how much detail he really hadn't understood before arriving in Washington. "I thought that I knew public policy issues reasonably well from reading

Canada's national newspapers every day, as well as the *New York Times* and the *Economist*. I was impressed at the magnitude of the issues and the many nuances in the [Canada-U.S.] relationship."

The embassy briefing books were divided into ten sections: Congressional Affairs; Political; Environment; Immigration; Canadian Defence and Liaison Staff; Trade Policy; Trade Development; Public Works and Government Services Canada (the department which contracts and procures for all embassy-related needs in Washington); Public Relations; Contacts. The Congressional Affairs section gave what was subtitled "U.S. Political Snapshot," while the most intensive (and no doubt interesting) was the Political section, dealing with such matters as the controversial BMD, NORAD, arms control, the Middle East, Iraq, Iran, Afghanistan, North Korea and what's called Four Eyes Intelligence Sharing (among the four English-speaking allies Canada, Britain, Australia and the U.S.). Second in terms of sheer volume was the Trade Policy section, the subsets of which would occupy most of McKenna's energy, time and attention—they included the softwood lumber file, the Byrd Amendment, NAFTA, the border, economic security, mad cow disease, the Alaska Pipeline and more than a dozen other elements. Tucked into the Environment section was one challenge which occupied an extraordinary amount of McKenna's time and which would become a key proving ground for how he would function on the U.S. diplomatic-political landscape: the matter of the Devils Lake environmental dilemma, which involved primarily the State of North Dakota and the Province of Manitoba. The briefing books became an important reference point during a year in which McKenna would read and consume reams of information.

Claude Carrière had already been at his senior embassy post since 2004; before that he had served in Washington and done a stint in Geneva, Switzerland. It was his job to "make sure the trains run on

Then ambassador Frank McKenna and Canada's former minister for advocacy in the United States at the Canadian Embassy on Pennsylvania Avenue, with the U.S. Capitol Building in the background. *Source: Canadian Embassy, Washington*

Frank McKenna on stage with presidents George W. Bush and Bill Clinton at the Metro Toronto Convention Centre on May 29, 2009. *Source: TD Bank Financial Group*

Frank McKenna, fourth from left, wades through hurricane- and flood-ravaged Gonaïves, Haiti, on September 14, 2008. Escorted by UN peacekeepers and Haitian police, McKenna, actor Matt Damon (*second from left*) and Haitian recording artist Wyclef Jean (*third from left*) were involved in relief efforts under the auspices of Jean's Yéle Haiti humanitarian effort. *Source: Yéle Haiti: Ron Haviv*

McKenna holds a news conference at the Canadian Embassy in Washington on January 30, 2006, to announce his decision not to seek the leadership of the Liberal Party of Canada. *Source: The Canadian Press* (AP: *Evan Vucci*)

Canadian Foreign Affairs and International Trade Minister Pierre Pettigrew and McKenna meet in Washington with U.S. Secretary of State Condoleezza Rice, October 25, 2005. *Source: The Canadian Press (Tom Hanson)*

McKenna and U.S. Ambassador to Canada David Wilkins attending the annual meeting of Eastern Canadian premiers and New England governors on August 29, 2005. *Source: The Canadian Press (Paul Chiasson)*

A not-so-cheerful ambassador-designate Frank McKenna is surrounded by media following his appearance before the parliamentary Standing Committee on Foreign Affairs and International Trade, February 22, 2005. The hearing erupted in a controversy concerning Canada's position on ballistic missile defence cooperation with the United States. *Source: The Canadian Press (Tom Hanson)*

Then prime minister Paul Martin officially announces Frank McKenna's appointment as Canada's ambassador to the United States on January 14, 2005. *Source: The Canadian Press (Fred Chartrand)*

Then president George H.W. Bush and Frank McKenna at a meeting of the Canadian advisory panel to the private equity investment firm The Carlyle Group, Royal Oaks Golf Course, July 9, 2002. *Source: The Canadian Press (Daniel St. Louis)*

The late Quebec premier Robert Bourassa, Prime Minister Brian Mulroney and Premier Frank McKenna chat during the Francophone Summit in Dakar, Senegal, May 23, 1989. *Source: The Canadian Press (Fred Chartrand)*

Frank McKenna agrees to play the cowbell as former Arkansas governor, one-time Republication presidential contender and FOX News/ABC broadcaster Mike Hucka- bee plays the bass guitar, with Utah governor Jon Huntsman on keyboards, backing Canadian country music recording artist George Canyon at the Canadian Embassy in Washington, February 25, 2006. A group of U.S. state governors in town for a national conference descended upon the embassy to help mark McKenna's depar- ture as ambassador. *Source: The Canadian Press (AP: Kevin Wolf)*

Frank McKenna joins world number-one-ranked male golf icon Tiger Woods for a Tiger Woods Foundation–Golf Canada fundraising evening at Fox Harb'r Resort, Tatamagouche, Nova Scotia, June 2009. *Source: Nike Golf Canada/Chuck Kochman*

Frank McKenna gets hands-on at a TD Bank Financial Group Summer Reading Club event, part of the bank's ongoing commitment to more than 1,700 libraries and programs involving the Canadian Children's Book Centre. *Source: TD Bank Financial Group*

The McKenna family at their Friel's Beach home in Cap Pelé, N.B. *Left to right, back row:* son-in-law Mike Smith with his and Christine's daughter Savannah; son Toby and his wife, Michelle's, son Jay; Frank McKenna and his daughter Christine; Toby and Michelle with their son Noah. *Seated, left to right:* Julie McKenna holding Toby and Michelle's son Connor and Mike and Christine's daughter Ella; daughter-in-law Renee and son Jamie and their daughter, Audree. Absent is newborn Sophie. *Source: The McKenna family*

time," as he puts it—the kind of analogy McKenna would appreciate. Carrière's role was especially important because the new boss had not come from either foreign affairs or federal government circles. With the benefit and value of his lengthy and impressive foreign service record, Carrière was there, among other things, "to protect his back and to make sure he didn't do anything stupid." Finally, after his rough segue into the job, McKenna had someone to watch his back.

Ottawa needs a seasoned bureaucrat-cum-diplomat in Washington because its embassy there is large, with more than one hundred Canadian citizens working there, as well as a couple of hundred who are locally engaged, most of them U.S. citizens. Carrière thinks that at first McKenna might have underestimated the size of the machine and the breadth and complexity of it all. "I don't think anybody who is not in the business [of the foreign service] would appreciate that." Plus the embassy has ties to the consuls general across the U.S., which, although they technically report to Ottawa, have many links to Washington. Furthermore, the ambassador is a public figure who can help temper what Carrière calls "some of the natural competitive juices that flow" among foreign service offices in the states. He is alluding, of course, to turf.

Because McKenna was not familiar with the embassy machine and all of the consular dynamics at play, it was Carrière's responsibility to make him familiar. This also meant ensuring the new ambassador had the type of access to the prime minister that would build his credibility in Washington.

Carrière considers McKenna a unique ambassador. One of the things McKenna liked to do, and did well, was simply talk to people at the embassy. He wanted employees to know he was in charge of the embassy, and as such was looking out for their best interests. "There was an unquestionable difference in presence," says Carrière.

But, as has been seen before where McKenna has led, there was a need to have someone—and this was Carrière's job as well—to go behind him and "dampen the enthusiasm." In McKenna's New Brunswick days, he was known for casually intercepting and interacting with midlevel civil servants in the hallways of the Centennial Building, using such occasions to pose direct, specific questions and rally enthusiasm on projects or files without departmental directors or deputy ministers being the least bit aware of it. The longer he was in office, though, the more he managed to transform the public service—eventually, no one dared to take things down a notch in his wake. As well, and whether they knew it or not, many found it irresistible to jump on his bandwagon. Dampening people's enthusiasm didn't mean undermining McKenna, according to Carrière. It was more a case of "let's see how we can manage that."

McKenna and Carrière would discuss the manageability of ideas the new ambassador was pushing. Carrière jokes that if he presented a logical argument against something McKenna wanted to do, McKenna would be as apt as not to say, simply, "Let's do it anyway." He was, however, prepared to listen, according to Carrière, and would take into account the explanation of consequences. It was Carrière's job to balance this fine line between the status quo and the range of new initiatives that were manageable.

Apart from the issues detailed in his briefing books, McKenna was also completely unprepared for the degree to which a Canadian ambassador in the U.S. has elevated status compared with how a Canadian ambassador is perceived at home in Canada. "That's something that I had no appreciation of when I started," he says. "People at the embassy would keep telling me this and I couldn't understand it." He thought that if the ambassador wanted to gain access to a senator from some state to discuss an agricultural issue, he had to call

Canada's minister of agriculture. "You don't seem to understand, ambassador," he was told. "The minister of agriculture is not going to be able to get through to senator so-and-so. You can get through to senator so-and-so. You're the ambassador." "The people at the embassy just started telling me constantly, 'You don't understand. You're the man. You're the guy that can get a meeting with anybody.'" It turns out the bureaucracy, the career foreign service people working for McKenna, were absolutely right.

When he finally realized he had that degree of access and influence, McKenna began to figure out how to use it. "I had thought that I could leverage all of my relationships in Canada and to some extent tried to do that, but I started to realize that I had power myself [in the U.S.] and that I had to exploit it." Ultimately, McKenna's political background would prove to give him an edge.

Bernie Etzinger says he was given a new lease on life by McKenna's arrival in Washington. After the significant gains that had been made by former ambassador Allan Gotlieb in working the U.S. Congress, the free trade advances overseen by Ambassador Derek Burney, and border security and 9/11's consequences in the eras of ambassadors Raymond Chrétien and Michael Kergin, Etzinger felt Canada's ambassadorial effectiveness had simply gone flat and its methods had become outdated. Up until that point, it was not necessarily the ambassador's job to be in the public eye. But it was clearly McKenna's job to be in the public eye. Suddenly there was a sea change.

"This was a guy who could get it," no matter what the file was, says Etzinger. "He could get it quickly, would understand the heart of a problem, would begin to talk about an approach and would develop a trust around the table. You could see it forming. When I was at meetings we started to talk about softwood lumber a little differently. We started to talk about Devils Lake a little differently.

And we started to talk about BSE [Bovine Spongiform Encephalopathy, better known as mad cow disease] and border issues differently. All of a sudden, you know, you were with someone who understood the art of the possible and someone who could figure out what the end-game was going to be, what it needed to be or even if there *should* be an endgame."

Etzinger sees public servants and career diplomats as people who are usually adept at babysitting bilateral relationships—but creating those relationships requires wholly different mindsets and skill sets. Etzinger says he went from feeling like a spectator or a member of the audience to actually being an actor in the show. The change gave him a better sense that he as an individual could contribute something more tangible and gratifying. One of the interesting effects of McKenna's first slew of meetings was what happened in the mix between Canadian nationals, who knew McKenna as a household name, and the American and third-country nationals who had heard of him only because of the buzz surrounding his arrival. Everyone had the same reaction, sensing that "this was someone when he started speaking whose life had been about connecting with people, because that sense of connection was apparent."

But the excitement had a downside. Etzinger called it the "demand equation," the sense that his workload seemed to double with McKenna there. It's a polite way of saying that McKenna was a slave-driver. "And he didn't trust the supply equation," says Etzinger, at least until he had a chance to assess the talents of people on his team.

The enhanced workload included more travel. Etzinger was astonished to experience that travelling with McKenna was "an exercise in Canadian celebrity." He recalls walking in Vancouver on their way to an appointment and getting stopped in the street so often that it took them triple their allotted time to get there. One can envision

Etzinger, as the aide responsible for getting the ambassador to his destination, constantly looking at his watch on a busy Vancouver street corner. "Everyone was somehow connected to the Maritimes," he says, "which made me think that maybe Canada's thirty million people were all living in the Maritimes. Like no one came from anywhere else. People enjoyed meeting him."

"Working for Frank was great fun," says Colin Robertson, the embassy's former minister of advocacy. "Frank ran the embassy like he was running a political campaign." Whereas New York is all about money and Los Angeles is all about celebrity, Washington, Robertson says, is all about power. "Frank comes in, a former premier, which they immediately see as a former governor, but also somebody who is seen as a potential successor to Prime Minister Martin." According to Robertson, an aficionado of Canadian history, McKenna was the first politician appointed to represent Canada in the U.S. since Vincent Massey was appointed Canadian Envoy Extraordinary and Minister Plenipotentiary to the U.S. by Prime Minister Mackenzie King in 1927. Although McKenna was the first black-and-white political appointment since Massey, Robertson says there had evolved a transition from pure career diplomats through to Gotlieb (who was known to be close to Prime Minister Pierre Trudeau), Derek Burney (who was in the political sphere as chief of staff to Prime Minister Brian Mulroney) and Raymond Chrétien (who was a career diplomat but was the nephew of Prime Minister Jean Chrétien).

Robertson recalls that some senior officials at the embassy—traditional foreign affairs lifers—had McKenna pegged as someone with a very steep learning curve ahead of him, which is something McKenna himself readily admits. In spite of what McKenna had to learn about his role, Robertson points out the side of the new ambassador which the foreign service lifers hadn't necessarily taken into account. "Remember, when Frank first meets you, part of Frank's appeal is that kind of folksiness, the kind of small guy from the New Brunswick farm and the rest of it," making it seem as though he's just been out milking the cows instead of pressing the flesh with President George H.W. Bush or Bill Clinton or Benjamin Netanyahu or the Secretary-General of the United Nations. Robertson thinks some people underestimated him at first, looking at him and thinking he'd need a lot of care.

Occasionally, he would even add to that impression by the way he drew people closer to him. New Brunswick-born author David Adams Richards has written that McKenna is not unlike the *Death of a Salesman* character Willy Loman, "or more to the point, an old-time southern politician from the thirties, Huey Long, comes to mind. That is, if his naïveté is somehow at times forgivable and charming, you can bet he plays it that way. You can also bet it is also encased in a will of iron."

According to Robertson, "McKenna would say to embassy staff, 'Look, you've got to help me, I'm brand new at this. I don't know this stuff.'" There were those at the embassy who thought they were going to be able to control the situation and do whatever they liked. But eventually, any doubters would discover there was "steel there."

Robertson knew better because he'd talked to former McKenna aide Francis McGuire, who knew every single angle of his old boss. Plus, Robertson had taken the time to read the 2001 McKenna biography, *Frank*, giving him strategic intelligence over his peers.

While some among the embassy staff were taken in by his folksiness, the politicians in Washington tended to take a more accurate read on the new ambassador. According to Robertson, the American politicians would meet McKenna and pick up right away that he was the real deal. "As opposed to a diplomat who always tends to hover more at the edges, Frank is right there and he's telling stories with the best of them. That's not classic diplomacy, but it is exactly how Washington works." He jokes that it is hard for traditional diplomats to transition to McKenna's style because they're more used to operating on protocol and by doing what he acerbically calls "European minuets."

THIRTEEN

Drive-By Diplomacy

"Keep the car running."

FRANK McKENNA'S COMMENT TO EMBASSY
CHAUFFEUR GEORGE DAWKINS AS THEY ARRIVED
AT OBLIGATORY WASHINGTON FUNCTIONS

THERE ARE LONG-STANDING patterns and traditions governing how ambassadors and their spouses move about and function in Washington. One of the most obvious is the cocktail and reception circuit, an almost incestuous, never-ending string of events where ambassadors and their spouses continuously see the same old ambassadors and their spouses, as well as politicians and their spouses. It's an endless merry-go-round of glass-clinking and palm-pressing, the likes of which turned McKenna off from the very beginning. "I concluded immediately when I was there, 'Look, I've got no future in a foreign service. I'm not going to have any other post. I don't need to know one other ambassador in the entire world, so that stuff's all bullshit to me.'"

Rather, McKenna wanted to meet people who could do things that fit into his mandate; business people, senators, congressional people, cabinet ministers, decision-makers of all types. The other most noteworthy ambassadorial couple of the modern era, Allan Gotlieb and, especially, his wife Sondra, became famous for embracing the Washington social scene. By contrast, the McKennas did only what they had to do in order to connect with the social "system." There are some Washington functions that are completely obligatory, but McKenna worked hard to avoid the drawn-out protocol stuff.

"If I was invited to something Condoleezza Rice had, I would tell my driver to keep the car running. I'd go in, breeze through the same way I would a political event, and I'd be out the door in twenty minutes," says McKenna. He calls these "drive-bys."

It was drive-by diplomacy as McKenna would stop and chat: "'Secretary, how are you? Good to see you. Good to see you, Ambassador.' And I'm gone." For the wing-footed Canadian ambassador, the typical reception might be one of four stops on a given night. "From my political background, I know that the importance is in being seen. It's not in hanging around for four hours." In one sense, he was playing the diplomatic role expected of him, being seen where he had to be seen, but then whizzing off to socialize with political power brokers or business people whom he needed to see to get the job done. In other words, he wasn't just working a room all the time; rather, he was working all the time. In his own way, he was reinventing the role of Canadian ambassador.

McKenna says that because of the way the diplomatic system has evolved in the U.S. capital, the role of an ambassador's spouse there cannot be underplayed. In spite of the initial problems she'd witnessed her husband experience preceding and concurrent with their arrival in Washington, Julie looked for ways to make things work for the best. One of the reasons she liked the Washington gig was that for the first time in their experience as a couple, her place in things was clear. "That's the first time I had a really defined role. So that was really quite pleasant," she says.

The role of a spouse in a U.S. diplomatic posting is very structured. Spouses handle all of the social connections through their involvement in a series of international clubs, groups of individuals who are connected informally but are clustered depending on how their personalities mesh. In other cases, the clubs are formulated according to "position." In the end, however, it always comes down to personality in determining one's degree of involvement.

The "club" to which Julie belonged included Alma Powell, the wife of former secretary of state Colin Powell, and Lynne Pace, the wife of former chairman of the Joint Chiefs of Staff, General (now retired) Peter Pace, as well as all the wives of the Supreme Court justices. In the ambassadorial community, spouses arrange dinner parties or receptions. "That's how it works," she says. "You're like a sorority sister."

Because of this, she recalls, at the McKennas' first functions she might know a good handful of people while her husband knew no one. For once, Julie lent a networking hand to her husband.

Frank recalls sitting at the ambassador's residence one evening thinking out loud about needing to get in to see the chairman of the Joint Chiefs of Staff. Julie remarked, "Well, I'll call Lynne [Pace]." Both he and Julie know that this kind of networking is not well understood or appreciated outside diplomatic circles. "She played a very important role in the success we started to achieve in Washington," he says.

At times, because of the schedule he adopted, it seemed McKenna was living in airports, or at the Canadian Embassy on Pennsylvania Avenue. His actual home, the ambassador's official residence, was like a time-share—except that the McKennas' share of time there was severely abbreviated. Ambassadors and their spouses are more like house-sitters for the Government of Canada, and the short-term occupants tend to inject very little of themselves into the property. Given an ambassador's fleeting time in an official residence and the fact that they have little more than their apparel and a few personal items in their possession, there is no point in making much of a tangible or emotional investment in the residence. And what most Canadians would never guess is that ambassadors actually pay a specified, regular allowance for their meals and certain other expenses. In other words, ambassadorial residency is not quite the free ride it looks to be from the vantage point of Canadian soil.

Rather than reflecting the style and tastes of its short-term occupants, the ambassador's official residence on Rock Creek Drive Northwest has a history and personality all its own. The Georgian-style red brick house was designed by architect Nathan Wyeth, a man responsible for bridges, monuments and buildings in and around the Washington-Georgetown area. Situated five miles from the Canadian Embassy, the official residence is a technologically secure, three-storey property in a quiet upscale neighbourhood. From the street, the residence is unassuming, but inside it is deceptively spacious. It also boasts a sprawling backyard featuring a large patio, a pool house and a pool that the McKennas loved to take full advantage of—even if it was only a half-hearted, tiled facsimile of their eye-popping view over Friel's Beach back home in New Brunswick. According to residence manager and embassy chef Thomas Naylor, whenever possible the two could be found poolside, enjoying the sun. They were like the proverbial Canadians in Florida who shamelessly wear shorts and a T-shirt so long as the temperature is above freezing. The couple made the best use of the yard and pool during the rare times that they got a chance.

The backyard and pool became McKenna's favourite spot for religiously tackling his beloved crosswords. "I am an avid fan of the *New York Times* Sunday crossword puzzle," says McKenna. "There was a time, if I didn't have access to the *New York Times*, I used to get it from the "New Brunswick Reader" [a Saturday feature of the *Saint John Telegraph-Journal*], even calling them to have them send it to me. When I really want to challenge myself, I take on the Friday or Saturday puzzles, which are much more difficult. I am a persistent puzzler and even if it takes many hours or days, I'm not content until I have finished the Sunday puzzle. There are a number of us who you might call nerds who are similarly obsessed. [We] have a very genuine respect for one another." Former president Clinton is one of those. In fact, he and McKenna's shared obsession is at times competitive and at other times collaborative.

The "nerd" comment is one McKenna's wife Julie has used in reference to her husband while reflecting on his time as a student at St. FX. While others were out partying, he was busy studying, immersed in student affairs, playing bridge or tackling a crossword.

In the job since the day after 9/11, Naylor lives on the third floor of the residence, while the ambassador's bedroom, several private guest rooms and an office are situated on the second floor. The bedroom adjoining the ambassador's small office is where current ambassador Michael Wilson gets his heart rate up on a gym-quality rowing machine. Another of these bedrooms can serve as the prime minister's quarters if he or she is in town.

The main floor houses the official dining hall, with a British-made mahogany table that seats twenty-four; a formal living room; a drawing room showcasing an ebony Steinway grand piano; and a den/library newly filled to the rafters with Canadian-themed books. Together there's enough open space to host one hundred–plus people for a stand-up reception. Throughout the residence are examples of Canadian art by such notables as Christopher Pratt, Jean Paul Riopelle and David Milne. Located near the pool is a sculpture by Inuit artist Kaka entitled *Mother and Papoose*, which was featured at the Canadian pavilion for Expo 67.

Julie says that at first it was "really very uncomfortable" living in a house where servants were constantly present. "We arrived there and they started unpacking our suitcases." This was unexpected and unnerved Julie a bit, as it might most people other than royalty. But she and her husband grew to love the people working there, including a butler, the kitchen staff, a maid, a groundskeeper and the person McKenna had the most contact with, chauffeur George Dawkins, a tall, dignified Jamaican whose responsibilities were split between general embassy duties and the specific needs of the ambassador.

Utterly polished, discreet and polite, Dawkins has been working for the embassy for thirty-seven years and is regarded as the elder statesman among embassy personnel. He has seen and heard it all, having driven every ambassador and prime minister, as well as countless ministers and other officials who have visited the embassy since 1972. He speaks particularly of the first prime minister he drove, Pierre Trudeau, as a magically charismatic man whom he admired immensely. McKenna says the staff almost cry whenever they see him and Julie on a visit back to Washington. Some even wanted to leave to work for them upon their return to Canada.

Given McKenna's schedule, the staff heard more from Julie, with requests regarding dinners and functions and the simple types of meals she and Frank looked forward to whenever they managed to dine alone. They could have had anything they liked on any given night, but Frank wanted to watch what he was eating and made a point of avoiding certain foods. It wasn't like they were going to have foie gras and lobster all the time. Dinner was more likely to be a chicken breast with potatoes and vegetables; no sauces and nothing very elegant.

Naylor remembers fondly that the first day the McKennas arrived at the embassy for a welcome dinner with the Kergins, McKenna brought his departing hosts a pack of smoked salmon from Oven Head Salmon Smokers in Bethel, on the New Brunswick side of the Bay of Fundy. "It's the best smoked salmon I've ever tasted," says Naylor, explaining that he won't use anything else now. The loosely connected fraternity of embassy chefs all over Washington agrees, and now they all use the same product. Even after all these years, almost nothing gratifies McKenna more than being able to promote New Brunswick entrepreneurs and companies wherever he goes.

It's not like the McKennas didn't rustle up their own grub whenever they felt like it. On the morning that Canadian comedian Rick Mercer arrived to do a segment for CBC's *The Rick Mercer Report*, the segment was filmed over an early breakfast that McKenna prepared himself, still dressed in his sweats, well before the staff were even up and around. It was five in the morning and still dark outside. After the breakfast segment was taped, Mercer and crew joined McKenna for part of his traditional walk to the embassy.

As it was for former Liberal leadership candidate Bob Rae when he agreed to jump with Mercer buck-naked into an Ontario lake, it was a stellar media moment that played very well back in Canada. Although situations like this are always staged, the point is that McKenna chose to be seen by Mercer's Canadian audience wearing sweatpants and preparing eggs rather than just wearing his blue pin-stripe suit walking down Pennsylvania Avenue.

For the most part, the McKennas railed against the traditional mould of ambassadors hanging out with other ambassadors. Two exceptions were Colombian ambassador Luis Alberto Moreno, who went on to become president of the Inter-American Development Bank, and Hungarian ambassador András Simonyi. They were more of McKenna's ilk than other ambassadors in that they made it known they too put their pants on one leg at a time. Of course, there were requisite people McKenna had to spend time with because of the commonality of issues, such as the British and Mexican ambassadors, with whom he would share breakfast once a month or so but with whom he did not establish close relationships.

When it came time for the McKennas to play the host role at the official residence, they went to great pains to create invitation lists focusing on people who were of use to their Canadian mission, not just whoever was fashionable or formed the standard Washington A-list of invitees.

"We even started preparing a list at the embassy, which I'm sure had never been thought about before, of who are the future leaders of America," says McKenna. "Who are the governors that are likely to move up? Who are the senators or who are the people that are likely to move up?" The idea emerged in a discussion McKenna had with Minister of Advocacy Colin Robertson, "the most entrepreneurial civil servant I've ever seen," whom others in the foreign service saw as more of a loose cannon than an entrepreneurial whiz-bang.

This "future leaders of America" idea was partly an exercise in guesswork and crystal-ball gazing. But, once seized by the idea, McKenna wanted to know who the people were who fit this mould and then to find ways to persuade them to become closer to Canada even before they'd established upper-echelon status. It was a strategic exercise in future as much as current diplomacy, intended as an investment. McKenna is the first to admit that he doesn't come up with nearly all of the ideas that have moved along his agenda in his various careers—but once he hears one, he can be relentless in seeing it through.

FOURTEEN

The Business Scene

"We were not creatures of Foreign Affairs."
FORMER NEW YORK CONSUL GENERAL PAMELA WALLIN
ON HER AND MCKENNA'S APPOINTMENTS TO THE U.S.
DIPLOMATIC COMMUNITY

AMONG THE MORE meaningful places to which McKenna was zooming off after his obligatory diplomatic-circuit drive-bys were two organizations which he believes are critically important to the future of Canada: the U.S. Chamber of Commerce and the Canadian American Business Council. Twigging onto the keyword "business" as the lifeblood of both organizations, McKenna made himself known to both in very quick order.

U.S. Chamber of Commerce president and CEO Thomas (Tom) Donohue has the kind of savvy, polish and directness it takes to tackle major issues like American protectionism and to advocate for business on any number of fronts all at once, from taxation to changes in transportation legislation to removing international trade barriers.

With his perfectly coiffed white hair, crisp two-tone shirts and ability to talk, Donohue looks and sounds like a U.S. television news anchor. He has dealt with a string of Canadian ambassadors since arriving at the Chamber in 1997, including Raymond Chrétien, Michael Kergin, McKenna and Michael Wilson.

"So McKenna shows up," he says, "and there are two or three things different." First, he's an entrepreneur in his own right through his involvement with Glenwood Kitchen. Second, he's a partisan politician, but one who knows how to compartmentalize partisanship away from his role as ambassador. And, says Donohue, "he's a fun guy." He describes McKenna as being the exact reverse of his successor, Ambassador Wilson, who is a "real serious financial guy." More important than being fun, Donohue says, McKenna "got it real fast about the business community" south of the border. "He understood capital, understood markets." Donohue says McKenna was pleasingly refreshing because he wasn't starchy and uptight the way so many in Washington are. "A lot of people are very tense in this town." He clearly sees McKenna as the opposite of that stereotype.

Donohue thinks of McKenna as a Canadian "poster boy," reflecting his image of Canadians as industrious people whose lives expose them to the wilds yet who have high levels of sophistication. "I mean, here's a guy who would be equally comfortable out in the back parts of western Canada as he would be sitting here in Washington having lunch next door at the Hay-Adams [the prestigious Washington hotel where president-elect Barack Obama resided with his family awaiting his January 2009 inauguration]. He's a genuinely nice man, clearly competent. The other thing I would say about him, no one could ever say that this is a one-dimensional person. You want to talk about government, 'I've been there,'" he says, mouthing the words for McKenna. "You want to talk about business, 'I've been there'; you want to talk about politics,

'I've been there'; you want to talk about finance, 'I've been there'; you want to talk about family and all that, 'Well, I've been there.'"

In a sense, adds Donohue, it's harder being an ambassador to the U.S. for Canada than it is to actually run the country or a large corporation. "Think about it. What do ambassadors do? They take the cables in the mornings from all the upstarts that work with the prime minister and from the foreign office, and then they go around and do all this shit around here, and then they go back in the evenings and send the cables back. Now some guys, and Frank was one of them, had really good relationships in the senior levels of government."

Donohue says that McKenna also understood the linkages between Canada and the U.S. "I spent a long time with all these ambassadors talking about what happens between the United States and Canada, because we're family. More than any other nations, we're family, so therefore we treat each other like family. McKenna's a guy who you would want to be your friend if you were sick. You would want him to be your representative or your ally if you were in trouble, and you would want him to be your partner if you were going to lay some money on the table. And I guess a lot of people think they might like him to be their prime minister."

Donohue understands that McKenna had a role to play, which sometimes involved acting tough. "You know, he knew how to get mad. He knew how to get frosted up about something." Donohue suggests that such situations among seasoned professionals involve more role play than genuine acrimony. "He knew how to get stuff done. I always looked down there [to the Embassy] and I'd say, 'Here's a guy that can run a company or a country.'" Donohue says he was sorry to see McKenna leave Washington.

The other key organization McKenna focused on was the Canadian American Business Council, whose executive director, "Scotty"

Greenwood, talks about McKenna as Canada's "entrepreneurial ambassador." McKenna, she says, was of a mind to try things that hadn't been tried before, which is one of the classic characteristics of entrepreneurship. She says his attitude was, if you have a good idea, bring it. He was prepared to take the position that if an idea works, great; if it doesn't, well, nothing ventured, nothing gained. The reason McKenna's entrepreneurial attitude worked in his role as ambassador is extremely simple: Americans love entrepreneurs.

Greenwood says it's not just Americans who love those who think and act like entrepreneurs. So do taxi drivers in Vancouver. She described an encounter with a cabbie there who, after learning in casual conversation why she was in Canada and that she knew McKenna, asked outright if he was going to run federally. "They knew the entrepreneurial side of him. That was the side of him they liked. They liked the fact that he was going into Ontario and stealing jobs. They liked that." The entrepreneurial aspect of McKenna aids and abets his continuing role as an advisor to the council that Greenwood oversees. That's because it is customary for both the sitting and former U.S. and Canadian ambassadors to sit on the council in an advisory capacity.

When McKenna first appeared and spoke to the council in Washington, U.S. Ambassador David Wilkins was also in the audience. Greenwood thinks it's noteworthy that McKenna spent the majority of his time at the podium focused on Wilkins and on the importance and influence in Canada of Wilkins and his predecessors Jim Blanchard, Gordon Giffin and Paul Cellucci. He consciously chose to do this rather than concentrate on his own agenda at his inaugural interface with the council. Greenwood says everyone in the room recognized the significance of what he had done.

And he did it with a blend of fact and humour. "Some of you, those that are north of the border would know," said McKenna, "but those from the United States probably wouldn't know, there is huge difference between being the ambassador from Canada to the United States and the ambassador from the United States to Canada. Nobody in the United States knows—quite frankly, nobody cares—who the Canadian ambassador is. That's fact. But what's also fact is that the United States ambassador to Canada is very quickly one of the best-known people in the entire country. And we've been privileged in the past to have people like the ambassadors who are here today. They are just so warmly received everywhere that they go in Canada. Gordon and Jim, they're almost hero status. They're much more popular, I can tell you, than Canadian politicians in Canada, much more respected too, I dare say. And I'm one of those Canadian politicians in Canada, so I think I can say that."

On message in a more serious if not sentimental way, McKenna talked about how he saw the relationship between Canada and the U.S. unfolding as he took the reins as ambassador. "We do have occasional differences," he said. "Mercifully, they are quite few. But that shouldn't be something that would surprise us, when you consider we have a relationship that's characterized by two sovereign countries, both of which have different historical antecedents, both of which have developed, and both of which have different constitutions. So it shouldn't be surprising that we would have the odd areas of difference. But those areas of difference are extraordinarily few, when you compare them to the overarching areas where agreement has always been reached and where goodwill and cooperation has characterized the relationship. So, speaking for me as a Canadian and, I think, probably speaking for a lot of people in this room, I feel very, very fortunate and well blessed to live in one of the countries of two large, robust, mature democracies—living side by side with each other, and having been good neighbours now for some two hundred years, and, let's hope, some two hundred years into the future. So, let's continue to work for and bless this relationship of ours."

The speech was characteristic in two respects of how McKenna used his own brand of diplomacy to get the job done: in the time he gave to the business community versus concentrating too much on the traditional diplomatic channels, and in the content of his remarks. Whether in stump speeches in a variety of U.S. cities or at the Canadian American Business Council, he was intent upon making his audience the focus of his attention rather than the other way around. It was a sleight of hand that made each audience member focus on everything he had to say—because their name could come up at any time. And everyone likes to hear their name, no matter how small or huge the personality. The point, of course, was to lure them into listening and learning about Canada.

Springboarding from elected officials to business leaders is effortless for McKenna. The U.S. Chamber of Commerce and the Canadian American Business Council provided countless opportunities for him to meet and hit it off with a long list of well-connected business people. One of them was Ron Covais, regional president for the Americas for Lockheed Martin Corporation, responsible for the company's western hemisphere (minus the U.S.) business development activity and international partnerships.

Lockheed Martin's business is aerospace and defence, and Covais's department focuses specifically on aerospace and defence as it relates to the U.S. and Canada. He also acts as corporate vice president for international business activity and government relations in Washington, and he orchestrates political activity with the U.S. government and international representation in the capital, which is how he first encountered McKenna. It's critical for Lockheed Martin to be highly active in government circles because its very business is governed by public policy. Almost nothing happens in the aerospace and defence trade that isn't subject to a wide range of government rules and regulations from both the U.S. and Canada. Covais says his company is always at the nexus of government policy and technology when selling products to modernize military forces, whether it involves the acquisition of a new C130 or the modernization of the Halifax-based frigate fleet.

Covais chairs the U.S. Chamber of Commerce Western Hemisphere Group for executive director and CEO Tom Donohue, and he sits on the board of directors for the chamber's international policy committee and is a board member for the Canadian American Business Council. With him as an example, it becomes easy to see how the inner circle in Washington tightens: the links from Donohue to "Scotty" Greenwood to Covais illustrate how the paths of the capital's power brokers intertwine.

WITH ABOUT FIVE hundred employees spread across operations in Winnipeg, Ottawa, Montreal, Esquimalt and Halifax, Covais's primary front is Canada; hence the link he enjoyed to McKenna and his predecessors Raymond Chrétien and Michael Kergin and current ambassador Michael Wilson. The company has been involved in Canadian defence matters for so long, primarily with the navy and air forces, that Covais coins it "a hundred-year relationship." The U.S. has more bilateral defence agreements with Canada than with any other country in the world, and it has pretty much been that way since World War II. Since 9/11 and the heightening of homeland security measures, Lockheed Martin's relationship has been expanded to help equip police forces, including the RCMP. But Covais says his job—and the relationship with Canada—is about more than manufacturing and selling aerospace, defence and policing apparatus. He says it is also about energy issues, environmental issues and social values.

Hard leftists would choke over such comments, branding them as propaganda, but Covais is trained to communicate as though he were selling sports cars instead of fighter jets and high-tech defence systems. His broader corporate responsibility calls for him to interact on any number of fronts if the need or opportunity arises. One example is Covais's involvement on the board of the Fulbright Program, the State department initiative which is active in 155 countries, including Canada, providing thousands of grants and scholarships annually to develop leadership through learning and international cooperation. McKenna, in his role as ambassador, headed the Canadian team involved in the program.

To describe McKenna's arrival in Washington, Covais uses the navy term "fleet up." He says McKenna "hit the deck running, running hard, taking and capturing the hearts and minds of a lot of people here in town very, very quickly. I think he did a really good job in the very short period of time because he understood business, he's a good politician and he clearly has all the character of a good statesman as well."

Covais makes a very interesting comparison between McKenna and former U.S. vice president Dick Cheney. Covais was Cheney's military assistant when Cheney was secretary of defence under President George H.W. Bush. Covais recalls that, for the longest time, Cheney wore cowboy boots, befitting his background as a Wyoming boy, until the time came he decided he'd better start wearing "the cordovans," the fine leather shoes. "I think Frank's nature, being from where he's from, is to be less formal," says Covais. But when it was time to put the pinstripe suit on, he adjusted to his environment.

McKenna, of course, was more than used to pinstripe suits long before he arrived in Washington, but there was a time in his early political days when he too needed grooming. Liberal political adviser John Bryden exemplified this once by recalling the moment at which he had to tell McKenna to start wearing interview-length socks so that his legs would not show below the hem of his pants in meetings or during full-body-shot television interviews. Francis McGuire loves to tell the story of getting McKenna's hairstyle changed to better suit what McGuire called his "block-shaped head."

Covais says McKenna was a straight shooter in an arena where not everybody is. "He said what he meant and he meant what he said, and you understood what he meant. He was a really straightforward guy, calling a spade a bloody shovel. And Canada stood tall under his watch."

This is how Paul Martin envisioned McKenna working when he first contemplated appointing him ambassador. "His straightfor-wardness made him a success," says Martin. "He would call me on issues and say, 'This is what you're going to get.'" Sometimes Martin would say "Go," and sometimes McKenna might be required to fur-ther persuade the prime minister, but it was a mutual back-and-forth, a mutual give-and-take. "My respect for Frank is based on us being equals."

McKenna explains his own perspective on how he approached doing business in the States: "You're going in and you're just having this straightforward conversation and you might say, 'Look, I know you've got to get elected and I know this is a bad issue for you,' and he'd say, 'Well, yeah, I know your background too. I know you under-stand what I'm going through here.'" So McKenna says he always played it straight. "And they knew that I knew where they were com-ing from." In this case, he's talking about dealing with a politician, but the model works in business as well, by understanding the constraints and possibilities facing the business person at hand—by *being* them.

It's been said that New York City is all about business and money, a premise that was well understood by Pamela Wallin when she served as Canada's consul general there (she remains in New York today as the senior advisor on Canadian affairs for the Americas Society). As a veteran Canadian celebrity journalist and television host, she interviewed McKenna while he was premier, and still recalls some of what she called "the breakthroughs" he made for New Brunswick.

Wallin recalls, for example, that he "skipped a twenty-five-year chunk of time" by overseeing the advance of broadband infrastructure and other forms of technology, a move which paved the way for his overtures to central Canada's CEOs to move their businesses east. "That was brilliant and smart. He knew he had to do something. He just got it. He raised the ire of some other premiers," she adds, "but he understood what he had to do for the future of his province." As consul general, she watched with keen curiosity as he landed in Washington in 2005 to begin his work as the gatekeeper for what she calls "the most important relationship in the world."

Wallin described him as "the Energizer Bunny" when he arrived in Washington and worked faster than any of his predecessors to leave his footprint on the city. She says it's unique that the Canadian diplomatic efforts between the consular offices in New York and the embassy offices in Washington meshed as well as they did. The two, she adds, haven't always clicked. Wallin thinks one reason is that neither she nor McKenna came from the traditional foreign service background, so they had no natural competitiveness or one-upmanship to preoccupy them. "We were not creatures of Foreign Affairs." It was a very important time for Canada-U.S. relations, as there was so much work to be done on some heady issues, especially the lingering aftertaste of 9/11 and related challenges such as border security.

Every business decision in the U.S. of any significance goes through the New York funnel, says Wallin, while political decisions go through multiple funnels—including Washington of course, but also including state governors. She believes that by spending time in New York as well as Washington (during his year as ambassador he visited New York about a dozen times), and by recognizing the importance of governors, McKenna was on the right path.

"Frank is somebody you can speak shorthand with," says Wallin. McKenna's was a useful style in New York, especially on Wall Street, where Wallin says people were engaged by his businesslike, non-partisan presence. He did not function as a Liberal, but rather as Canada's representative, realizing that in one way or another, whether it's the energy sector or manufacturing, nearly all Canadian businesses of any importance are linked to U.S. interests. He understood and acted out what Wallin says former Chrétien cabinet minister John Manley had earlier put into words: that Canada needs to grow up and be a contender in what is a very complicated world out there.

For his part, McKenna enjoyed working with Wallin and found her to be the most useful and effective of the Canadian consuls general in the U.S. during his time there. They both understood where their turf boundaries were and they both allowed space for each other's strong personalities to play themselves out. "We got along famously," he says. "We were both battling Ottawa on a lot of issues, so we were simpatico in that respect and we worked together." But the typical consul general, he says, "would normally have a resentful relationship with Washington."

Outside the direct Washington and New York spheres of influence, McKenna is said to have worked the other side of the political "street" too. "He knew and understood the most important thing" about the significance of governors, according to Wallin: "He had that north/south experience. He understood the basic premise that governors are important and that trade links north-south are important. And he understood how Washington operates." She thought it was important for Canada to have someone with McKenna's style in Washington, adding that his short time there and his choice not to run for the federal Liberal leadership were both losses for Canada. She understood these decisions, though: "Sometimes you have to go earn a paycheque"—which is, after all, what being in business is all about.

FIFTEEN

The Impossible Deal

"He and I were both frustrated we weren't able to close the deal."

U.S. TRADE AMBASSADOR SUSAN SCHWAB
ON FRANK MCKENNA AND THE CANADA-U.S.
SOFTWOOD LUMBER AGREEMENT

ONE OF THE high-visibility files McKenna dealt with in Washington was the pursuit of a lasting softwood lumber agreement between the U.S. and Canada. In April 2005, just weeks after his appointment, he stood before the Council of Forest Industries Convention in Prince George, B.C., where he pledged that softwood lumber was his number-one priority as ambassador. He prefaced his remarks by underscoring that the file was a political minefield because of the ongoing bilateral relations, because of an impending provincial election in British Columbia and because of the threat of a federal election in Canada. He would therefore, he said, not get immersed in discussing with the conference the fine details of the negotiations that were under way. "So, as Henry VIII said to each of his wives," McKenna quipped, "I won't be keeping you very long."

But in fact he did keep them long enough to deliver a noteworthy speech which reinforced Canada's rights in the dispute. He outlined ways to sell the importance of trade between the two nations—not just to the politicians in Washington, but also to the industry interest groups within the U.S. Here he had begun the trend of comparing the Canadian and U.S. political systems, which he would do frequently over the coming months, referring to the U.S. system as being more chaotic than Canada's.

A few months after McKenna spoke to the B.C. forest industries delegates, he went before the annual awards gathering of the Woodrow Wilson International Center for Scholars. There he talked about the general health of the Canada-U.S. trade relationship. Central to his speech was the matter of what was known as the Byrd Amendment. The amendment was just another chapter in an incredibly lengthy dispute that had gone on for more than two centuries, beginning in 1789 when Massachusetts timber merchants persuaded a relatively new U.S. government to place a 5 per cent tariff on imports of New Brunswick timber. Since that time, McKenna claimed, there had been more than thirty different flare-ups between the two nations involving softwood lumber. "In fact," he wrote, "softwood lumber had to be excluded from the Free Trade Agreement or it would have been impossible to reach a deal."

The Byrd Amendment, or the Continued Dumping and Subsidy Offset Act of 2000, had been put forward by veteran U.S. senator Robert Byrd. It provided for the annual distribution of anti-dumping and countervailing duties. (Anti-dumping actions prevent imported goods being sold at an unfairly low price, or "dumped"; countervailing duties are imposed to offset the subsidies granted by a nation to its own producers.) The distribution was available to "affected domestic producers for qualifying expenditures," defined as manufacturers, producers, farmers, ranchers and workers. Effectively, the bill encouraged protectionism by giving a double reward to the complaining party. In the case of softwood lumber, the amendment caused the accumulation of approximately $5 billion in Canadian-paid duties held back.

McKenna has explained publicly that the amendment came to be when Byrd, as a master of Senate rules, "surreptitiously" inserted language into an agricultural appropriations bill. Because that bill carried the promise of money for a wide swath of U.S. farmers, politicians could ill afford to vote against it. "It was an extraordinarily egregious piece of legislation," says McKenna. "President Clinton was put in the unfortunate position of being unable to veto this provision without vetoing the entire spending bill. It is a classic example of one of the great problems of the United States Congressional system." McKenna was outwardly campaigning to remove the amendment because it maintained what he called a "bounty" on trade disputes such as, but not limited to, the softwood lumber issue.

McKenna delivered his speech at a very critical moment in the negotiations to settle softwood lumber. A U.S. coalition of special interests representing part of the U.S. softwood processing industry, he said, threatened to destabilize relations on other fronts, such as energy. He blamed the coalition and the U.S. congressional attention to it for bringing American market access to Canadian energy into play, because Canada is the most important provider to the U.S. of virtually every category of energy, including crude oil, natural gas, electricity and uranium. "And this coalition is putting in play the United States's reputation on trade matters throughout the entire world."

Here is one instance in particular where McKenna was extremely persuasive about Canada and its place as the most important neighbour the U.S. has in the entire world. He said at the time that if the two countries didn't get it right, then there would be diminished hope for international cooperation anywhere in the world. "We are the exemplar," he said of Canada and the U.S. "We are the model. We are the best example that anybody can find of a civil, harmonious, friendly, respectful, neighbourly relationship going back for hundreds of years without a shot being fired in anger."

Even before he'd arrived in Washington, McKenna had commented on the problem of the Byrd Amendment in February 2005 before the parliamentary Standing Committee on Foreign Affairs and International Trade. "I, like you," he told the committee, "am very, very concerned about the application of the Byrd Amendment. To me, that represents the confiscation of property and violates the rule of law. In all of the other disputes that we've had with the United States, if we were proven to be correct, those moneys had been returned to us." He called the Byrd Amendment's impact on the softwood lumber situation an anomalous situation. "We don't know definitely yet whether it will ultimately prevail and they will attempt to confiscate these moneys. I think that this would be a major breach of international law. It would entitle us to retaliation." Fortunately, the Byrd Amendment was repealed in 2005 after being declared illegal by the World Trade Organization.

A softwood lumber deal was officially announced the following April after McKenna's departure from Washington. By then, Michael Wilson was in the ambassadorial chair and British Columbia Conservative MP David Emerson was minister of international trade in the Stephen Harper government. Although McKenna was long gone by then, there are those who say it was he who actually sealed the deal.

The final agreement was eventually signed for the U.S. side by Trade Ambassador Susan Schwab, who returned to the University of Maryland when the Bush administration folded in January of 2009.

Schwab met often with McKenna. The two oversaw the detailed negotiations conducted by two key individuals and their teams. Those trade negotiation officials included James Mendenhall, former general counsel to the Office of the United States Trade Representative (who has since gone with the Washington law firm Sidley Austin LLP), and embassy operational chief Claude Carrière. "I spent many, many hours with Frank over at the Canadian Embassy," says Schwab. "And he came here. We sort of took turns, but by and large we ended up spending rather significant chunks of time together."

With or without the Byrd Amendment, the softwood lumber file was complicated by its very nature. Consider that there were no fewer than ten parties involved in the negotiations: the U.S. trade office; the Canadian Embassy, the provinces of British Columbia, Quebec and Ontario; the Maritime lumber provinces; the British Columbia Lumber Trade Council; and the forestry corporate giants Canfor, Tembec and Tolko. Adding to the challenge, each of the parties had a different position.

Neither a career academic nor a career political appointee, Schwab shares McKenna's understanding of the business world because of her time in the private sector. "He thinks like a business person *and* like a politician, and to a degree, I do too." McKenna adds to this that his U.S. counterparts, like Schwab, had him elevated in their minds because he was talking so frequently to the prime minister. "When we were negotiating softwood lumber, the people I was negotiating with knew the prime minister was talking to me as many as five times a day. We would be at the table and an issue might come up and they'd say, 'Well, look, we can't move unless you can move on that.' I'd say, 'Look, I'll talk to the prime minister' and two minutes later come back in and say, 'Yeah, we can move a little bit.'" It was real-time negotiation.

Schwab compares the softwood lumber dispute to the feud between the Hatfields and the McCoys. "I mean, there was just a lot of bad blood over the decades," she says. The time and energy which McKenna, Schwab and their teams invested in the file took them to the threshold of an agreement, but due to political events in Canada, they weren't able to actually finish it. "He and I were both frustrated we weren't able to close the deal. I suspect, and this is just purely speculation on my part, but if it had been up to him, he would have closed the deal."

Schwab believes one of the key reasons they got to the point of an agreement is because of McKenna's ability—"I mean I was just very, very impressed"—and because of his style. "Frank was so down-to-earth and so practical and quite frankly, when you are negotiating trade agreements, or any kind of agreements, when there are points of contention that need to be resolved, the single most important piece of the equation is being able to develop a personal trust and respect. And it's really easy with Frank McKenna. He was representing his side and I was representing my side, so it wasn't as though one or the other was somehow squishy, but he was very up front about what he needed to accomplish, and I was very up front."

She also says McKenna was a bit of an oddity as a politician because one normally expects to be contending with someone always needing to score points. "We've seen Canadian politicians in the past, trying to damn the dog or to try and score points under these kinds of circumstances, political points for an audience back home." McKenna, Schwab says, "was smart, clear in his ability to communicate his political imperative, Canada's political imperative and commercial imperative. He had a real desire to get the job done and not score points." Schwab could not seem to overstate the significance of the softwood settlement to the overall health of Canada-U.S. relations, particularly in view of what took place in the economy beginning in the fall of 2008. "I cannot even imagine how awful it would be right now [January 2009] in terms of Canada-U.S. relations if we didn't have this agreement in place." She claims that putting the agreement to bed stabilized relations to a greater degree than most people would appreciate. Having it off the radar has allowed leaders to focus on other matters.

Jim Blanchard says McKenna has not received the credit he deserves, together with embassy staffers like former embassy chief Claude Carrière, for his instrumental role in the softwood lumber agreement. "The deal was done," says Blanchard, "and then before it could be announced or finalized, the Parliament was dissolved and an election was called." As a result of the writ being dropped, Martin couldn't go out and announce the deal. Did it bother McKenna when Emerson, Wilson and Prime Minister Harper ended up taking all the credit? Blanchard is unhesitating in his response: "I don't think it bothers him one bit."

SIXTEEN

The Duel

"My appreciation for his talent grew with every opportunity I had to work with him."
MANITOBA PREMIER GARY DOER ON
FRANK MCKENNA'S APPROACH TO
SOLVING THE DEVILS LAKE ENVIRONMENTAL
CONTROVERSY

THE DEVILS LAKE environmental dispute perhaps best typifies McKenna's effective style as ambassador, calling into play his combination of communication skills and political intelligence. Devils Lake was the water diversion project in North Dakota that would have violated the Boundary Waters Treaty and threatened to harm water quality and plant and aquatic life in the Sheyenne River, the Red River basin and ultimately, because the Sheyenne flows north, Lake Winnipeg.

"I think the serious way he went after the Devils Lake thing was impressive," remembers Roger Noriega. "I mean, that's real tough stuff, going up against senators." He says there were players involved in Devils Lake, specifically Richard Armitage, who "didn't give a damn about that lake" and "didn't give a damn about what was right." Noriega was told at the time by his contacts at the U.S. embassy in Ottawa that Canada was in the right on Devils Lake and that McKenna was on the path to getting a deal. Armitage wasn't concerned with truth and justice regarding what could happen environmentally; he was concerned with money and expediency. "McKenna went after it, and it was a hard, tough issue." But McKenna was determined to turn the tide.

A significant part of that turnaround involved somehow getting through to North Dakota senator Kent Conrad. As it turned out, McKenna didn't have to pursue Conrad because Conrad was already in pursuit of him. McKenna was summoned one day to Conrad's office after Winnipeg South MP Reg Alcock made the senator furious by remarking to some of the Washington-based Canadian media that Conrad was contemptuous and wouldn't see him over the Devils Lake problem.

Alcock at the time was president of the Treasury Board, the minister responsible for the Canadian Wheat Board and the minister in the Martin cabinet responsible for Manitoba affairs. McKenna later learned that Alcock's outburst was unfounded because he more or less cold-called the senator's office while he was absent.

Conrad's summons arrived while McKenna was in the middle of a meeting: "I want to see the ambassador," he reportedly chimed. "So I go up the Hill," says McKenna, estimating that he was probably there in less than half an hour, "and walk in. He's got all the North Dakota media there, all of it; the cameras, everything. And he just proceeds to ream me from asshole to appetite, right there in front of the press."

"This was terrible what your minister did," Conrad said. "I didn't have a meeting set up with him. How can he say I stood him up?"

McKenna felt Senator Conrad was in the right, so he decided to tell him so, right on the spot. "Look, you're right," McKenna recalls saying. "It's just inexcusable and shouldn't have happened and I'm going to get you an apology from the minister. So you have my apology." Conrad was completely taken aback. Then McKenna persuaded the senator to take advantage of the fact the two were in the same spot by getting rid of the media and by agreeing to sit down together to discuss Devils Lake face to face.

By the time they sat down, Conrad had already softened up. "Look," he said according to McKenna, "I just want to start off by saying this. I don't have anything against Canadians. In fact, if you want to know the truth, my great-grandfather was a Canadian. In fact, he was a pretty well-known Canadian. He was the last guy in Canada to be in a duel and he actually was a lawyer. He killed a guy on the courthouse steps over a case. And then he went on to become a Supreme Court judge."

McKenna responded immediately, "You son of a bitch, you [your grandfather] killed my wife's great-great-grandfather!" Conrad said, "You're kidding!" McKenna said, "No shit. You owe me you son of a B!"

When Conrad confessed he thought the story was mere family lore, McKenna told him there was such an event and promised to get him the whole story. It involved an 1821 pistol duel at dawn between Fredericton lawyers George Ludlow Wetmore and George Street. Wetmore was the brother to Julie's great-grandfather, Medley Wetmore. There are several versions as to what exactly prompted the confrontation. According to one account, the disagreement stemmed from an onerous courtroom conflict.

Exactly what the true story is, or whether or not Conrad and McKenna were connected by an old-fashioned duel at all, is really pointless. The real point is that in that instant at the Capitol building, the two men put a halt to the media duelling and discovered that they had good personal chemistry. "The relationship became the basis for a solution to Devils Lake," says McKenna, "because we started to talk." Before McKenna left the senator's office that day, the two were poring over maps of North Dakota and Manitoba, discussing what to do about the Devils Lake dilemma. When McKenna's time in Washington was finished, Senator Conrad had the flag pulled down off Capitol Hill and gave it to him as a going-away present.

Although the Conrad connection was highly unusual, not to mention unlikely, McKenna found it, and it serves as a lesson in relationship building. The switch was immediately flipped when McKenna spontaneously apologized and then suggested they sit down and talk. It was a very disarming outcome, even for such a politically experienced senator. Not every encounter offered the ambassador two or three degrees of separation involving family folklore, but with everyone McKenna met and spoke to, he always sought some kind of common connection. In politics, connections are all-powerful. "If you notice—and we think it's bullshit—but every time a politician goes into a community, they say, 'Look, it's nice to be back here in Upper Hooterville,'" says McKenna. "'I remember driving through here twenty-five years ago and the guy at the gas station did such-and-such.' And the next thing you know, a connection is made."

McKenna discovered connections everywhere, including with Massachusetts governor Mitt Romney, a candidate through much of the 2008 Republican primaries. "When I found out that he'd spent every summer of his life in Ontario, I knew instantly we had a friend in Romney. Or when we talked to [Republican presidential candidate] John McCain and he told me his daughter was in Toronto—he's a big fan of Canada—we knew we had a friend. John McCain is a big friend of Canada's." When they first met, McCain told McKenna the only thing he had to read when he was a Vietnam prisoner of war was a copy of Canadian Robert Service's "The Cremation of Sam McGee," providing them with an obvious Canadian connection. "He memorized every word of it," McKenna recalls. Once, to prove it, McCain began reciting the poem over the telephone. Then there's Vermont senator Patrick Leahy, who's married to a French-Canadian. The discoveries go on and on.

The first time McKenna met Vice President Dick Cheney was at either the annual Alfalfa or Gridiron Dinner; McKenna can't exactly recall. Strangely enough, although Cheney was sitting at the head table, nobody was talking to him, so McKenna went up and introduced himself. "I like Canada," Cheney said. "I go there a lot. I love to fish up there. Did you ever hear of a place called the Miramichi?" Given the fact that McKenna's provincial constituency of Chatham formed part of the Miramichi, that link allowed the two to establish a dialogue. The weekend Hurricane Katrina hit, obviously causing a change in plans, the two had been scheduled to go hunting together for four days in northern Alberta.

So, McKenna concludes, two people often have an affinity that lies just under the surface. "It just needs to be mined out." He admits that in Washington, there is an awful lot of mining to be done, with more than five hundred independent elected thinkers in the city, most having some potential link or memory to their northern neighbour.

According to Colin Robertson, the Devils Lake environmental story shows how McKenna's natural, no-bullshit negotiating style could achieve results. He credits McKenna with creating a war room with daily meetings and personally intervening with the North Dakotans, including Governor John Hoeven, senators Byron Dorgan and Kent Conrad, and the White House through Council for Environmental Quality director Jim Connaughton. The whole while, McKenna kept in close contact with Manitoba premier Gary Doer. "Success in finding the solution, especially when the State Department proved unwilling or inadequate to the task, goes appropriately to McKenna." Robertson says it was the same approach McKenna used in bringing resolution to the softwood lumber dispute.

Premier Doer had had peripheral encounters with McKenna during the Meech Lake debates, when Doer was Manitoba's leader of the official opposition and Gary Filmon was premier. He had strongly advocated a McKenna type going to Washington, recommending to Paul Martin at a first ministers' conference that Canada needed someone in the U.S. post who was skilled at dealing with the media. He talked about how former U.S. ambassadors like Jim Blanchard and Paul Cellucci knew the political and business games and were skilled at communicating with the media. So Doer was happy with the choice of McKenna long before he even had a full appreciation for just how effective McKenna could be. "I was personally delighted when McKenna was appointed," says Premier Doer, "because he was arguably one of the best communicators in Canada and demonstrated the ability to work with a lot of people and be credible with a lot of individuals."

The two men met to discuss the Devils Lake file between the time of Martin's ambassadorial announcement and McKenna's departure for Washington. During the briefing, according to Doer, McKenna was calling matters the way he should have been calling them; he "wasn't there with any sugar-coated optimism." Doer recalls being surprised at how McKenna already seemed to have a sense of what awaited him in the U.S. capital. Once established in Washington and with his hands all over the file, Doer says, the ambassador developed a dogged determination to see it go in Canada's favour. He recalls meetings with U.S. and Canadian officials that would last until two in the morning, and an episode when McKenna worked non-stop through a scheduled vacation in New Brunswick. "My appreciation for his talent grew with every opportunity I had to work with him," says Doer, adding that McKenna was a quick study whose passion for solving the Devils Lake issue was infectious. "He was knowledgeable, tenacious and charming. He had a lot of credibility with the Americans, even while the governor and senators were not agreeing." He says McKenna had a way of making his point with people he was disagreeing with, using a combination of charm and communication skill. "He's got an energy level too. He persuades people not just with intelligence—there's an energy to his passion—and he's also funny. He uses humour effectively."

Doer was further impressed when he was invited to attend McKenna's going-away function at the embassy, which happened to coincide with a national meeting of U.S. state governors taking place in Washington. A slew of them, including former presidential candidate and current talk radio personality Mike Huckabee, showed up at the party. Huckabee even picked up a bass guitar and sat in on an impromptu set with Canadian country singer George Canyon and his band. Pictures show McKenna in the middle of the ensemble, moving to the music and playing a cowbell. Doer sees it as "a real sign of respect" that those governors set aside their own social agendas to see McKenna off.

SEVENTEEN

The Arsenal of Persuasion

"It sounds kind of simple and hokey, but he was so proud
of Canada, and when you are a professional representing
Canada you lose touch with that sometimes, and then
you walk into someone who is such a natural."
FORMER CANADIAN EMBASSY PRESS SECRETARY BERNIE
ETZINGER ON HOW FRANK McKENNA CHANGED HIM

WHILE IN WASHINGTON, McKenna returned to several of the old habits
he had developed as New Brunswick's premier. This is especially true
of his work ethic, his communication style and the manner in which
he formed a team around him. Most of the players at the Canadian
Embassy were already there and had their own predictable foreign
affairs habits, but McKenna had been faced with leading change before.
In the early television western-themed sitcom vernacular, he had
formed an F-Troop ('F' for Frank) in New Brunswick out of a combination of hand-picked loyalists like Francis McGuire, Maurice Robichaud,
Charles Harling, Steve MacKinnon, Nat Richard and many who

formed part of the provincial bureaucracy—a bureaucracy that, before his arrival, had its own dyed-in-the-wool manner of doing things. The same would be the case with the staff in Washington. Neither they nor McKenna knew at the beginning what changes would be in store at the embassy, but McKenna had an instinctive sense that it would involve selling ideas as he had back home in the 1990s. And he was eager as can be to figure it all out and get the job done.

Although he was closest to the political support group surrounding him in New Brunswick, he felt over time that the platoon was growing. He began to sense that his deputy ministers and senior public servants were following the code of the Musketeers—all for one and one for all. It's true that at least senior public servants in New Brunswick were generally caught up in McKenna's mobilization effort. He could feel that people working in their various roles and jurisdictions across the province were on the same page. "The bottom line is, I felt like by luck or good management we ended up getting a huge force-multiplier out of the public service."

In Washington, the only long-time loyalist he had at his side was Richard, whom he called a "very good soldier" who lives and breathes politics and public service. Although he wasn't directly in McKenna's Washington office, he still served as a useful set of ears and eyes for his old boss. This doesn't mean he was a mole. Having Richard there just added a sense of familiarity to McKenna's daily endeavours. "It was a comfort to have somebody whose first allegiance is probably to you rather than to the foreign service."

Richard became a soldier in the Washington version of F-Troop after he got a call from Ruth McCrea shortly before the official announcement proclaiming McKenna's appointment. Since leaving the premier's office concurrent with McKenna in October of 1997, Richard had not worked with McKenna. "He seemed keen to have someone to come down who had known him or had worked with him in the past," says Richard. The move required a fairly routine secondment from the Atlantic Canada Opportunities Agency to the Department of Foreign Affairs and International Trade. Richard believes that the relative ease of seconding him was a key reason why he got the nod instead of others who he imagined might have been more helpful given their breadth of experience and authority.

The requisite security checks, red tape and other logistical issues meant that Richard did not actually arrive on the ground in Washington until August 2005, some five months after McKenna had started on the job and just seven months before he would resign—a turn of fortune that abruptly ended Richard's brief time there. When he finally did arrive, he became involved in public affairs, including all of McKenna's Canadian outreach projects. He was also heavily involved in logistical planning for the new ambassador's travels. Working closely with McKenna's officially assigned executive assistant Rob Sinclair, Richard was not surprised to see that his old boss was still approaching work with the same "drive and gusto that he did everything else in his life." He was the very same Frank McKenna with whom Richard had worked day-to-day during the final year and a half of the premiership.

The ambassadorial role, however, is quite different from that of a premier. The ambassador is a political appointee who, by necessity, has to talk to the boss in Ottawa once or twice a day and who must check in with the foreign affairs minister. Even more cumbersome, files such as softwood lumber involved a multitude of partners to check in with. This was a clear change in the operating environment for someone with McKenna's independent style of leadership. "Given his personality," says Richard, "he would have found that a bit frustrating." Richard estimates that there were probably fifty hot files when McKenna arrived in Washington, although some were obviously hotter than others. And Richard believes that the reporting to Ottawa must have been even more acute than normal given the pins and needles Paul Martin's minority government was sitting on.

McKenna wished he could have had his entire team from the premier's office, including former aide Francis McGuire. "Francis would have been terrific." He hesitates for a moment and then jokes that he's not sure the U.S. would have been ready for McGuire and his often over-the-top style of doing business. Replacing McGuire to a degree was Colin Robertson, who has a similar rogue, exuberant, idealistic style and is just as cerebral as McGuire. By chance, McKenna did end up having staff close to him who had solid Maritime connections, including his two successive executive assistants, Christine Hanson and Rob Sinclair, both of whom happened to be from Halifax. His secretary, Lolie Acorn, surprised him by being a Prince Edward Islander, as her surname would attest.

The rest of F-Troop would have to evolve in ways similar to how the bureaucracy evolved under his watch in New Brunswick: the foreign affairs bureaucracy would, over time, be drawn into the vortex of his working style and enthusiasm. It took weeks, if not months, but change eventually came about. "I felt like we all coalesced into a real strong fighting unit," he says. "And you know, when I left, I had some awfully hardbitten people in the embassy who have been around for thirty or forty years who'd never said a good word to me all the time I was there." Those people formed the old foreign service guard and had made a critical miscalculation: that McKenna was just in from "Upper Hooterville." By the time McKenna was readying for his departure from Washington, some of even the hardest-bitten individuals had buried their belief that McKenna was naïve. They opened up and told him on a personal level that he was the best ambassador they'd ever worked for, that even though they'd had him for only one year, it was the best year they'd ever had.

He is convinced the Washington F-Troop formed into a fighting platoon because they got excited about the success they were seeing themselves achieve on major files and because of the forays being made into major media outlets like CNN, FOX and National Public Radio (NPR). Everyone at the embassy was affected when McKenna made news on the major cable news networks and NPR because those are such mainstream and penetrative media forms; their families, friends, colleagues and associates would see or hear the broadcasts and talk about it. Some staff also liked it when McKenna would say "to hell" with the traditional ways in which Ottawa and Washington had been dealing with something like the softwood lumber file. "The problem is eating us up," he would tell the troops. "Let's fix it." Next thing he knew the troops were charging over the barricades. His "damn the torpoedoes" approach was a breath of fresh air within the normally staid and cautious bureaucracy.

The bottom line is that what McKenna discovered in Washington was a deeper talent pool than what he had anticipated. "I thought we had a kick-ass team in New Brunswick," he says. "At the end of the day, when I left there, I thought I had just about as good a set of people to go to war with as you could have. And I didn't believe I could ever have that again. But in Washington, when I left, I felt that we had a team like that." McKenna believes that Canada takes its foreign service in the U.S. somewhat for granted, as he once did. "Let me put it this way. There's a talent pool that's very deep. So is it fair to say we don't exploit them properly? That's a different issue from, 'Do we recognize the depth of our talent?' I don't think we recognize the depth of our talent. I think that's categorically true. I felt like I probably wasn't exploiting those talents well enough when I started, but by the time I ended, I really felt like we had a pretty turned-on group of people."

McKenna believes that the cost of having a foreign service team running in the U.S. at full amperage is linked to how well-prepared the political and bureaucratic leaders are to accept mistakes. Federal governments, and especially government diplomatic environments, are very risk-averse. "But I was lucky enough that I had a prime minister who covered for me and was prepared to give me a lot of latitude." (McKenna continues to make this point in spite of having been caught in the crosshairs of the ballistic missile defence issue when he first landed in Washington.) In order to be effective as an ambassador in the U.S., he says, the ambassador needs cover. "You need a minister or a prime minister who is prepared to say, 'Yeah, look, if you screw up, it's on my account. But I want you out there.'"

McKenna was barely through the front door on his first day at the embassy when he was warned about Colin Robertson. Arriving in Washington in September 2004, Robertson earned a reputation as being too off-the-wall to remain in a senior foreign affairs role at the embassy. The warning came because, as McKenna puts it, some of the senior people in Ottawa "were trying to rip his ass out." McKenna makes a point of saying that an exception was Foreign Affairs and International Trade Deputy Minister Peter Harder. But most others in the senior ranks in Ottawa, McKenna says, were acting like, "Let's get this guy. He's a rogue. He shouldn't be in there." There was a point at which McKenna was nearly convinced that Robertson was dangerous and totally off the range all the time. But what the warnings really served to do was pique McKenna's curiosity. According to Robertson's wife, Maureen Boyd, it took about two months before McKenna was sure about his new minister of advocacy—he then spent the rest of his year in Washington defending Robertson and his footloose style.

To say that McKenna was satisfied with his decision would be a gross understatement. "After a month or two of watching, I started to realize that this is a person that is an enormously creative talent," says McKenna—which is not to deny that Robertson didn't need some control and discipline. Directed rather than constrained, he could do "massively important things." It wasn't as though McKenna had not operated with the likes of Robertson in his previous life. He'd had a similar character in long-time Liberal political operative and former deputy minister of economic development and tourism Francis McGuire. McGuire is renowned in the Maritimes and elsewhere as a fearless trailblazer who relishes breaking the rules to get the job done: it's all the more fun that way. McKenna may have instinctively cued in on Robertson's McGuire-isms, motivating him to keep the "rogue" close at hand. In fact, Robertson would become the ambassador's new foil, a player McKenna had been without during the eight-year bubble after he left the premiership.

McKenna has told McGuire to his face that 80 per cent of his ideas are brilliant and the other 20 per cent are "just pure foolishness." The great thing was that McKenna could always just say to McGuire, "Francis, I think that's really stupid," and McGuire would usually agree, and the two would move on the next solution or idea. "When you shoot off that many creative ideas," says McKenna, "they can't all be great." He admits that he likes having people around him who push the boundaries the way that McGuire and Robertson did. "Sometimes my job is to pull them back," he explains, "but I would rather be pulling them back than pushing them out."

McKenna and Robertson had the same tendency to be frank about matters, and they had something else important in common: both had ties to Liberal icon Allan J. MacEachen, the man whom McKenna describes as his mentor and protector. Working on Parliament Hill as a young point service officer, Robertson used to provide briefings to MacEachen at the very end of the Trudeau era, so he learned how Canadian politics work at a fairly lofty level. This is similar to what McKenna had experienced when he worked directly for MacEachen just a few years earlier.

Robertson's time as a foreign service officer—in New York, Hong Kong, at the UN and as consul general in Los Angeles—taught him how U.S. politics and business function. He also was part of the team that negotiated the Canada–United States Free Trade Agreement and NAFTA.

It should be noted that McKenna had before him two key people who had worked together for years: Robertson and Bernie Etzinger worked in the communications bureau of foreign affairs in Ottawa and then again at the Canadian consulate in California. Because they'd known one another for so long and shared philosophies regarding how to get things done, they were the proverbial "partners in crime."

The Washington Advocacy Secretariat Robertson ran was created by Prime Minister Paul Martin as part of his intended formula to improve Canada-U.S. relations. The idea of an advocacy unit was partially in response to pressure from the Canadian business community and the provinces to better penetrate the houses of power in the U.S. capital. Some of the provinces, Alberta and Quebec in particular, had threatened to heighten their own presence in Washington if the embassy didn't agree to step up the tempo of advocacy and lobbying. The point was for Robertson to develop a methodical, in-your-face presence on Capitol Hill. This approach was not classic diplomacy, but rather what Trudeau-Mulroney-era ambassador Allan Gotlieb described as "public diplomacy," a style perfectly suited to a freethinker like Robertson. He credits Gotlieb with having pioneered the approach for Canada. Robertson coined the title "Advocacy" because it was more honest about what the job at hand was.

In fact, the Americans have been associated with the concept of public diplomacy since long before Gotlieb; McKenna wanted to play them at their own game. In 2008, on the seventh anniversary of 9/11, U.S. Undersecretary of State for Public Diplomacy and Public Affairs James K. Glassman spoke publicly about public diplomacy as "the arsenal of persuasion." He very simply described public diplomacy aimed at publics, as opposed to officials. "While some people associate public diplomacy with commercial marketing—that is, with building a national brand—the truth is that public diplomacy, like official diplomacy and like military action when it becomes necessary, has as its mission the achievement of the national interest. Public diplomacy performs this mission in a particular way: by understanding, informing, engaging, and persuading foreign publics." The aim, he said, is to engage foreign publics to make it easier to achieve U.S. foreign policy goals. Public diplomacy has a long-standing tradition in the U.S.: Glassman said that during the Cold War, the United States became very good at it, with such institutions as the Congress of Cultural Freedom and Radio Free Europe.

While Canada via McKenna would have its own less grave reasoning and objectives for wanting to conduct public diplomacy—mostly trade, economic and environmental matters—the key goals of the U.S. effort are to diminish the threat to Americans and the rest of the world posed by violent extremism and weapons of mass destruction. These goals are linked to the entire U.S. national security strategy.

Before McKenna's arrival, Martin's commitment was stalling: the foreign affairs bureaucracy was not conditioned to this new form of advocacy, leaving Robertson in a state of limbo. The traditional foreign service folks didn't like the idea of proactive lobbying and did everything they could get away with to create obstacles. Even if Robertson had met or had established a contact with a U.S. senator, he was prohibited from speaking to that senator. Protocol had it that only the ambassador was allowed to speak to senators. Robertson calls this the "Upstairs-Downstairs" effect. "The prohibition order was, I wasn't to talk to [U.S.] elected officials because that's really only for [Canadian] elected officials. Well, none of the elected officials from Ottawa were coming down, so this position I knew wasn't going to work. So I was starting to just do it anyway, because if you go up on the Hill, that's how it works. Then Frank comes, Frank gets it immediately and says, 'Of course this is what you should be doing.'"

Whenever colleagues frowned upon Robertson's advocacy agenda, he would have to actively defend what it was he wanted to do. "I would go in and explain why, and [McKenna] would give a fair hearing. And what he decided, he was the boss. Most of the time, I was able to make a positive case. There were not too many cases where we weren't able to find a way to do what we wanted to."

But when McKenna arrived and embraced Robertson's way of doing business, things ramped up to "super-speed." He not only gave Robertson the green light to get going, he also delivered a clear set of instructions. It was McKenna's view that so long as Robertson didn't break any overt rules and so long as he knew generally what was going on, then "get off and do your thing!" On the flip side, McKenna told Robertson he was going to ride herd on him. He acknowledged that there could be both advantages and disadvantages to Robertson's reputation.

Whenever McKenna did have to rein Robertson in, it was for good reason. One example was softwood lumber. Robertson thought he should embark on certain lobbying activities on Capitol Hill regarding the long-standing lumber dispute, but McKenna told him to contain those activities. "I don't want us to be out there as aggressively on that," he would say, based on his political instinct and the sensitivity of the file at a given time.

As far as McKenna was concerned, if Robertson had a contact — a senator or otherwise — he should milk it the same way people at the U.S. Embassy in Ottawa would milk it if they'd established a contact with an MP or someone else up the ladder. Of course, depending on the issue, there were instances when it would still be more appropriate for McKenna to be the guy on the phone, but at least Robertson was no longer under a sort of gag order. Even with the new ambassador's stamp on the initiative, though, there were still those who attempted to smother Robertson's activity in ways that were semi-clandestine. "There were some rocky times," says Robertson.

He recalls how a colleague fought an initiative called Connect2Canada, a virtual network for Canadians and friends of Canada in the United States, which was launched on Canada Day in 2005. The colleague was pointedly asking what a thousand Canadians could possibly do that three hundred embassy diplomats couldn't. Another example involved efforts by some foreign affairs people to discourage or stifle an event designed to promote the Province of Alberta on the National Mall in Washington because it was felt Alberta would get too much prominence over the federal government.

For the files he was permitted to act on, Robertson's advocacy and lobbying focus was on Capitol Hill. Once set loose, he quickly learned that the underlying preoccupation among members of Congress and their teams was security, whether it involved the border, Iraq, Afghanistan or elsewhere. He had neither money nor votes to sell. He just had messages from Canada, messages which had to be delivered in quick pitches rather than lengthy briefs. He calls it the proverbial "elevator pitch." With security as the underlying issue for Americans, Robertson began taking a fully uniformed military officer on his scheduled calls because it signified to some and reminded others that Canada was militarily engaged, if not necessarily in Iraq.

The officer's name was Major Jamie Robertson (no relation), a one-time NORAD public affairs source said to be comparable in creativity and imagination to embassy press secretary Bernie Etzinger. Major Robertson created Canadianally.com, a website that explains Canada's varied military commitments. He was more than just a prop for Robertson's lobbying effort: he had an actual role to play in the brief pitch they made while going door-to-door on the Hill. He would also bring along a specially minted Canadian coin as a souvenir of Canadianally.com, a simple yet effective idea which appealed to many of the elected officials they were targeting. According to Colin Robertson, one-quarter to one-third of people in Congress and the Senate have had uniformed service in the U.S. military, so for them, anything smacking of military had great appeal. On some days, they would conduct as many as six calls, which civilian Robertson described as exhausting, each one requiring an energetic ramp-up. For more selective, penetrative targets, the Robertson duo would pave the way and then involve McKenna in more in-depth discussions with congresspeople, senators or state governors.

Robertson wasn't just lobbying for some kind of generic Canada entity or angle. He had substantive, specific issues in his portfolio that defined whom he should lobby, an example being the devilish Devils Lake environmental issue. Every day for a period of about two months, Robertson was focused on lobbying that single issue on Capitol Hill, specifically targeting the North Dakota congressmen and the two senators for whom it was a critical matter. Then Robertson zeroed in on politicos from nearby states such as Minnesota with peripheral interests in the matter. On those days when he was able to be at the embassy, McKenna held his morning "war rooms," ticking off agenda items like Devils Lake and making sure the various elements of the embassy were all singing from the same hymn book. Robertson's work was designed to supplement what the Canadian government was doing with the State Department and the White House. "And Frank got all that. It was his modus operandi, like he really is the CEO who entrusts his people and the more you were able to accomplish, the more work he would give you." And he seemed to love it when unorthodox ideas were raised—which of course was a specialty for Robertson, McKenna's risk-taking foil.

When McKenna resigned as ambassador and announced he was leaving Washington, the writing was on the wall for Robertson. One colleague said to him at the time, "I guess you'll have to go too," recognizing that the resistance to their lobbying and communication tactics would likely return to the embassy ranks. Robertson left within a few short months of McKenna's March 2006 departure and took up his new responsibilities back in Ottawa. It was all just as well, as the air had pretty much gone out of the embassy, at least for Robertson, when McKenna left. "You really felt that you were performing on all cylinders and you were moving forward," he says of the time with McKenna. "We were doing stuff which hadn't been done before. We were experimenting, but we were experimenting with effect. We were actually moving the yardstick forward instead of just holding or playing defence."

Since McKenna and Robertson left the embassy, the minister of advocacy position has, predictably, been scaled back to a more traditional, bureaucratic foreign affairs stance. Because the previous title "got up the nose of some," as Robertson puts it, it's now called federal-provincial relations and congressional relations. How predictable was that step backwards? In the absence of someone pushing the limits the way Robertson had done and McKenna had endorsed, you can also bet that the day-to-day tasks have grown more bureaucratically benign. There is probably less penetrative, in-your-face lobbying taking place on the Hill in favour of something more traditional and desk-driven.

Desk-driven bureaucracy would drive McKenna clean out of his mind. He likes to operate expeditiously, with the fewest number of obstacles in the way. And to be sure, bureaucracy in the federal government context can turn ideas and programs into processes so weighed down with caution that things spin and spin and spin until no one knows who is responsible for taking any form of action. If you think this sounds like a ridiculously critical overstatement, just show up as a fly on the wall at any normal meeting of a federal government committee and see what goes on. Senior federal bureaucrats, while largely dedicated and hard-working, are also extremely formidable when it comes to building and protecting domains, creating process and maintaining their status quo. The higher up the chain of command one goes, the more formidable are the individuals. In this light, McKenna may have added ten years to his life with his decision not to seek the job of prime minister and instead to try to create legitimate change.

Robertson's wife, Maureen Boyd, couldn't avoid being a devoted McKenna-watcher because his presence had so much effect on her husband's day-to-day life in Washington. With a background as a CBC national television reporter and communications consultant, Boyd has worked with three different Governors General at Rideau Hall and now does strategic communications, media relations and fundraising. She describes McKenna as "clearly superior in terms of tracking media, in knowing what the story was and knowing how, I think, to be the most effective at using contacts." She says he was much more of the Gotlieb school than other ambassadors she's watched. Because he was a politician, he was comfortable in the media milieu and punched according to his weight and, sometimes, above his weight. "I think it is kind of sad now," she says, "that the present ambassador [Michael Wilson] is muzzled the way that he is, because today you have to be out there and be in public and doing the interviews."

McKenna admits that Ambassador Wilson's style is more understated than his own. But he's quick to focus on what he considers one of Wilson's great strengths, and a key component of an effective ambassador: that he has the ear of Prime Minister Stephen Harper.

There's a yarn McKenna has used as an icebreaker in speeches to audiences in Canada. He talks of being back home in New Brunswick and leaning over his fence to talk to a local lobster fisherman. McKenna says he likes to ground himself by reaching back into the world of the local lobstermen, who he says always seem to have a greater grasp of what is going on in the real world than people elsewhere. "I said to him, 'Look, I'm working in a place that's self-absorbed, doesn't know anything about us, doesn't know anything about me, that's totally inward looking, totally indifferent to the fact that I or we exist.' He looked at me with total puzzlement. He said, 'Are you still working in Toronto, Frank?'" But McKenna wasn't talking about Toronto, of course. He was referring to Washington.

When Roger Noriega thinks of Americans and their view of Canada he is reminded of a view he once heard expressed: that the worst thing about Canadians is not that they don't understand the United States but that they think they do. You can't watch American television and really hope to understand Americans any more than you can look at Montreal and say, "Oh, Canada is so European." "That's not really Canada," says Noriega, a relentless Canada-watcher and CBC television viewer. The degree to which Noriega understands Canada probably makes him very rare among Americans. "This is going to come across as really stupid," says Noriega, "but it [Canada] is a different country. It is organized around a different sort of values. We have a lot of things in common, but a different set of values."

He describes the key difference as Canada's "social mission," something which irks Americans, particularly when Canada is not marching in lockstep with the U.S. agenda, be it the Iraq War, taxation policies or health care. He characterizes Americans as locked into such a rigid jingoistic pride over their nationhood that if the president is not wearing a U.S. flag lapel pin then he is judged unpatriotic. Noriega knows that Canadians don't operate on that level, but do have a sense of pride in nationhood. It's just approached differently. "I'm one of those, I'm one of a very few conservatives, who sees Canada in a very positive light," he says. The reason: whether from watching *The National* or listening to CBC radio, he is informed. "Listen to *As It Happens*," he says. "There is something different about the calls." Noriega's observations go to the heart of McKenna's desire to conduct a Canadian campaign in the U.S. with the intention of dispelling the Canadian myths and bring the two nations closer together.

Once it became clear to McKenna that it was necessary to find a new way of telling Canada's story—the identification of key strategic messages—he followed the same tactic used while premier of New Brunswick: find out what resonates, and stay on script. In New Brunswick the message had to do with the province's surprisingly advanced broadband infrastructure and what that meant for the attraction of call centres and technology companies needing broadband to do business effectively.

FRANK McKENNA ·

The simple idea of re-employing his own tactic would have eluded McKenna if not for an accident of fate. He had just finished sitting in on an open-line call-in radio show. He and Bernard Etzinger were in the back of their car when it occurred to McKenna what had just happened on the air. A female caller had gone off on a tangent about Canada's failure to support the U.S.-led war in Iraq, about terrorists coming into the U.S. from Canada, about the porous Canadian border, about drugs arriving into the U.S. from Canada, and about the legalization of marijuana in Canada. "McKenna looks at me with this look and he says, 'It was like she was reading that.'" It occurred to Etzinger that McKenna was right. "It sounded like it was a script. It sounded like talking points." It was clear to both men that the negative view of Canada existed in the form of a standing mantra that almost anyone could use to paint Canada black.

"Do we have anything like that?" McKenna asked. "What do you mean?" Etzinger responded. From that exchange came the decision to fight back with Canada's own story, its own speaking points, its own mantra, researched, formulated, written and distributed in such a manner that anyone could understand it and use it effectively.

In Washington, McKenna and his F-Troop began to conduct research toward developing a script that would be repeated time and time again to Americans who had a tangible economic or emotional vested interest in Canada. First, they decided to seize on the economic facts about Canada and its relationship to the U.S., especially focusing on border states. Even knowledgeable embassy staffers were astonished at what they were able to mine from the statistical base that had been simply sitting there. Second, with the tangible facts in hand, the strategy called for shaping and communicating them in a fashion that followed the "all politics is local" philosophy of former U.S. Speaker of the House Tip O'Neill. McKenna and his F-Troop team would especially channel those facts toward senators, congressional representatives and governors in their home constituencies.

Together with other public affairs staffers, it was Bernie Etzinger's job to search for those tangible facts about the Canada-U.S. relationship which could provide new fuel for their communications effort. The embassy team would investigate the impact of Canadian businesses or purchases or energy deals on a particular state or district and they would begin to use the revealed data in a seamless storyline that everyone could understand. "He started all of that with this notion that we would leverage the message and reach out to the individual in a way that we were able to explain all that stuff." Etzinger says the embassy team developed a new grassroots marketing capacity to communicate the Canadian message in a new and meaningful light.

From the Canadian conferences McKenna spoke at, to the podiums he spoke from in the U.S., to the cable news network interviews he gave, McKenna was what Bernie Etzinger calls "a press secretary's dream." Having a dream communicator changed Etzinger's philosophy about where and how to channel messages. Suddenly, it was logical that the Canadian ambassador should be on the air with FOX News' Bill O'Reilly or CNN's Wolf Blitzer. So long as McKenna was the messenger, no longer would there be general "trepidation" inside the embassy over going on such shows—with the possible exception of the show hosted by the veteran broadcaster who has branded himself as "Mr. Independent," CNN's Lou Dobbs.

Etzinger describes the Dobbs opportunity, which opened up quite suddenly with a call one morning in June 2005 from one of the show's producers. The program had been doing a series on U.S. border issues and wanted to do a segment that focused on Canada.

"Dobbs was worrisome," says Etzinger. "This was someone who a lot of Canadians thought really didn't like Canada. There were a lot of people" both at the embassy and in Ottawa "who really thought he shouldn't go on Lou Dobbs." Etzinger says this wasn't a lack of confidence in McKenna's ability. It was more a fear of being seen to validate a world view that Lou Dobbs projects. It was an easy trap to fall into. "What I often saw during that period of time when Canadians would go on air was them being very defensive, that played right into the [host's] talking points. Frank McKenna was never defensive." Etzinger says you're either going to go on shows like Dobbs or O'Reilly and be their puppet for eight to ten minutes or you're going to leave them saying, "That guy was a good interview."

It was a good couple of hours before everyone agreed the interview should go ahead. Next thing you knew, on the very same day, McKenna was on the CNN set and Lou Dobbs couldn't seem to help but be nice to McKenna. "We knew that this was a real moment," says Etzinger, "a real moment on a number of levels."

It started off plain and blunt enough. With ten seconds to go before they were live-to-air, Dobbs was being plain nice, when he suddenly turned to McKenna and blurted: "Don't you think Bush is the biggest fucking idiot?" The blurt jarred McKenna, but not enough to throw him off his game. When they went to air, Dobbs took on his television persona and spent much of the segment exploring border issues with McKenna, comparing the Mexican border situation with that of Canada. McKenna politely challenged him on the comparison, saying that the controversy over the Mexican border has to do with illegal immigration. "On the northern border, that's just not the case," he told Dobbs. "You don't hear of Canadians trying to get under barbed wire fences to get to the United States. We admire the United States, but we have a great deal of affection for our own country as well." He stated Canada's case that issues on the Canada-U.S. border are dramatically different from the border to the south. "And our concerns on the northern border are two: respect the legitimate needs of both countries to be secure, but at the same time maintain what is the largest trading relationship in the entire world."

Dobbs then told McKenna that he'd been "stunned" during a recent broadcast interview when a Texas state senator had said the U.S. should be more concerned about the Canadian border than the Mexican border because that's where the 9/11 hijackers came from. Dobbs and McKenna's conversation put to a rest the notion that the terrorists had come across the border. McKenna and his people had encountered that claim prior to the Dobbs interview. In fact, two months beforehand, Robertson and Etzinger were tracking U.S. media accounts when they discovered Newt Gingrich had been the source of such statements. One of the programs he made the claim on was the FOX News program *Hannity & Colmes*. Expressing how surprised he was over the comments, McKenna wrote the former Speaker of the House asking him to set the record straight and retract his statements. "Are you aware," he wrote, "that former Attorney General John Ashcroft has said on the record that none of the terrorists from the September 11 carnage came to the United States through Canada?" He went on to refute the myth by referring to *The 9/11 Commission Report*, which detailed how the hijackers entered with U.S. visas and that none of them entered from Canada. McKenna's well-researched letter played to Gingrich's ego: "Unfortunately, your comments perpetuate an urban legend that can take on a life of its own, especially when repeated by people whose opinions are deeply respected in the United States, such as yours. As a historian, you know how important the facts are."

Gingrich admitted to espousing these theories, claiming he had heard them from Senator Hillary Clinton. According to Robertson, Gingrich actually likes Canada, having attended the inauguration day event staged at the embassy in 2004. Gingrich was good enough to issue a news release retracting the statement and reiterated the point on CNN's Lou Dobbs program.

When Gingrich made his retraction, it became fodder for Connect2Canada, the online forum for Canadian expats and others with an interest in Canada. The Gingrich episode was an example of McKenna's style of immediacy in contrast to previously typical embassy activity, as characterized by Manitoba premier Gary Doer: "like sending a letter down Pennsylvania Avenue by carrier pigeon." Robertson closed the loop on the matter by using the next possible opportunity to get to Hillary Clinton to ensure she was not espousing the 9/11 theory any longer.

In response to Dobbs's comment, McKenna said the myth had hurt Canada "terribly," and he reinforced that none of the terrorists had entered the U.S. from the north. "All nineteen were legally present in the United States," he insisted. "I guess what hurts us," he continued, "is that we would never want to contribute in any way to anything that would harm our neighbour. The United States is our only neighbour, you know. And we take it very seriously, the security. We take our own security very seriously because we're also on the al Qaeda hit list and we want to protect Canadians."

McKenna recalls the Dobbs interview as being an important moment in relaying key points he wanted to make to a wide U.S. audience. At the same time, he seemed to have developed a relationship with a very widely exposed media personality, which, if he'd remained in Washington, might have proven worth its weight in gold. The transcript of the show reveals that Dobbs repeated one phrase over and over: "We love Canada. We love Canada." When McKenna squeezed between Dobbs's endearments and made points about being the biggest energy supplier to the U.S., Dobbs kept on: "Did I mention I love Canada?" McKenna kept on selling. "You've got me convinced, Mr. Ambassador," said Dobbs, a journalist who typically takes no prisoners and who rarely passes out accolades. "Canada is and has been and I'm sure will always be a great friend of the United States." After the apprehension they'd felt about agreeing to the interview, Etzinger and everyone else who watched at back at the embassy and in Ottawa could hardly believe what they had heard.

The porous border issue also arose on the FOX News program *The Big Story*, with host John Gibson. When Gibson quoted a Canadian intelligence report as admitting that Islamic terrorists were congregating in Canada after being sponsored and trained abroad, McKenna responded by saying that of course it is possible for terrorists to squeeze through the Canadian border, suggesting that no border security plan is going to be perfect. But he then countered with a series of questions and answers: "Were any of the September 11 terrorists from Canada? The answer is no. And do we care about protecting the border? The answer is yes; emphatically, both countries care a great deal about protecting the border and I think are doing a very good job of it." Gibson suggested that terrorists can get off a plane from Afghanistan claiming political asylum and be welcomed into Canada. McKenna wasted no breath in saying such myths were "categorically not true."

When it came to Bill O'Reilly's show on FOX, McKenna was intent on presenting what Canada had done to help victims of Hurricane Katrina in New Orleans. He wanted to make good and sure the message got out. When briefing notes for the show were presented to the ambassador, he was very hands-on, according to Etzinger, saying "put this in, put that in," the notes serving as preparatory reminders for the interview. He didn't want a stone left unturned in terms of what Canada's relief response effort had been. He used the same spiels on other media too, including on the New York City Public Broadcasting System affiliate WNYC-FM, where host/interviewer Melissa Block introduced McKenna's hurricane relief story interview by saying, "So now we know what it feels like to be a country that receives foreign aid."

Jim Blanchard recalls how McKenna handled his TV interviews and convinced Gingrich to retract his 9/11 statements. For Gingrich to back off like that was "unheard of," according to Blanchard, who is always astonished at how Canadian federal cabinet ministers are always facing demands to apologize for everything, even things someone else did while occupying the same ministerial portfolio ten years prior. "I've never seen anything like it. That was significant. You know, he was just handling that media presence with great savvy. And he was very proactive with the media. I think that was helpful. That's really important here because we are so insular."

Canadian Embassy staffer Nat Richard says his boss loved to engage in this kind of media battle. "He was very aggressive in knocking these things back," says Richard, "getting on programs like Lou Dobbs and Bill O'Reilly. I think he enjoys that, but he was extremely good at it and he's a natural at it."

One of the side benefits of getting McKenna on such high-profile U.S. television programs, apart from the obvious penetration of the U.S. audience, was the spill into Canadian households. Canadians, who regularly form part of the major U.S. news network audience, liked it that their ambassador was appearing on shows of that type because they instinctively understood the potential impact. It wasn't like speaking to an audience in New York or Philadelphia and maybe getting picked up by the flagship local daily newspaper, which might get read by a fistful of readers.

One of the things Etzinger liked about getting on Lou Dobbs was that Dobbs doesn't just attract an audience of cable news network junkies but actually attracts a sound base of business people. So here was a chance to talk to a slice of the U.S. and Canadian business hierarchy. It was a certainty that there would be a buzz in offices the next morning. In the U.S., the chance was that business people would be talking about "that Canadian guy on Lou Dobbs last night" while in Canada they'd be talking about "McKenna being on Lou Dobbs last night."

The effectiveness of McKenna's high-profile television exposure was not lost on the *Toronto Star*'s Tim Harper. Four months into the new ambassador's term, Harper characterized McKenna as a warrior doing battle over the airwaves with the U.S. behemoth. "The legendary elephant keeps rolling over, just as weighty and indiscriminate as ever," he wrote (without specifically mentioning the government or politicians; it was more a description of Americans in general). "It spreads myths, protects its own industries, threatens to ignore environmental treaties and is often oblivious to the neighbour it is squeezing, unwilling or unable to listen to cries of protest. But Frank McKenna keeps pushing back. Pushing often enough, the thinking goes, that the American elephant might even notice." Harper detailed the fact that McKenna was active on several communication fronts in his effort to undo some of the damage done by myths and inaccuracies about Canada—popping up on the op-ed pages of big-city papers such as the *New York Times,* penetrating cable news "gabfests," playing the major network television game and even using the old tried-and-true medium of letters written to perpetrators of such misinformation. "He's a man who never bothered to absorb the small print in the diplomat's book of etiquette, a politician in a diplomat's suit."

Explaining his proactiveness on so many fronts, McKenna reportedly told Harper that Canada cannot afford to let negative information be perpetuated in the U.S., whether through media or in political backroom chats, because once the myths are out there, they take hold.

Early in McKenna's Washington tenure, Harper was among the first journalists to record growing speculation that McKenna might be using the ambassadorship as a launching pad to a career in federal politics. "The McKenna style has also led to speculation that he may be trying to disprove the old truism that a future leadership campaign can't be built from outside the country." The irony, of course, is that this is not what McKenna was doing, but it is what Michael Ignatieff did.

Etzinger says it should not be underestimated how appearances on high-profile cable news shows play to the most senior people in Washington—even the president, vice president and secretary of state—who might see the broadcast personally, or read about it in a briefing note or transcript, or hear about it from staff. Being on those shows wasn't just a way of getting the Canadian message out, Etzinger says. It was also a way of getting into the right circle.

Few Canadians had a better independent bird's-eye view of Frank McKenna in Washington than veteran television journalist Henry Champ, now retired. Relaxed in his Washington home in sweats and a baseball cap, Champ is tall, imposing, affable, charming and humorous in an old-school journalistic way—he could have played opposite Jack Lemmon in the movie *The Front Page*. He's the kind of guy who invites someone on first meeting to feel free to come back to the house in the evening to watch an NHL game on TV and have a beer, and he means it.

Champ has pretty much done it all since his first overseas posting in 1972: he's had stints in Washington, Warsaw and London, then a respite in Halifax and an eventual return to Washington, where he settled in for fourteen years. He is married to Karen DeYoung, an American who shares his profession as a former editor of the

Washington Post. He also is part of a small fraternity of Canadians who made their mark in U.S. television media, including Peter and Arthur Kent, CNN's John Roberts and the late ABC anchor Peter Jennings. Champ's U.S. exposure happened with NBC before his eventual return to the CBC.

Champ describes McKenna as one of the more "free-form" ambassadors to come to Washington from Canada—but compliments Raymond Chrétien as a bit free-form in his own right, thanks in part to his comfort level in being Jean Chrétien's nephew. Champ said that because of the obvious access to his uncle, the politicians in town loved Raymond Chrétien. In fact, Champ gives Chrétien more due as ambassador than do most people interviewed for this book.

"Frank was in the same mould," says Champ. "When you're working Capitol Hill or the White House and you can say I ran an election or I was elected, that carries a big weight down here, because the foreign affairs guys, they're fine, but they don't scratch your back, they don't tell you dirty jokes." McKenna, Champ says, knew how to do things with a wink and a nod when it was necessary—part of that secret handshake thing.

"I was doing broadcasts there, and he hadn't been there three days," says Champ about McKenna's arrival in Washington, "and I looked over and he's coming in the West Gate [of the White House], he's coming with James Connaughton, who's the environment and energy czar, but was also in sync with the boss [President George W. Bush]. When the boss had other things to do, Connaughton was a troubleshooter. And here was Frank, and it looked like he owned the place. They were just walking in the door. The guys before Frank, some of them, may never have gotten to the White House and he was over there right from the beginning. He was a great favourite on the Hill because, well, Frank's Frank."

Champ says that it was a "tragedy" when McKenna left Washington. But isn't "tragedy" a little overstated? "No," says Champ, "it was a tragedy. It certainly was because look at what happened." Free of his journalistic obligations to be impartial, Champ goes freewheeling. "You had Michael Wilson coming in and you had the Harper government with their pants down." Everything had to be channelled through the PMO, which in Harper administration terms has tended to mean Harper. "Wilson can't make a move without the PMO. But things were different during McKenna's short time there. I've talked to Frank about this a number of times. As far as he was concerned, if the PMO didn't like something, they just sent him a note, because he was smart enough as a politician. He's not going to make any mistakes anyway. You know if you're in politics as long as he's been, you're not going to blurt out something stupid. Even the couple of times he did get in a bit of a trap," says Champ, "he cleaned it up immediately." But wait a moment. Michael Wilson's been around politics as long as McKenna. The difference is Prime Minister Harper and the PMO's lock-hold on information flow, which simply drives ministers and bureaucrats in his government insane—which it probably does to Wilson as well, especially given all of his credibility and experience.

Champ tells a story about a call he got from McKenna one day during his Washington stint. It was in follow-up to an invitation from Champ, who had actually played in the minor leagues during the 1950s and loves baseball, to take advantage of Champ's season tickets to see the Washington Nationals play. McKenna explained that New Brunswick native Rhéal Cormier, then a pitcher with the Philadelphia Phillies, was going to be playing that night and McKenna wanted to know if there was a chance to get to the game so he could host two guys. "Shit, I've got four seats," says Champ, "so it's fine, let's go!"

To Champ's astonishment, McKenna wasn't trying to garner favour with a couple of Washington influencers. He hadn't inquired and really didn't care, but that was his assumption. "No, he had two New Brunswickers, a farmer and a clothing salesman." This was not McKenna carding favour with a lobby or interest group. "This was Frank taking care of friends," says Champ. "We had a great day. I don't think anybody talked politics. There was a sense that I saw at the baseball game, a sense about him that you don't see in many politicians, that he was an Everyman." Then Champ comments on his broader relationship with McKenna. "I always treasured his company more than I treasured any information I got."

"In Washington," he says, for a journalist to be effective, "you need to know about seven or eight people. You know a couple of people at the State Department on the Canada Desk. You know a couple of people at the White House who know Canada. You get to know them and get them to trust you. If you've got the embassy, either the ambassador or a senior designate, you keep your strength, because you are being lied to all the time by the Americans, so you start by saying, 'Listen, they're telling me this. Where are we? You don't have to give me a secret. Just keep me straight.'" And vice versa applies as well. Champ says that under McKenna's regime, that was all okay. It's not as if McKenna was in the business of phoning journalists and giving them scoops. "But," adds Champ, "if I was going to go the wrong way [on a story], he would straighten me out. And I also knew that he wouldn't lie to me." Rather than lie, McKenna would refuse to divulge something if the situation demanded he do so. Sometimes he would say he just couldn't talk about it.

For a string of television journeymen like Henry Champ, Don Newman and Mike Duffy, there was absolutely no hesitation—in truth there was a keenness—to talk about McKenna in interviews for this book. One reaches a point after decades in journalism, says Champ, where if one hasn't figured out the ethics and the rules about speaking openly, then what's the point of being a journalist?

Champ is careful not to overstate the relationship between himself and McKenna. They were not buddies in the true sense of that word. "But we were good friends, and I loved going to events where I knew he was going to be, because it was fun. He was informational and he was funny. I'm not making this up," says Champ, "but it's my side of the story. I think he liked me as much as I liked him." Champ throws in a caveat regarding his own likeability: "I think he probably liked everybody. That is the thing about Frank. He likes everybody." But says, Champ, he picks his friends. "And I'm sure on the media he thinks that most of these people are dipsticks." This is purely a hunch—Champ stresses that McKenna has never said or done anything to reinforce it. Whenever Champ gets asked by people how to treat the media if they're entering a job or a situation where media contact will likely occur, he says "avoid them."

Champ says McKenna's relationship with the media, especially the senior media players, was unusual. "I'm not dissing the younger people, but senior people in the media have learned by the time they get to be senior that you have to know people. Younger people don't do that. They get on the phone and they always think they know someone. It doesn't work that way. You have to build bridges to people. Conversely for politicians, they have to let the media representatives see them for who and what they are. "You have to let them look at you. That was easy to do with Frank."

Asked who in public life he would compare McKenna to, Champ wastes no time answering. "My favourite politician ever is Hubert Humphrey," he says, referring to the former senator and one-time presidential candidate in the 1970s. When Champ was a young Canadian journalist, Humphrey treated him honourably and directly. He was gracious and human. Champ says there is something about McKenna's qualities that brings Humphrey to mind. In a Canadian context, when Champ thinks of McKenna he is reminded of former NDP leader Tommy Douglas, who had different politics but the same kind of approachability. Champ had a close relationship with Douglas because they'd both attended Brandon University in Manitoba and Champ had covered him in Ottawa. "That's the kind of guy that I would put McKenna in with."

Champ's long-time CBC colleague Don Newman says that McKenna has an odd form of charisma which somehow works even in today's hot media environment. "The interesting thing about him is that he doesn't stand out, but he has this kind of ongoing pleasant demeanour that everybody likes, and he is good company. But, you know, he doesn't look particularly different than anybody else. He's some sort of pleasant, ordinary-looking guy." Like Champ, Newman was the CBC's Washington correspondent, spending seven years at the post in the 1970s, and his program *Politics* includes quite a bit of reporting on U.S. affairs.

During Newman's days in Washington, the Canadian ambassadors included familiar names like Jake Warren and Marcel Cadieux, traditional career diplomats in an era when the succession was typically from the job of High Commissioner in London or foreign affairs deputy minister and on into Washington. Newman says the U.S. posting was considered the pinnacle, the pre-retirement job within the Canadian foreign service. He notes how there has been a gradual shifting away from the career diplomat personality in Washington, who would report through traditional foreign affairs departmental lines of authority to the personal representative of the prime minister. This has become gradually more emphatic with the appointment of Raymond

Chrétien, McKenna and Michael Wilson. Even though predecessors Allan Gotlieb and Derek Burney both had diplomatic backgrounds, they also clearly represented Prime Minister Brian Mulroney. Newman says the Americans give their key ambassadorial posts to people who have a direct relationship with the president, which has a direct psychological effect on politicians and the bureaucracy in Ottawa.

BERNIE ETZINGER SAYS that one of the most enlightening initiatives started under McKenna became known around the embassy as the Trade and Security Partnership Map, a state-by-state examination of what was described in embassy communications materials as "the world's largest trade and security relationship." This gave McKenna's F-Troop a platform upon which to identify the Canadian presence in a Congress or Senate member's district, illustrating how Canada truly mattered to that politician's constituency. Produced in both electronic and hard media, the map illustrates and explains from two directions a compendium of facts and data on what's really relevant about Canada to each of the fifty states.

In addition to the map, individual fact sheets were produced for each of the states, providing more intensive detail. The facts and data touch on everything from electricity to potatoes to aerospace to facts versus fiction regarding the border. When visitors walk into the Canadian Embassy, they are welcomed by the map and a wall of fact sheets. Visiting Americans are irresistibly drawn to their own state, and visiting Canadians to the states whose business prospects interest them the most. Iowa's fact sheet, for example, says that 78,000 Iowa jobs are supported by Canada-U.S. trade, that Canada is Iowa's largest foreign export market, and that Canadians make nearly 100,000 visits to Iowa annually, representing $19 million. It breaks down the export types to Canada, the import types from Canada, agricultural connections and business success stories that link both countries. When you multiply this story times fifty, it's absolutely huge—just as it was a huge task to assemble it all into a uniform storyline.

With this kind of information and tools in hand, McKenna's script began to take shape. It began by relating stats that swept across the U.S. as a whole. As he would profess in speech after speech during his year as ambassador, no relationship comes even close in importance to Canada as that with the U.S. "Forty per cent of our GDP crosses the border every single year," he told audiences from New York to Los Angeles, "so 40 per cent of our wealth is associated with trade with the United States." He would then point out the simplest, most obvious, but critically important and often-overlooked fact: "We don't have any other neighbours." As he told the annual meeting of the Canadian Chamber of Commerce in Charlottetown on September 26, 2005, the commercial exchange between the two countries amounted to almost $2 billion per day, the biggest trading relationship in the world. A truck passes through the shared border every 1.2 seconds. "Just colossal numbers reflecting the robustness and the value of this great relationship that we have." This data helped form McKenna's evangelistic message about Canada's relationship to the U.S. throughout the year he was in Washington.

During that speech, which McKenna repeated in front of Canadian and U.S. audiences every time he had a chance, he said that in spite of all the interaction and goodwill that exists, "the biggest problem we have in terms of the bilateral relationship is the sheer lack of knowledge, the sheer indifference that Americans have toward us."

He told a story he'd heard on the way to one of his corporate directorship meetings in Australia. During a stop in New Zealand, he learned that everybody there loves to complain about Australians. The typical New Zealander's viewpoint was captured in the line, "If you don't like the possums here, blame the Australians. They're the ones who brought the damned possums here anyway." The same was said of all the rabbits hopping around New Zealand. McKenna saw sweatshirts in local stores supporting the New Zealand rugby squad and any other sports team that aspired to kick the stuffing out of Australia. When he mentioned this to a colleague during the board meeting in Australia, the response was: "That's funny. We hardly know they exist." For McKenna, the lesson came to symbolize Canada's relationship with the U.S.

"We have an asymmetric relationship," says McKenna, "and if you want to know what asymmetric is, it's the relationship PEI has with Alberta, for example. It's the relationship between parties of different size. We have an extraordinarily asymmetric relationship with the United States of America." He said it begins with the differing population, which goes on to be reflected in trade figures and percentages, with between 35 and 40 per cent of Canada's GDP tied to U.S. activity, while only between 3.5 or 4 per cent of the U.S. GDP is tied to Canada. McKenna likened the situation to Canada having "all your eggs in one basket," which is only okay as long as you watch the basket very, very closely. He considered it part of his job as ambassador to watch the basket.

To compensate for such an extreme asymmetric situation, McKenna feels, Canada needs to develop strong and close personal relationships built on finding and acting upon the American self-interest. Canada needs to find the emotive trigger which can cause Americans to come to the realization that the Canadian relationship is more valuable than they'd ever understood.

In May 2005, McKenna took his campaign to destroy myths about Canada to the Canadian Association of New York, giving a speech in which he talked about everything from his list of leading

Canadian companies with a presence in New York, employing what he estimated to be 30,000 people, to the fact that Cy Young award-winning pitcher Éric Gagné is Canadian. This approach formed his communications style in the U.S., drawing audiences in with a name-dropping list of Canadian sports and pop culture stars such as multiple National Basketball Association MVP winner Steve Nash and singers Bryan Adams, Shania Twain, Sarah McLachlan and Céline Dion. This may sound crassly commercial, but McKenna insists that in the U.S. market "the cult of personality is all-powerful," so one of the best ways to appeal to the Americans was to play their own game: that of talking celebrity. It was how he baited his audiences. Once he had their attention, he could put forward the political, economic and security-related facts which put valid stock behind his argument that the U.S. and Canada are completely interdependent and that Canada is the best neighbour Americans have.

"We produce so many interesting and wonderful goods that people take for granted," he said in New York, referring no doubt to both Americans and Canadians. He couched the story in a simple exchange he'd recently had with a businessman in Washington. All McKenna did was impart a few facts: that the train the man took to New York was made in Canada; that the Four Seasons and Plaza hotels he stayed at were Canadian owned; and that the increasingly revered BlackBerry was the offspring of a Canadian company. The man came away with a different point of view.

Central to much of McKenna's public speaking activity was the fact he campaigned relentlessly, as though he was in elected office again, working hard to get votes. Whether it was just an old habit dying hard or a purposeful, hard-nosed strategy he'd actually mapped out, McKenna found himself doing what he did when he was New Brunswick premier: infiltrating his way into the business community to prospect for opportunities. Prospecting became an important byword of his decade as premier. "Everywhere we would go we'd try to get in to see industry." On a typical prospecting day in Toronto, McKenna would swoop in from New Brunswick and go either to Canadian corporate head offices or international corporate offices situated in Toronto, or invite CEOs to meet with him at his home base, the famed Fairmont Royal York Hotel. He did the exact same thing in the U.S. "I'd go see the president of DuPont. I went to see the president of Campbell's Soup. I went to see the president of Pitney Bowes."

What becomes clear is that even between the premiership and the ambassadorship, McKenna had never stopped this relentless business interventionism. Even with his multiple mandates while in the eight-year bubble, he always had the same thing on his mind: attracting industry.

One on one, McKenna launches into a philosophical lesson about how people can overcome a lot of disadvantages through sheer hard work and perseverance. He's referring not only to individuals, but also collectively to the province of New Brunswick. Explaining why he's been so successful banging on corporate doors, he says he's learned over the years that business leaders exhibit a normal reaction to being pursued. In short, they like it. Next to imitation, it's probably the greatest form of flattery. "And I find the business community like people who are making sales calls," because it shows an aggressiveness and a forward momentum that they can appreciate and oftentimes become swept up in.

McKenna loved giving these speeches. Nat Richard recalls one in Philadelphia that simply wowed the crowd. "I think at the time they had a New Brunswick reporter accompanying him, and he was just floored." The reporter wrote about how McKenna's speech grabbed his audience. There would always come a point in McKenna's speeches where, if he was following a prepared text at all, he would just start winging it and take off up to his oratory plateau. He would speak from the heart. "There are a lot of politicians who would kill to have that ability," says Richard, "but I've seen him do it many times."

Once the speeches were over, though, McKenna did not take time to bathe in the success of the moment. He and Richard would get in the car and McKenna would simply get back to business. "It was like, 'Did you talk to the office? What's going on?'" He couldn't shut down even after a great speech without thinking about what was coming up next.

Inside the embassy, one of the cases being made by Colin Robertson and his colleagues was for the previously mentioned Connect2Canada initiative. Still in effect today, the network was designed as a way of putting accurate information into an environment that was accessible to anyone online, but particularly to target and mobilize people with an interest in the affairs of both nations. Because the network is interactive, it also serves as an idea-exchange environment. It was never intended to merely be a one-way flow of information out, but also to obtain feedback from subscribers. "They would start as your eyes and ears," according to Robertson, "and they become your voice—and we are directing the voice."

The Connect2Canada idea was spawned by Bernie Etzinger while he and Robertson were working together in California. According to Robertson, the prevailing view was that that the expat Canadian community consisted of a bunch of "cocktail slugs" who showed up at events but didn't really serve much purpose. Etzinger's assignment at that time was to focus on Silicon Valley, which gave him a lot of exposure to Canadian expats in the high-tech community. So he spearheaded the creation of the Digital Moose Lounge. In its early form this was just a loosey-goosey beer-and-hockey-themed website, until the California consulate started collecting the names of site visitors with a more serious interest in Canadian affairs. So when Etzinger and Robertson ended up at the Canadian Embassy and McKenna came on board, a new opportunity came to light to tackle the question, "What can a couple hundred thousand Canadians do that three hundred diplomats can't?" The answer, they determined, was: "A tremendous amount."

Backed by the Connect2Canada initiative and working the Canadian diaspora, McKenna had "all the right kind of celebrity for us in terms of the marketing," says Etzinger. "Plus he understood that the U.S. is a land of fifty states and Canada is a land of various provinces and territories, so he knew he needed to get out on the hustings in the U.S., like you would for any other campaign, and he understood that the provinces also bring something to the international arena. "Often, you know, DFAIT [the Department of Foreign Affairs and International Trade] is asleep at the switch when it comes to that reality, especially internationally."

Too often, DFAIT's preoccupation is who gets to represent Canada, which leads to a constant jockeying for supremacy or positioning. "Who has power internationally," Etzinger says, "is very much an aggregate of the federal and provincial areas of jurisdiction." McKenna, he believes, "was just the perfect package" to break that predictable DFAIT cycle of events.

The vision was that the network could grow to involve up to two million people. Unfortunately, as of early 2009, only about 43,000 people had joined, a clear sign that the project has grown dormant. If it had expanded as envisioned, it might have been a powerful advocacy force for Canada.

In a way that is clear only in retrospect, the underlying principle of Connect2Canada—the strategic, advantageous use of technology for spreading and sharing knowledge—ties directly into the "My Canada" speech McKenna gave at St. FX University in November of 1998, when he spoke about Canada competing in a modern world via a new national agenda focused on the pursuit of knowledge. That Connect2Canada, as a microcosm of what he was talking about, didn't take shape until seven years later, says one of two things: either McKenna and the sources of his "My Canada" theories were ahead of the philosophical curve, or Canada's Department of Foreign Affairs was behind.

EIGHTEEN

A Diplomatic Debate

*"What we have learned from Mr. Martin's government
is the art of how not to manage Canada-U.S. relations,
in seven easy lessons."*

FORMER CANADIAN AMBASSADOR TO THE UNITED STATES
ALLAN GOTLIEB ON THE DIPLOMATIC PHILOSOPHY
OF PRIME MINISTER PAUL MARTIN

NOT EVERYONE WAS impressed by McKenna's tenure as ambassador.
Allan Gotlieb, the man regarded as having made perhaps the most
indelible mark ever as Canada's ambassador to the U.S., has some
critical things to say. In a biting speech delivered to the Royal Society
of Canada joint conference on Canada-U.S. relations at the University of Western Ontario after Paul Martin's 2006 election loss,
Gotlieb took the prime minister—and by extension McKenna—to
task for their management of the relationship with the U.S.

The speech was echoed by a near-simultaneous op-ed piece
Gotlieb authored for the *Globe and Mail*. In both, he lined Martin up

behind former prime ministers John Diefenbaker and Pierre Trudeau for squandering the state of Canada-U.S. affairs, claiming Diefenbaker had made a mess of the defence relationship, Trudeau the economic relationship and Martin "the relationship as a whole."

He even links the fall of Martin's government to the fumbling of U.S. policy, even though Martin went to greater lengths than other prime ministers to make the relationship prosper: creating the special cabinet committee on Canada-U.S. relations, creating the unit in the PMO to supervise the relationship, opening the advocacy secretariat in the Canadian Embassy, tripling the number of consulates in U.S. cities, and dispatching politically astute Frank McKenna to Washington. Nevertheless, Gotlieb had lots to say. "What we have learned from Mr. Martin's government," said Gotlieb, "is the art of how not to manage Canada-U.S. relations, in seven easy lessons."

In lesson one, Gotlieb condemned the campaign-waging mentality aimed at local congressional constituency interests, advocating instead the more traditional diplomatic approach of working primarily with the executive wing.

Lesson two slammed Martin and his team for overplaying their "all politics is local" hand. He claimed that there is no substitute for treating the president as the single most important player in the U.S. political arena.

Gotlieb then levelled four other points of criticism: the Martin government's emphasis on lobbying, undertaken most vociferously by Colin Robertson; the Canadian diaspora approach so strongly advocated by McKenna; the government's underestimation of the importance of defence and security, especially in the aftermath of 9/11; and finally the open criticism of the U.S. and its policies. No doubt this was a finger-wag at McKenna's Empire Club of Canada speech and Martin's electioneering at the expense of the American relationship.

When I spoke to Gotlieb, a contradiction emerged. Although in his speech and op-ed piece he criticized with specificity several of the strategies employed by McKenna in Washington, in dialogue he said he had no issue with McKenna's handling of the post. He emphasized that he was questioning Martin's actions.

He explained that for the fifty years preceding the Vietnam and Watergate era, Canada had, diplomatically speaking, virtually ignored the U.S. Congress, concentrating instead on presidents and their administrations. In his book *I'll Be with You in a Minute, Mr. Ambassador,* he explains how and why Canada "forbade our people to go to Congress." What he attempted to do, beginning with his 1981 appointment by Prime Minister Trudeau (he continued as ambassador under John Turner and was reappointed by Brian Mulroney) was to correct that imbalance. His shift in tactics more or less mirrored what was actually happening in Washington, which Gotlieb describes as influence having "devolved to power units on the Hill." He called it "the doctrine of the sub-separation of power" which gives chairpersons of committees in the Senate and Congress more power than federal ministers in Canada because they can originate legislation and they have huge staff allocations to conduct research and investigations.

Not allowing modesty to get in the way, Gotlieb accepts credit as Canada's "godfather" of modern advocacy. He says that while it's true that power resides in the two houses of U.S. government, you can distort the White House perception of your intentions if you create too much distance from the presidency. This is what happened under Martin, the very leader who initially seemed most likely to improve Canada-U.S. relations after the chill or "drift" of the Chrétien years.

Rather than warming up, relations with the U.S. grew even chillier under Martin.

"Nobody thought that the relationship [with President George W. Bush] was cozy or good or great. He might be one of a thousand players," says Gotlieb, "but he is still the most significant player."

As for waging a campaign like Connect2Canada, or building the Canadian diaspora, or any other Brand Canada initiative which McKenna envisioned or supported, Gotlieb says it sounds nice but is not sufficient. "If the administration is against you, you can't win. If you have the president on your side, you might be able to turn the tide in Congress, but if he's not, you don't stand a chance. You can't win a war by attacking or defending on one front. You have to be on all fronts. Martin's approach was to say, 'It's the Congress, stupid.' But it wasn't."

As for his personal take on McKenna, the two have been associated only fleetingly. When Carlyle Group chairman Frank Carlucci asked Gotlieb to put together the Canadian advisory board for the firm, it was Gotlieb who approached McKenna. So they saw one another at the advisory board meetings, but their paths never really crossed in Ottawa, and Gotlieb was nearly done as ambassador by the time McKenna was elected premier in 1987. Whatever Gotlieb does know about McKenna is pretty much second-hand. "My impression was that he was impressive in Washington and was doing a good job, and that he was being effective on the Hill and was well respected," he says.

But Gotlieb disagrees with those who've advocated political types like McKenna or Michael Wilson versus a career diplomat such as himself. For one, career ambassadors are far less likely to get caught in the change of government, as happened to McKenna with Stephen Harper's election as prime minister. Gotlieb believes McKenna did the right thing by resigning, but that doesn't mean it was a good thing for the continuity and momentum of initiatives at the embassy. He was no sooner in Washington than he was packing to go home and Wilson had to start all over—not a great scenario for a milieu where access to power is based on developing and maintaining personal relationships. Leaving was never an issue for Gotlieb after Trudeau or Turner because he had no political profile one way or the other. "Washington takes many years to establish contacts because power is so dispersed."

It's different in Ottawa—where, Gotlieb jokes, if you know four people it might be three too many. But he's not joking when he says that if the U.S. ambassador to Canada knows the prime minister and the foreign affairs minister, he or she is all set.

Conversely, when McKenna got to Washington, he was given a memorandum titled "The American Political Firmament—Who's Who." It had four parts: the estimation of who would run in the then-upcoming presidential contest of 2008; the list of Congressional representatives who would be stepping down to seek election as governor of their respective states or to land a seat in the U.S. Senate; the list of likely candidates for House leadership positions for the second session of the 109th Congress, and the list of the top seventy-five members of the House and Senate who bore watching because of their accomplishments and potential influence.

McKenna describes himself as "sanguine" about Gotlieb's views, adding that a number of people inside the Department of Foreign Affairs are less tolerant of the former ambassador's critical viewpoint—they believe it's been so long since Gotlieb worked in Washington that he's out of touch with what's really happening on the ground there. McKenna is referring no doubt to Colin Robertson and Bernie Etzinger, among others.

"Relationships tend to wax and wane depending on the issues of the day, and the issues of twenty-five years ago are clearly different from the issues of today," McKenna observes. "The methods of advocacy are also clearly different, and people who served in the embassy during his time frequently told me that there is no comparison in the Washington of that era and the Washington of today."

McKenna admits that the Martin government deserved "some gentle chiding" for its handling, or mishandling, of the Canada-U.S. relationship. His feelings were anything but gentle on that first day on the job as ambassador when the ballistic missile defence issue blew up in his face, but McKenna likes Martin immensely on a personal level and would always avoid being critical of him. "The last months of the Martin administration were characterized by a high level of political anxiety, and the Canada-U.S. relationship occasionally became a victim of that partisan atmosphere."

McKenna was right about how some foreign service people regarded the tone and content of Gotlieb's intervention. Unable to stand idly by at the time, Robertson decided to debate Gotlieb via email. Robertson is one of those who have long considered Gotlieb to be the "godfather" of Canada's approach to using the power and influence of Congress and the Senate. So when the former ambassador came out swinging in his speech and op-ed piece, Robertson admits to being momentarily confused. "Advocacy is not an end but rather another means to an end," he wrote to Gotlieb. "The end, of course, is to advance Canadian interests. That's what our diplomacy has always been about. Advocacy does not replace the kind of high-level diplomacy that you underline—tone at the top does matter—but rather complements it by giving us another, highly effective arrow in our diplomatic quiver."

Robertson defended the value of having a politically experienced ambassador in Washington. "Frank McKenna is a 'political' ambassador. His political experience earns him acceptance and access among the elected that those who haven't been in the political ring don't enjoy. It's like being part of a club, and I've concluded that in Washington, for an ambassador to have held senior elected office increases your capacity for success. And because Washington is a political town, I don't think we can over-emphasize the importance of lobbying and advocacy and building relations."

As for McKenna's diaspora vision and the Connect2Canada initiative, Robertson defends it as right for the times. He and Etzinger—and, in a way, McKenna—see Gotlieb as an ambassador from another era when, as Etzinger put it, notification of Washington parties and functions was still issued on paper invitations that were mailed or hand-delivered.

"The Internet and the rise of blogs have further democratized the political process and put even greater reliance on the need for rapid response," Robertson wrote to Gotlieb, estimating that there are now more than 33,000 lobbyists in Washington, whereas in Gotlieb's time they numbered in the hundreds and "you could meet the dozen that counted." Robertson wrote about the tools at foreign affairs' disposal to respond to these changing times: "Did you know that we now have the capability of showing a [Congressional] representative a map of their district with exact locations of Canadian firms and jobs in their territory?" He referred to the value of relationships outside of Washington at the state and sub-state level as being "the hidden wiring" of the relationship between Canada and the U.S. The Canadian diaspora must also form part of this hidden wiring. And there is the expediency, immediacy and rush of modern news media such as CNN and FOX, which McKenna demonstrated a comfort with, if not a mastery over. Robertson said it is important for the Canadian mission in the states to be able to play by American-led rules, providing rapid response to keep pace with the news cycle. The producers for the Lou Dobbs show called in the morning, and before the day was out

McKenna had spoken to millions of Americans in one fell swoop with his own targeted message.

Etzinger elaborates on Robertson's points. Often, the person receiving a tactical Connect2Canada message would be inspired to forward the message to their own network or community of friends or business associates, which could bring hundreds of other faces on board. What McKenna's messages said to individuals, believes Etzinger, was: "I know you may be some middle manager in some corporation somewhere, but I know that you have influences and I know that you will have contact with people who will matter for us and so I'm going to reach out because of that."

Before that, says Etzinger, the foreign affairs department was "completely dismissive" of the network power of the expatriot Canadian population around the world. "Allan Gotlieb thought that they were just the hangers-on at cocktail parties," he says. In fairness to Gotlieb, that again was in an another era. "But the idea of a highly networked expat community is one that, had Frank McKenna stayed, we would have taken to a global level." The trick to such a network's global reach, Etzinger says, is tailoring its content for local consumption, state by state, town by town, community by community, affinity group by affinity group.

The post-McKenna levelling-off of Connect2Canada and Michael Wilson's more subdued approach to changing Canada's image mean the Brand Canada campaign was essentially lost. Gone from Washington and thrust back into the Canadian corporate machine, McKenna realized immediately that the ambassadorial pulpit had been the only place from which he could evangelize effectively. No matter how many speaking engagements he accepts south of the border, neither his individual brand nor his weight is the same if he's not the ambassador.

This is all the more unfortunate, as McKenna believes that the election of President Barack Obama in 2008 improves the climate in the U.S. for delivering the Brand Canada message. "I think we should be all over them," says McKenna, referring to the new Washington personalities riding into power on Obama's coattails. "As Canadians, we need to be getting them across the border [into Canada], but we know we need to be going to see them as well. Ministers should be down there getting to know all the new folks and getting to know the folks who may be the power brokers of the future."

What about business leaders such as himself trying to fill the void should the Canadian government not take full advantage of the change that is so obviously occurring in Washington? McKenna is not delusional. Even though corporate Canada is active in certain ways on certain fronts, it cannot match the profile of Pennsylvania Avenue and the resources and protocols that go with the embassy. "I think you have to be conscious of the limitations. At the end of the day, the United States will deal with ambassadors and deal with premiers and deal with prime ministers, but they are not going to deal with has-beens"—including himself.

There were signs in the spring of 2009 that Stephen Harper's Conservatives were starting to pick up on the need to communicate better in the U.S. In mid-April, the government actually admitted publicly that they were paying lobbyists to try and smooth the way for more Canadian exposure. Just a week or two prior, the prime minister had suddenly begun to appear on major U.S. talk shows similar to the ones McKenna had been chasing four years prior. There was, however, something institutional and robotic about Harper's message and delivery compared to the impassioned style of McKenna.

The debate over McKenna's effectiveness as Canadian ambassador continues with the boyish, if not impish, Chris Sands, a regular go-to guy whenever the media are looking for analysis on Canadian affairs in Washington. He looks amazingly like the straight-laced PC guy in the Macintosh computer commercials; he also has the wholesome look of a man of the cloth—and, in fact, teaches young people at his suburban Washington-area church. Having earned his PhD from Johns Hopkins University specializing in Canada, U.S.-Canada relations and North American economic integration, Sands seems like he's everywhere: an adjunct professor at the American University School of Public Affairs; a senior fellow at the American University Center for North American Studies; a member of the advisory committee to the U.S. Section of the North American Competitiveness Council; a lecturer at the Foreign Service Institute of the U.S. Department of State for the Department of Homeland Security; and a senior fellow at Washington's Hudson Institute, a public policy research organization that forecasts trends and develops solutions for governments, businesses and the public at large. You know the company you're about to keep by the photographs on the wall of the institute's lobby. With the likes of Ronald Reagan and Dick Cheney among those prominently displayed, everything looks and feels Republican.

Sands is a talking machine who especially appreciates being interviewed about Frank McKenna, if only because it gives him a chance to discuss Canada. Hardly anybody at the institute talks about Canada because most things there are so American-centric. Calling McKenna the first truly "political ambassador" to the U.S. in Canadian history, Sands reinforces the sharp contrast with previous ambassadors, especially Chrétien and Kergin. "Kergin was an inside guy, just as Raymond Chrétien had been, but McKenna came in with the political skills," says Sands. By "inside guys," Sands means that the two were too low-key for Canada's good. The problem was exemplified by President George W. Bush's oversight in not thanking

Canada in the immediate aftermath of 9/11 and of his failure to speak publicly when a U.S.-led friendly fire incident in Afghanistan ended up killing four Canadian soldiers (even though Bush had carried out the proper protocol of calling Prime Minister Jean Chrétien in the middle of the night to advise him of the incident and to express his regret on behalf of Americans). Canada was not on the radar at a time when Canadians felt they were involved in U.S. causes—and Canadian citizens became incensed about it.

So along comes McKenna riding on expectations that, because of his political background, he would be the salesman for new Canadian policies that Prime Minister Martin had promised would be more pro-American. But the Martin government, rather than shifting to a more pro-American stance, "became extremely ambivalent about whether it really wanted to get close to this [Bush] administration," Sands explains. He believes the Martin government saw that domestic polls did not support U.S. policies such as BMD. "They were willing to be in Afghanistan. That was a big commitment, but they went in a little bit tentatively and then with the wrong equipment and they had a lot of issues trying to get organized there." These conditions created an overall drag on the U.S. attitude toward Canada, which spun off into issues such as border security. For example, while the Martin government thought Canadians would be exempted from passport requirements for entry into the U.S., the Americans were in no such frame of mind. Canadians became subject to this requirement on June 1, 2009.

Sands disagrees with the many who believe McKenna was effective during his year in Washington and could have been the right guy to improve relations if he had not been crippled by policy in Ottawa. Instead, he believes, both McKenna and Martin fell short because they were unable to make a breakthrough on the issues Americans were most concerned about, especially BMD and border security.

Sands thinks McKenna's tactics were superficial. "He met people, he was friendly, he was more outgoing, but in terms of Washington public diplomacy, it was a little underwhelming. He didn't do a lot of the think tanks, he didn't talk to the universities. He wasn't snubbing them, but he just wasn't doing much in the way of public outreach." The plan to infiltrate Congress could have been a good strategy, Sands agrees, but only if McKenna had something tangible to offer congressional representatives when he did manage to get an audience with them. He needed something more tangible than just glad-handing and goodwill.

Sands is not unaware that at least some of Martin's policy positions had to do with the minority government situation he was caught up in, hence the poll-watching on BMD and Martin's thumbs-down on Canadian cooperation in that area of security. The Americans could sense that Martin was in a weak position when it came to policy development.

Sands said that McKenna's "sunshine" on Canada wasn't necessary with the Washington crowd who already know the country. It was not going to be effective in the face of the Martin policy gap, no matter how well-built initiatives like Connect2Canada were. Sands likens Connect2Canada to a pub night party where Canadians get together to do things like watch election results from home. He called the project just another form of spin.

Sands's view on the McKenna team's diaspora approach pretty much matches that of Allan Gotlieb, who says that "star-spangled Canadians do not and never will form part of a legitimate Canadian constituency. They will not pressure congressmen to be nice to their former fellow countrymen. They will not rise up against the nasties who want to restrain Canadian exports into the United States. Canadians who are now American citizens will act like Americans."

FRANK McKENNA ·

Bernie Etzinger disagrees, believing that the information gleaned and delivered through mechanisms such as Connect2Canada was both meaningful and effective. A chunk of their audience were CEOs, VPs, entrepreneurs, people inside the political systems. As well, the initiative was never seen through to its envisioned scale and therefore was never permitted to take flight in the way that was intended.

Much more effective, Sands says, was the more natural lobbying effect of Canadian-owned businesses near the Canada-U.S. border. He compares the effectiveness of their lobby to that of the Mexican-American lobby. Quite apart from any previous embassy activity, Sands says, the Canadian business community was already into free trade long before the Canada-U.S. free trade agreements were signed.

"Governments follow, [they] don't lead," he says. "I don't think in North America that trade follows the flag. It never has. Canada-U.S. free trade did not open up Canada-U.S. trade for big business. They were already there. What it did, it generalized the benefits and simplified things for the businesses that had already made their investments and decisions about where they wanted to go." In that sense, the agreement served to ease along or perhaps accelerate the activity already taking place between the two countries. The same was true of Mexico-U.S. businesses and their trade relations. If the Canadian government really wanted to be effective, all they needed to do was watch where the business community was going and invest more energy in that direction.

Sands says that although it was good that McKenna placed considerable stock in relations with the U.S. Chamber of Commerce and the Canadian American Business Council, he thinks McKenna may have put too much stock in the singular, one-by-one approach to the Canadian diaspora, who really don't present a voice or form a lobby with any real sense of glue.

Sands has firm theories about ambassadorial effectiveness. "If you're McKenna or you're whoever, how do you engage with your maximum leverage?" Sands says you do this by getting inside the headspace of the business community, which is already so far advanced in terms of cross-border integration. The North American auto industry would be a classic example, says Sands, as well as the Wal-Marts and Campbell's Soups of the world. (Another example, closer to home, is McKenna's TD, which is aggressively expanding its U.S. activities while maintaining its footing in Canada.)

Sands believes that by focusing more on the business community as an ally, the Canadian government would have greater success grabbing congressional as well as administration attention when issues demand. "That is arm number one of what I would be doing," he says. This sounds like the kind of philosophy McKenna could easily buy into.

"Arm number two" is the state governments, which Sands says are underestimated. This too matches McKenna's way of thinking. "We have found in the last ten years or so—and you have probably observed it as well—that while the federal governments fiddled and were unable to really connect, the states and provinces have stepped forward and filled the vacuum and started dealing with things," says Sands. Governors and premiers see themselves more or less as equals, while the U.S. president and the Canadian prime minister are far from equal. One reason the states and provinces can have greater success is because they are closer to their voters. "That's the whole idea of federalism, you know. And we are pragmatic federalists in both our countries, which is to say we have two [levels of] governments that work for us, at least—not counting mayors—and we don't care who does it. Whoever gets the job done wins points." Sands agrees that McKenna was focusing on the "second arm" by dealing directly with governors and by encouraging the opening of thirteen new consular offices across the United States.

Although Sands thinks McKenna "had the ability to be maybe a bit of a game changer," he inherited an embassy that was going through a sea change away from a group of foreign affairs career people who he says "didn't like the Americans very much." Sands says it was a particular problem during the Jean Chrétien era. "McKenna was good at his job. He just needed to do it longer."

"It's so ironic," he says. "Canada is a country full of people who get along with Americans, I'd say the majority. Maybe they don't love us and don't always love George Bush, but they get us." Sands contrasts some of the embassy's foreign affairs people with former Alberta energy minister Murray Smith, whom the Alberta provincial government sent into Washington as their "mini-ambassador" to represent their interests stateside. "He's great, you know, he's a back-slapping guy who seems like he belongs in the States. He's really easy to deal with. You have tons of them. And what you [the Canadian government's Department of Foreign Affairs and International Trade] were sending down were really odd ducks and people who in the embassy just stewed over the fact that the red carpet wasn't rolled out, that Canada wasn't getting enough credit."

Sands says that some of the embassy staffers were antagonistic toward what they saw as the "anti-internationalist Bush administration with its six-guns blazing. And it was hard for McKenna, because it was a problem under [Michael] Kergin; it had been a problem before that, where even under Raymond [Chrétien] you had people who were seen around town as being not very friendly; I mean, just not liking us. Canadian diplomacy was oriented around a lot of complaints, a lot of laundry lists of things we were doing wrong. The number of Canadian delegations coming down [to the U.S.] is numerous as the stars—chambers of commerce, groups or whatever. And they all complain."

Sands calls this phenomenon "Canada fatigue on Capitol Hill." Other countries, such as Denmark or the Netherlands, operated on a much more balanced agenda, occasionally raising an issue, but Canada was on all channels all the time. True, Denmark and the Netherlands don't share a border with the U.S. and aren't linked to it in the same way Canada is, but the difference was just too extreme.

Pamela Wallin agrees with Sands that there is no point in battling with the U.S. on every issue that comes along. "We can't always go to war with Americans whenever it suits us politically. We need to get past all of that. We have a geographic position everybody else envies. We could be the access point if we weren't so busy trying to say we're not to be identified as Americans." She says that McKenna understood this opportunity well.

Rather than complaining all the time, the way to be effective in Washington is to come and say, "Here is what we're doing for you," Sands says. "Because if you can do that, then we're listening, because you just did us a favour." He admits that for some Canadians who are just too sensitive, that kind of approach might sound too much like paying "tribute to the empire," but he defends it as at least a strategy.

Henry Champ agrees. He's had leaders from the Hill tell him that dealing with Canadians is impossible. Not to say that the Americans don't push hard and try to get what they want on a consistent basis as well, but they're not as "bloodthirsty" as most Canadians would perceive them to be. "I think Americans know very little about Canada except some key issues. They are our friends. We can trust them when we need them. They don't cause us shit. The Canadians, meanwhile, are always suspicious that they're being short-shrifted. And the

Canadian media tends to mirror this attitude too, amplifying and exacerbating the perception about the complaining Canadians."

It's not that the Canadian media shouldn't analyze the two-dimensional topic of Canada-U.S. affairs, "but there is a reality" in the U.S. that has many more complex dimensions. With all the problems that country has—the economy, the war on terrorism, Iran, North Korea, the Middle East—NAFTA and mad cow disease and softwood lumber are not exactly always the most threatening or burning issues of the moment.

Backstabbing or reneging has also been something ambassadorial entrants like McKenna have had to contend with. Sands used the example of attempts supported by Canada to enact an international land mines treaty. The Clinton administration and other countries said they would play ball but would have to maintain exemptions in places like Korea. For the Finns, an exemption would involve their border with Russia. Sands said that at the last minute, Foreign Affairs Minister Lloyd Axworthy said no to the idea of exemptions and the Clinton administration felt terribly betrayed. The Canadian move created a lot of bad blood. "You used to hear about three things: you used to hear about that [the land mines treaty], the Iraq decision and missile defence, as three areas in which Canada said they were willing to work with us and at the eleventh hour stabbed us in the back and complained loudly that it was a matter of principle and the Americans were being unfair in demanding more."

Sands believes that by changing the complaint rhetoric, McKenna could have emerged as a rare bilateralist, one who can be pragmatic in understanding both the Canadian and U.S. points of view. Brian Mulroney was close to being a bilateralist because his U.S. business experience gave him different insights from those of other significant

Canadians. But, Sands says, drawing on his in-depth knowledge of Canadian affairs, no one in Canadian history played the bilateralist role as skillfully as Sir John A. Macdonald. "He was the last great bilateralist." Sands believes that McKenna, even as ambassador versus as prime minister, could have become the great modern bilateralist because of his experience as New Brunswick premier—in which capacity he dealt with a string of New England governors—and his business experience on both sides of the border.

McKenna says that his most comfortable and successful experience working bilaterally was not in Washington, but rather with politicians and government officials he met from the states bordering Canada, beginning naturally enough with those closest to Atlantic Canada. "It's funny how you realize very quickly how values line up," McKenna says. "When I was in New England, it was like being back in Canada."

He established close friendships in particular with Vermont governor Jim Douglas and lieutenant-governor Brian Dubie. He also enjoyed effective and memorable relationships with Vermont senator Patrick Leahy, Maine senators Susan Collins and Olympia Snowe, Washington State senator Patty Murray and Minnesota's Norm Coleman, to name a few. And McKenna thinks the affinity was mutual.

He thinks in some ways these border state politicians feel closer to Canada than they do to Washington, D.C., and some other American states. "They just were totally aligned with Canada on all the issues. They have a lot of Canadian values and a lot of Canadian attributes. All the border state people would actually tend to be more liberal, more Canadian in their outlook, than their fellow countrymen."

All of the debating among Gotlieb, Sands, Robertson, Etzinger, McKenna and other interested players is purely rear-view mirror stuff, having no possible consequence for the future. When Paul Martin's government went down in defeat to Stephen Harper's Conservatives on January 23, 2006, McKenna knew immediately he had no choice but to resign. He did so within forty-eight hours. That sequence of events, leaving him as one of the most briefly serving ambassadors in the history of Canada-U.S. relations, meant that no one would ever know for sure how effective McKenna's diaspora, Connect2Canada and Brand Canada initiatives would have been. As it turns out, McKenna's bilateralist tendencies would have to be attempted through some other means—unless of course he decided to continue playing a role in public life.

IV · Public Candidate

NINETEEN

Escaping the Trap

*"I just want you to know, I'm here for one term and I'm going
to run like hell and at the end of that term, we are going to
have a leadership convention and I'm going to be replaced."*
WHAT FRANK McKENNA SAYS HE WOULD HAVE TOLD
CANADIANS HAD HE BECOME PRIME MINISTER

McKENNA FULLY ADMITS that he found his year in Washington as deeply
engaging, if not quite as satisfying, as his ten years as premier. "Everything else in between wasn't," he says, referring to the eight years he
spent out of public life. He describes the lure of public life as an
"intensity of emotion" that he likens to the kinship of soldiers in com-
bat. "Different stakes, obviously," he adds, "but the camaraderie and
the sense of mission is quite similar, in the sense of satisfaction for
accomplishment."

Every day that he worked as premier, McKenna felt intensely that
the work he was doing was important in a very tangible way, that it

really made a direct difference in the lives of people. "I just felt profoundly satisfied and moved by the experience and I hadn't had that during my eight or nine years in the private world. I was very well compensated and had very interesting challenges and it was an exciting and stimulating life, but it did not have the same degree of intense satisfaction. That was revived for me at the ambassador level. It was, for me, the equivalent of being either a premier or the prime minister of Canada, the level of power and the level of ability to influence."

McKenna thinks that in order to have been a truly effective ambassador, to have left a legacy, he would have needed at least four years on the ground in Washington, perhaps five. "I really would have liked to have had more time," he says. Still, he says that a year in that role was better than not having done it at all. "In a year we got a hell of a lot of interesting things done." And although he did not know exactly what he was going to do with his career, he did know what he was *not* going to do.

On January 30, 2006, just five days after he'd resigned as ambassador, McKenna convened a news conference (which was also carried as a teleconference) at the Canadian Embassy in Washington, during which he quickly put to rest the reams of speculation that he would seek the Liberal Party of Canada leadership following the federal general election defeat of Prime Minister Paul Martin just a week earlier. Flanked by wistful embassy staff and a backdrop of Canadian flags, he spoke to reporters.

I wish to formally advise that I will not be a candidate for the leadership of the Liberal Party of Canada.

When I left the job of premier of New Brunswick in 1997, I had spent fifteen years in public life: twelve years as leader of the

Liberal Party of New Brunswick, two years as leader of the opposition and ten years as premier.

This period was the most intensely fulfilling time of my life. Unfortunately, it was also the most completely absorbing experience of my life. I became addicted to my responsibilities—seven days a week, twenty-four hours a day. I was unable to find the appropriate balance then, and I am certain I would not be able to find the appropriate balance now.

I reminded myself this week of my vow upon leaving office that "having escaped the trap, I wouldn't go back for the cheese."

Contrary to the belief of some, being prime minister of Canada has not been a burning ambition for me. I didn't accept the position of ambassador in Washington to create a platform with such a motive. It was simply an opportunity to provide four more years of public service to my country.

Similarly, I did not resign from my position in Washington to pursue this goal.

This week, the result of the federal election and the resignation of the prime minister have forced me to give serious and immediate consideration to this opportunity.

I had to balance the enormous sense of obligation I felt to my party, my country, friends and supporters, with what was right for me and my family. It was clear that any aspirant for this office must look at a time commitment of eight to ten years.

I love my country and would do anything for it, but I am not vain enough to believe that I alone can provide the leadership that our great country and party need at this time. I've dedicated almost sixteen years to public service, and I was proud and humbled to do so. I have done my share.

Having made this decision, I feel an enormous sadness at being unable to honour the support and aspirations of so many close friends and supporters.

I know, however, in my heart, that I will have no regrets.

Like so many other Canadians, I stand ready to serve my country in other ways.

The delivery of these remarks, more than at any other time, vividly marked a change in Brand McKenna. Up to that moment, he existed in the eyes of most as a man with a purely political brand. Sure, he'd been out in the private sector for eight years and had played the role of ambassador for only one, but he still had a full-body political tattoo which not even his blue pinstripe suits could hide. But on that day, delivering his remarks from a carefully prepared text rather than winging it, Political Brand McKenna began to fade from view. The candles flickering for his leadership in the minds of his most fervent loyalists were being extinguished.

Nat Richard, who was present for McKenna's Washington announcement, says it was a heady, emotional time when his boss not only pulled up stakes in Washington but turned down the leadership opportunity, both events occurring within a heartbeat. It was emotional for the McKennas, for people like Richard, Steve MacKinnon and Ruth McCrea who were close to McKenna, for many of the embassy staff and for the staff at the ambassador's official residence.

"I was disappointed, but I also understood his decision," says Richard. "You know, I had just seen the guy go a hundred miles an hour when he was in the premier's office. Imagine what it would have been like in a [national] leadership campaign and then the [election] campaign and the toll it takes on a family." He knows that it is "unfair to expect more of someone who has given so much. But at the same time there is a kind of sadness."

On their last day at the residence before leaving Washington for Toronto, McKenna gathered the staff for a brief, informal gift-giving ceremony. After each was presented with a personalized gift, the group was shocked when McKenna suddenly jumped impromptu to his feet and announced, "I'm going to do a dance for you guys." With that, right out of the blue, "He got up, I swear, and danced a jig," says head-of-house Thomas Naylor. They all looked on in disbelief.

When asked about it, McKenna says that he is actually a terrible dancer. "I have no rhythm and no ear for music, but I absolutely love to dance and find it hard to keep my body still when music starts playing. All the time I was campaigning in the Province of New Brunswick, I used to dance my way down the aisles and later on stage. My wife and children have begged me not to do it, saying that I look absolutely ridiculous. However, it feels good and gives me a chance to express some of my joy at being in the company of people that I like." There exist a sufficient number of photographs and video clips of McKenna's public dancing outbursts to verify that what he says is true.

It seems nearly everyone shared the belief that McKenna would take a run at the leadership, but at no time had McKenna fully shown his cards. Richard says it was impossible to know what kind of thought process he was going through. "He never seemed to me that he was the kind of guy to just jump into things. He was very methodical, very rigorous in his thinking. There was a lot of speculation; I would talk to them [Steve MacKinnon, Ruth McCrea, Maurice Robichaud and Francis McGuire] on a regular basis on weekends and just compare notes on what might happen. I guess I always thought to the last minute that there was a chance."

There even came a point where, according to Richard, MacKinnon called McKenna and more or less implored him to run. When MacKinnon called Richard and Robichaud back, he was resigned. "Well, so much for that," he remarked. MacKinnon was very disappointed. Although he would go on to become national campaign director for Liberal leader Michael Ignatieff, MacKinnon would have quit his job in 2006 to support McKenna. He believes that if McKenna had chosen to run, his victory "would have been a slam dunk" at the 2006 leadership convention, which instead blundered into Stéphane Dion emerging as the winner.

As Nat Richard attests, MacKinnon called McKenna many times in both 2006 and in 2008, intent on persuading him to run. "The line that stayed with me was that there was no political reason for running that outweighs the personal reasons for not running," says Richard. Beyond that, the only specific reason MacKinnon could guess at would have to do with McKenna's being "spooked by Quebec" as a result of his involvement in the Meech Lake Accord and his lack of proficiency in the French language.

MacKinnon adds that, in spite of any concerns about McKenna's French or about Meech, "he was confident throughout all of our conversations that the political viability was there. I can tell you there were hundreds of Liberals who were phoning and emailing and urging him" to run. Many of those pleas were made directly to and through MacKinnon. He says that Frank McKenna has a vast fan club even though he never set down deep roots in the Liberal Party of Canada. "The irony is that the very party he would have had to lead didn't know him very well. People had this intuitive sense about him."

McKenna had somehow even managed to transcend some of the ethno-cultural differences existing in Canada. MacKinnon points out McKenna's specific ability to rise above the political divide between Canada's Jewish and Muslim leadership, both of which were calling upon him to run.

In one in a string of personal calls he made to friends and associates following his leadership announcement, McKenna reached former U.S. ambassador to Canada David Wilkins before it could be heard on the news. "Damn, Frank," said Wilkins, "you're the only guy in Canada that likes me and now you're leaving." McKenna laughed. A few weeks later McKenna was in Ottawa and made a point of calling Wilkins to say: "I'm looking for a job. You know of any? You got any good tips for me?" "He left me laughing," says Wilkins.

Just after McKenna tendered his resignation to Prime Minister Stephen Harper, he and Julie enjoyed a dinner with Jim Blanchard and his wife. Blanchard recalls McKenna talking about the reasons he would not run for the Liberal leadership: his age and the possibility of being stuck as leader of the official opposition for four or more years. Blanchard understood completely, recognizing that for some people sixty can be among the most productive years of one's life, while sixty-five or sixty-six may not offer the same energy level. "Meanwhile," McKenna told Blanchard, "I'm missing my family, my wife, I've got grand-kids and I'm not prepared to give up the best years of my life as a leader of the opposition."

Blanchard understood McKenna's wisdom. He knows that there is a cycle to politics in Canada and that the cycle had turned to the Conservative party. He also realized McKenna would have to kick his way through the leadership race. It wouldn't just be handed to him. Everybody would be trying to knock him off. He'd be the definitive front-runner and they'd all be taking shots at him, framing him as being too pro-business, not liberal enough, from a small province, an "Ameriphile."

Other friends and associates at home in Canada were wistful, contemplative and deeply sad over McKenna's decision. David Peterson says he was mad, then quickly changes his verbiage. "I was *sad* at him," he says.

The McKennas and the Petersons now live within a breath of one another on the same Rosedale street. But they represented wholly separate and different parts of Canadian society when they first met after Liberal leader John Turner was wiped out in the 1984 federal election by Progressive Conservative Brian Mulroney. The talk in political circles was that the various provincial Liberal interests were going to be wiped out too. In spite of that prediction, Peterson managed to get elected as the only Liberal premier in Canada within two years of Mulroney's rise to power. He was followed into office by Quebec premier Robert Bourassa, then McKenna, then PEI's Joe Ghiz. "There was this inevitable sort of curve" which formed, Peterson says, with the trend swinging toward Liberal politics in much of the country.

Peterson knows what it's like inside the vortex of provincial politics—but on a much larger scale than McKenna, Ontario being the big provincial enchilada. "It's fun having the power, although I don't miss the lifestyle at all," he says, echoing McKenna's own distaste for certain aspects of the political game. "But it is awfully exhilarating to have the power to do good things and do what you want to do. I understand that there's a half of Frank that was just like a dog ready to run because he's competitive and he's aggressive and he cares passionately about public policy and he likes the life." But then there's another half to McKenna, who Peterson believes can find stimulation in areas beyond front-line politics.

Peterson adds that McKenna didn't need to run to feed his ego. "There are some people in the race that are needy. They need absolution. That is not Frank. He's been there, done that. He's had his fair share of success and he's very at peace with his own ambitions and his own ego and his own self-esteem." He also talks about McKenna's focus on his children and grandchildren to the extent that "he is depressingly normal. Frank enjoys the benefits of having power, but he is not one of those guys hanging on by his fingernails. He understands the cycles of life and the evolution of life. And he will go to his next thing with grace, not kicking and screaming."

Peterson says there is no end to the things people like McKenna are asked to join or commit to or support because "he's a big league guy." One has to make choices by being selective and keeping a little space open for something really interesting, something that really appeals to you personally. "You always keep a little emotional and intellectual space in your life so if something comes along that's really fun, well..." Clearly, if one becomes a head of state, not much emotional and intellectual space is left in one's daily life beyond what the job occupies. If Peterson is correct, then the predicament of being prime minister would not have appealed to McKenna.

Before he dispelled it, everybody had been talking about Frank McKenna and the federal Liberal leadership. Columnists, reporters and editors across Canada seized on the prospect of a McKenna candidacy faster than you could say "coronation." Paul Martin's defeat in the January 2006 federal election brought about not only McKenna's resignation as ambassador (which L. Ian MacDonald, in a *Montreal Gazette* op-ed piece, called "elegant"), but also an avalanche of spontaneous speculation about his plan to run for the national Liberal leadership. Saint John *Telegraph-Journal* columnist Carl Davies aptly coined it "The McKenna Watch."

Globe and Mail columnist Jeffrey Simpson wrote about McKenna as having "gravitas." Others agreed that his seriousness, virtue, sense of duty and ability to garner respect could have combined to reset the standard for Canadian politicians. Political, business and media heavy-weights examined and offered their opinions on how and why he was able to leave public office on such a high road, and many offered their theories about what they think drives McKenna and what makes him so apparently different from other politicians of his generation.

In the business section of the Moncton *Times & Transcript,* journalist Alec Bruce said that after resigning McKenna would return to Canada with a unique combination of electoral success and foreign policy acumen, and a record of economic expansion. "He remains the finest stump speaker of the past twenty years, a considerable asset given the shrill fare that has passed for passion among electoral contenders over the past eight weeks." He then foretold what was about to happen in reaction to McKenna's forthcoming decision not to seek the leadership. "If in the end," wrote Bruce, "McKenna chooses not to run, it will be to the astonishment of exactly everyone."

The Saint John *Telegraph-Journal* editorial writers had appealed directly to McKenna's heart in their estimation of events to come in Ottawa. The editorial appeared under the headline "McKenna: Go for it." "Timing is everything in politics," it read. "And Frank McKenna has the impeccable timing of a ballroom dancer...Mr. McKenna will make an excellent candidate. He has the vigour and the vision to provide a necessary contrast with Stephen Harper and the Conservatives. We encourage him to enter the leadership race whenever it commences."

But the *T-J,* as it's affectionately known in New Brunswick, was also quick and careful to point out that a Liberal coronation would not be a healthy outcome, citing Martin's slide into the Liberal leadership as "an inside job." The paper reflected on the aging anecdote that for his first election campaign, at Sussex Regional High School in New Brunswick, McKenna's campaign slogan had been "More dances with Francis." "It appears likely New Brunswick and Canada will get at least one more dance. We expect Mr. McKenna's timing will still be there."

Carl Davies was one of the earliest journalists on the McKenna Watch. A full year before Martin's fall and McKenna's resignation, Davies had written in his "Capital Notebook" column in the *Telegraph-Journal* about Martin and McKenna at former New Brunswick premier Louis Robichaud's funeral, where they had dodged questions about the possibility of McKenna being named ambassador. Davies noted that, earlier, Martin had envisaged McKenna in federal politics as his lieutenant. But, after a very public, patient period of waiting, McKenna chose not to run after Moncton MP Claudette Bradshaw's decision to keep her seat rather than vacating it to make space for him. Martin's luring of McKenna to run federally seemed "prescient" by the time Martin was on his way out and the McKenna Watch was on. If McKenna was going to play a role federally, it was certainly not in the fashion that Martin had imagined.

Davies went on to say that one factor attracting people to a McKenna candidacy was his reputation for standing up to any challenge. "If there was ever a job for Frank McKenna," Davies concluded, "this is it." On the other hand, Davies ably predicted what would eventually happen in the 2006 Liberal leadership race, with a battalion of contenders lining up for what in hindsight was a disastrous convention outcome with Stéphane Dion as the chosen one. "Every contender can expect to take their lumps in such a contest," Davies predicted, "and Mr. McKenna has to decide whether he wants to put himself and his family through the public wringer." One might think McKenna had read Davies's column and taken it all to heart.

Of course, the McKenna Watch was not all one-sided. *Ottawa Citizen* writer Susan Riley disagreed with most other pundits, calling the prize Ignatieff's instead of McKenna's. "The job belongs to

Ignatieff," she wrote. "According to an ancient, sacred narrative that governs all of these contests, he is destined for greatness." Riley also quipped sarcastically that if McKenna were chosen leader and elected prime minister, he "could do for the country what he did for his province: make Canada the call-centre capital of the world." This was framed as a dig against the strategy employed by McKenna, the New Brunswick Department of Economic Development and Tourism and NBTel in the mid-1990s to attract call centres to the province, a move criticized by some for bringing low-paying jobs rather than providing a bigger boost to the manufacturing sector in areas such as value-added wood products.

This mountain of media attention would never have happened if not for one undeniable fact: Frank McKenna has charisma. Only when pressed will he discuss it: "I think it's passion, and passion is not something you can put on and take off, so you can't just tell somebody, 'Become passionate.' I've always been really passionate about the things I believe in. And so when I speak, I wouldn't have the soaring rhetoric of an Obama. For me, it would always tend to be, what's in there just pours out. That's why I very seldom read a speech. It's just kind of a stream of consciousness. What I think is what you're going to get."

The McKenna Watch aside, though, there is plenty of first- and second-hand evidence that he was seriously considering a run at the leadership. "Scotty" Greenwood thought for sure that McKenna would run—and with good reason. In 2006, the two had a dinner together during which they talked about politician and journalist Carole Taylor. Under completely differing circumstances, each of them had been in Taylor's hometown of Vancouver that same day. Greenwood remarked to McKenna on what a remarkable talent Taylor is, adding that she imagined McKenna running for the leadership with the likes of Taylor on his team. Greenwood and McKenna went on to list others who would fit the bill. "And," recalls Greenwood, "he goes, 'Yeah, totally, I was thinking the same thing myself.'"

Just as she was perplexed on first meeting him that a politician would voluntarily leave office on such a high, Greenwood was just plain puzzled that McKenna—so ready-made for the role of prime minister—would not chase the prize. She says she continually asks herself: "What is his agenda?"

His box of Washington records and memorabilia from his year as ambassador contains a set of revealing handwritten notes illustrating his thought process surrounding the leadership question. The notes are scrawled in erratically written columns headed by the under-scored words "Pros," "Cons," "Reasons" and "Vision." Also scribbled in and around the columns are familiar but unexplained names such as (former U.S. secretary of state) Colin Powell and (Quebec premier and former national Progressive Conservative leader) Jean Charest. He was obviously thinking about these men in the light of their respective one-time federal leadership prospects. Some of these lists and notations are hard to decipher, but together they provide a clearer picture of just what McKenna was thinking at the time.

The "Pros" column is the most brief of the four:

- Excite friends, family and supporters
- Honour and reputation
- Chance to do great things for Canada
- Satisfaction

The "Cons" list by far outstrips the foregoing:

- Financial
- Lack of French
- Referendum
- Leader debates

- Endless campaigning
- Scrutiny of private life
- Scrutiny of finances
- Limited opportunity for vacation, travel and family
- Baggage—N.B. record, French businesses
- Unrelenting negativity
- Loss of respect and reputation
- Can't do a lot of things want to do
- Leadership, two elections, 36–48 months
- Referendum
- Minority government

The "Reasons" column includes:

- Private life
- Heart-breaking decision for me of disappointing people who believe in me
- I've contributed my share
- Save the country—I haven't seen evidence it needs saving
- Compelling—country at risk—Party not enough

The "Vision" list appears on a separate page and includes items listed under three headings:

- Environment—(words are obscured); AITA technologies
- National—Energy grid; Highways; Trails; Health Technologies; Single
- Securities
- Health—World class technologies covering everything; Competing at service delivery level, Liberal Party and universality

It should not be forgotten that the McKennas had gone through a good deal of personal upheaval by moving to Washington and then moving back to Toronto, all within the course of a year. And it involved more than moving just the clothes on their backs. In order to clear the decks for Frank's appointment, the McKennas made huge sacrifices by ridding themselves of stock options, selling shares in companies and putting everything into trust. So was the job really worth all that trouble and cost? "We really didn't care about that as much. I mean, the interesting nature of the work and the potential for a whole different kind of life was much more than compensation for the financial changes," says Julie. "But we couldn't afford it again, not at this stage of our lives."

McKenna concurs. When you grow up a little bit poor, you always want to make sure there's enough to look after yourself. "I still look for golf balls because I don't know when I'm going to get my next free ones," McKenna half-jokes. In fact, he does have a tendency to wander and scout for balls on the fringe of a course while other players are lining up and taking their shots.

But of all the items that appear in his lists, the most intriguing may be the simple word "compelling." It speaks to McKenna's remarks about the differences between the U.S. and Canada when it comes to the gravity and magnitude of events that shape each country. In U.S. politics, there's a constant: what McKenna refers to as "a searing trauma" which he says is always at play, making it irresistible for men and women of a certain political ilk to chase the U.S. presidency. In Canada, there is rarely such drama or distress by which to create "an emotional framework" to compel leadership or "to judge our leaders." The question re-emerges as to whether—after the variety and depth of issues he confronted in Washington, the stimulus he felt, the people he encountered and the world of possibilities at his feet—McKenna saw becoming prime minister of Canada as less compelling by comparison. Two and a half years after writing those notes, McKenna remains clear about both his decision and his rationale. In a May 2009 interview on CBC's *The Hour*, he told host George

Stroumboulopoulos that he would consider a run at federal politics only if the nation were in crisis.

But there was so much more to consider, McKenna says. "You'd have to go through rebuilding your party. You'd have to do all of the finances of the party, which are in terrible shape. You'd have to go through an election where you may end up in a minority situation. You'd have to devote two, three or four years of your life to getting this thing in the right place. You'd have to go across the country and go to every country fair and be in every parade and shake every hand and do all of the stuff that I had to do in New Brunswick."

He says that for some who are enamoured with politics, those actions are reward in themselves: the attention and the spotlight, the ego stuff. For them, just winning an election is enough. Some, he says, revel so much in winning elections that the moment they win, they begin their campaign for the next election. "For me, that was just totally irrelevant. That was all part of getting there to be able to do what you wanted to do, and I've always been clear about that. To me, the day the election was over, it was: 'In the office, start working and we don't have time to waste.'" Although he loved the contact with the people, the rebuilding and fundraising and campaigning simply take valuable time away from getting the job done. If McKenna had believed for a moment that the track to the actual job of prime minister might have been shorter than what his analysis showed, he probably would have leapt at the job.

Richard remembers McKenna asking him to investigate the history and precedents of minority governments in Canada, including details like their duration and the circumstances leading into and out of minorities. "I think he was trying to work into his mind what the various scenarios might be." One of the key points that his research revealed was that of the nine minority governments since

Confederation up to 2006, most had followed with a majority prize in the subsequent election, an exception being Paul Martin's campaign in 2006. The suggestion that Stephen Harper would likely take a majority as a result of his second election run would not have turned McKenna on about his own prospects. He had no desire to sit in opposition for a week, let alone potentially years. It would have frustrated the hell out of him.

Another observation in the document Richard prepared for McKenna was that the current situation resembled the volatile period between 1957 and 1963, which saw four elections in just six years, three of which produced minority governments. Interestingly, the paper subtly shows a slight bias on Richard's part: he notes that in spite of all the seeming reasons not to wade into a minority government circumstance, "No one predicted the historic 1987 clean sweep in New Brunswick, either." It was as though Richard was hinting to McKenna that he should ignore the facts and go with his gut.

As he examined the Liberal leadership question, the matter of Meech Lake and its potential impact on his candidacy in an election had to have been lurking in the back of McKenna's mind. Brian Mulroney believes McKenna would have suffered in Quebec at the hands of the media and intellectuals, who could have persuaded Quebeckers to vote against his team. "Look," says Mulroney, "[Justin] Trudeau got killed" in the riding of Papineau by francophones during the 2008 election, and only the multicultural elements of the riding allowed him to win his seat. "Justin is a fine man, but people don't forget" something like the position Trudeau's father, Pierre Elliott, took on Meech. "It will come to light. It'll bounce back any time there's a crisis."

Nevertheless, Mulroney believes that if McKenna had run for the Liberal leadership, he would have been "a formidable force in federal politics." But he understands the choice McKenna made. "You have to be careful you don't throw away a lifetime of achievement just to lead a party."

Steve MacKinnon agrees that McKenna's linkage to the Meech failure would have come back to haunt him in Quebec, coupled with his limited capacity in the French language—and McKenna would not have relished having to devote six or seven months to improving his fluency. Jeffrey Simpson also thought McKenna's lack of proficiency in French was a detriment to his candidacy, but not to the degree that he thought he wouldn't win.

MacKinnon says McKenna now sees that he should have ratified Meech immediately in 1987. "I think it haunts him. I know it haunts him," just as it haunts Mulroney. "I think it intimidated him and he is not easily intimidated. Even though Frank did everything he could to save it and Mulroney owes him a great deal for even getting it to where it got, Meech Lake would have been a big problem."

So why was MacKinnon so confident of a McKenna Liberal leadership and election as prime minister? He responds with a question of his own. "How did Stephen Harper—who had a bigoted, narrow, small view of Quebec during that episode—get to be prime minister? Harper said and wrote things about Quebec and bilingualism, and the list goes on, that would make you shiver. But somehow he managed to skate by all of those things to become prime minister." Surely McKenna could have overcome his two obstacles to election success in Quebec.

McKenna agrees. He says he knew who, during a leadership race or election campaign, would have tried to stir up the Meech topic in Quebec, but he believes he could have managed to clarify publicly that he actually signed Meech Lake and always supported Quebec's aspirations. "Stephen Harper was totally opposed to Meech Lake, as was Jean Chrétien. So how could it hurt me?"

FRANK McKENNA ·

MacKinnon says that the bar is traditionally higher for Conservatives in Quebec—"It's expected you're a bigot"—whereas Quebeckers don't have the same suspicion of Liberals, even in the context of a discussion about Meech.

Henry Champ weighs in on this point, recalling how Harper's pollsters mined the right emotional messages to use in Montreal-area ridings in the 2006 federal election. In spite of some of the perceptions of him as a western bigot, Harper was able, for that moment at least, to sway enough voters to help him in Quebec.

Nevertheless, Champ doesn't buy MacKinnon's notion that Meech would have hurt McKenna had he chosen to run. "I don't think that's a big deal," he says. "I don't think Meech kills anybody anymore. It's my guess, but I think his popularity and the fact that he's a nice guy would have carried."

Don Newman concurs. With McKenna still topical as a candidate when the second window for the Liberal leadership opened in the fall of 2008, Newman had spoken to people in Quebec who'd been around for a long time and knew the turf. It was their consensus that most people had forgotten about Meech. "I don't think it matters so much," he says. He even adds that, in an odd way, McKenna's national celebrity is partly owed to Meech Lake. "And by and large, maybe with the exception of Quebec, he was seen as playing a positive role on Meech Lake, even though Meech Lake wasn't very popular. But he kind of got it both ways, right? Because he didn't go along with it in its pure form, but his changes were seen as improving it. Plus, I think, the political landscape in Quebec is such that the Bloc Québécois is going to win a lot of seats no matter who the Liberals and Conservatives put forward." No matter what, the competition is for only about twenty-five seats.

But then Newman turns to the very existence of the Bloc Québécois—to which, strangely enough, he sees a clear McKenna tie-in. The succession of events from New Brunswick's failure to ratify Meech to the drafting of the companion accord triggered federal Progressive Conservative Lucien Bouchard's departure from Ottawa and his subsequent formation of the Bloc. "I'm not blaming him," says Newman of McKenna. "I'm just saying it's interesting, but it also illustrates how the country is so different, even in neighbouring provinces like New Brunswick and Quebec."

With the hard fall of Liberal leader Stéphane Dion following his October 2008 election defeat to Conservative Stephen Harper, McKenna was again faced with an onslaught of telephone calls, emails and public calls for him to reconsider the conclusion he'd drawn just twenty-one months earlier. The leadership question loomed large again.

TD Bank vice-president James Dodds accompanied McKenna to California that fall, when front-page stories at home were declaring McKenna the front-runner in the Liberal leadership race. "Thousands of emails and endless telephone calls were coming in. It was great to get away for a day or two," says Dodds. The bank was deluged with calls.

Although he joked that he would vote for McKenna, Dodds knew it was not in his bank's best interests to lose him. Although he does not pretend to have influenced McKenna's decision in any way, he did offer just one bit of advice. "My only comment, passed on to him several times," says Dodds, "was that everyone always thinks you can only contribute to public policy and public life through politics. Don't underestimate the contribution you make now."

McKenna wasted no time ending the speculation. This second time around, on October 28, 2008, he answered his suitors with only a brief written statement. There was no news conference, and the release closed with the resolute message that he would not be available for media interviews.

"Although I have been deeply moved by expressions of support for me from across the country, I have not been persuaded to change my long-standing resolve to exit public life for good. My only regret is that I cannot honour the expectations of friends and supporters who have shown enormous loyalty to me. The challenge of winning the leadership, restoring the health of the Liberal Party and returning a Liberal majority government requires a longer time commitment than I am prepared to make. There will be an ample number of well-qualified candidates to do this important work."

One of the first people to call McKenna after this announcement was Bill Clinton, who was in Pennsylvania campaigning for Barack Obama at the time. "Look," he said, "the bad news is, the country is not going to have you. The good news is, I am going to have more time with you." McKenna will never forget receiving the call, one of a number of interactions and gestures demonstrating that their relationship goes well beyond the events they have staged together. "The Clinton relationship is real," says Dodds, an observation he makes after having logged many hours flying with the two on Clinton's plane.

When McKenna chose for the second time not to run, Michael Ignatieff assumed front-runner status. "So what happens to the front-runner immediately in this country?" asks McKenna. "We try to bring the front-runner down. Everybody gangs up and they do what they have to do" to try and win for themselves. For McKenna, a leadership run, a convention, a campaign and the fixing of the party would have amounted to one thing: "a painful exercise." Some suggested that if McKenna had chosen to run, people would have stepped aside for him. But he knew that that type of thinking was delusional. "So you'd get to the convention floor and you'd have no idea. Two or three people could conspire with concessions that you have no idea about," which is exactly how the Liberals ended up with Stéphane Dion as their leader in 2006, when no-name leadership contender Gerard Kennedy walked his delegates across the floor.

Concerning his decisions not to run, McKenna said at the time: "Well, to somewhat paraphrase and perhaps mangle Mark Twain, the prospect of success does wonders to fixate your mind. I've never been more humbled in my life than [by] some of the kind things that were said to me this week. But it does require that you concentrate on it very, very quickly and it is emotional just because so many people seem to hold such high hopes for me. But, at the end of the day, I've been there. I've been at the centre of the storm a long time. I'm a veteran of the free trade debate, of Meech Lake, of [the failed] Charlottetown [Accord], of [the] Calgary declaration, of some of the great debates of our time. And I know what it takes from you. And I had to balance that against the opportunity to spend more time with friends and family, to watch my grandchildren grow—you know, to do things that are meaningful and to do things that would be good for my country but perhaps not at the level of service."

In fact, McKenna says, he would have gone for the job if not for the campaigning, the daunting party-rebuilding and the prospect of winding up in a minority government for several years. So McKenna's real addiction to politics is in doing the job, not in getting the job, whereas some politicians relish the adulation of being at the centre of a campaign. For McKenna, campaigning was just a necessary require- ment, a necessary evil almost, for earning the chance to be premier.

Nat Richard knows one thing for certain: one of the most diffi- cult things about the career decisions McKenna has made during the past two years has been his inner sense of letting people down by not running. Julie shares this sentiment, saying it was very difficult for her husband to say no because of other people's belief in him.

"He was under a lot of pressure, and from people that he loved. A lot of people very close to him put a lot of pressure on him, and that's why he even took the time to consider it, because he felt he owed them that."

There are, no doubt, those who immediately assumed that Julie was one of the obstacles, or perhaps *the* obstacle, to his running for the leadership, but she swears nothing could be further from the truth. "You'll be very surprised at this," she says, "but I had no part in this latest decision. I was like, 'Do whatever you want. If you want to go for this leadership, go for it. If that's what you want to do, you should do it.' But I knew he was never going to do it." Julie says it's something nobody else understands unless they have lived the life of a political junkie or been married to one. She says residing at 24 Sussex Drive was never in the cards for them. "He wanted to be premier, but he never wanted to be prime minister. I never heard him say it. He knows what the job is. It is not a fun job. You see, you have to really want to do it. In the end, he did not really want to do it. This has never been a burning ambition for him."

If her husband had gone for the leadership, Julie says, she would have simply adjusted to it like she has every other situation they've experienced as a couple. Sometimes such decisions are undertaken on blind faith. McKenna's decision to take the ambassadorship and move to Washington, she adds, was more or less like that.

McKenna says Julie would have been fine with him running federally and even being prime minister, "but it wouldn't be what she wanted." At the end of the day, he also swears not running had nothing to do with any opposition from her. As evidence, he points to the effort she put into her roles as a premier's and an ambassador's wife.

McKenna talks about his friend David Wilkins who, in an interesting parallel, had to announce in the fall of 2008 that he would not be seeking the governorship of South Carolina after he left his ambassadorial posting in Ottawa. "He said the most painful thing for him was making the twenty-five phone calls to people who were really invested in him doing that."

That is exactly how McKenna felt. "These were people who don't want anything" for themselves, he concluded; they wanted him to run for the sake of the country. He named businessman Wallace McCain as one of many examples: it broke McKenna's heart when he had to call him to say it was a no-go.

Like so many others, McCain had tried to persuade McKenna to go for it. "I'd like you to do it, but it's your call," he told McKenna. He says that everywhere he travelled in Canada during the past few years, people from coast to coast, "no matter where you go," always wanted to know, "When is Frank going to run?"

McCain says that if elected, Michael Ignatieff will do a good job, but "Frank is a better vote-getter, including in Alberta. He would have picked up two to three seats in Alberta." McCain still believes in his heart that McKenna will never leave politics behind entirely. "Count on it," he says. "Guaranteed."

Mike Duffy didn't see McKenna organizing and winning quite so easily. He recalls how Paul Martin had eight to ten people working with him for a decade, visiting every riding association and visiting every prominent Liberal in existence, to position him for the job. "Frank hasn't spent the last ten years with a secret army on the ground," says Duffy. "There is no secret society of underground workers in Timiskaming and High River." He added that the "hoops and contortions" McKenna would have had to go through to win against the long term party-building of Bob Rae and Michael Ignatieff would have been monumental. Duffy is right: this second time it was different because Ignatieff and Rae had built up organizations and equity, and they weren't about to give them up.

David Peterson admits that McKenna did not organize for a campaign because he never intended to run. A lot of people asked Peterson if he was going to run the McKenna campaign. "No," he told them. "'Is there an organization?' they asked. 'No.' 'Could one be formed?' they asked. And I said, 'It would only take half an hour.'"

Organization or no organization, Duffy says there were other potential obstacles to winning. "Trudeau could not win today the way he won before unless something dramatic were to happen at the convention floor." He said these are the reasons Newfoundland's Brian Tobin did not run. "He discovered he couldn't win. I'm a huge Frank fan," adds Duffy, now able to say so after his media career, "but I do not underestimate the obstacles," including the fact that Ignatieff would never give up easily to McKenna's popularity. But, Duffy says wistfully, "Without Frank, what are we left with?"

Don Newman thinks McKenna was feeling the pull to look at the leadership question out of a sense of duty. "He does have a sense of duty to do it because people are telling him that he has a duty to do it." But is that the right reason for someone to commit their lives to a task so large? "I counsel anybody who is told they have a sense of duty [that] if they don't *feel* they have a sense of duty, then they probably don't." Newman believes McKenna spent a lot of time wondering whether he felt a powerful enough sense of duty. "But I think, bottom line," he says, "if he thought (a) that he would win and (b) that the party would win the next election and hopefully with a majority, then he would have had a hard time saying no. But you can't guarantee anything." Newman talked about the unpredictable and odd dynamics of a nominating convention, which, if you take the 2006 version as an example, is like a crapshoot with all the names and games involved. The thing Frank McKenna would not want to have done was spend the precious decade he is currently in—leading to his seventies—fixing the Liberal party for some successor.

McKenna believes he could have won the leadership. He stresses that this belief is not derived from vanity, but rather a lesson learned early on in provincial politics: during his run at the New Brunswick Liberal leadership against favoured front-runner Raymond Frenette, he learned to read polls and become an effective campaigner. Although the lesson is not a direct parallel to winning the federal leadership and then the job of prime minister, it did teach McKenna to examine things from more than one perspective. Doing so allowed him to see that he could win, but not necessarily a majority. And that became the turning point in his decision not to run.

On a CBC political panel in 2008, when McKenna's name was again being bandied about for the federal leadership, pollster Allan Gregg told national news anchor Peter Mansbridge that he felt McKenna did not have the stomach for the job. McKenna says Gregg was partially right. "I couldn't disagree with him. I don't have the stomach for the process to get to the real job I would want. I would have liked to have gone in. I would have liked to have gone into that job and announce right at the outset, 'I just want you to know, I'm here for one term and I'm going to run like hell and at the end of that term, we are going to have a leadership convention and I'm going to be replaced.'" Unlike other politicians, he would likely have been believed: such a scenario would have mirrored the promise he'd made and kept when elected premier of New Brunswick—his unheard-of and now-legendary ten-year pledge.

McKenna explains that a federal fixed-term pledge would have been used as an instrument in focusing the entire energy of the public service and the political apparatus. By creating his own built-in limitation on his time in office, he would not be doing things for the express purpose of seeking re-election. So it wasn't about politics. It was about providing a service.

After Michael Ignatieff was crowned Liberal leader, no contest, in 2009, McKenna said that what the Liberal party now has is "clearly the most cerebral leader that we have had since Pierre Trudeau. He is very intellectually curious, grasps complex policy ideas very quickly and is working assiduously to rebuild the party from the grassroots. He has a large appetite for work and has proven very adroit in managing various political constituencies. He has the makings of a very strong political leader."

V · The Public Eye

TWENTY

Banker's Hours

"He was so unusual for a politician. He delivered
everything he said he was going to deliver."

TD BANK PRESIDENT AND CEO ED CLARK ON HIS FIRST
ENCOUNTER AND BUSINESS TRANSACTION WITH THEN
PREMIER FRANK McKENNA IN THE MID-1990S

SO MUCH FOR the myth of "banker's hours." Now that he is deputy chair of TD Bank, McKenna's days are chock full of meetings, travel and speaking engagements.

As evidence of just how busy he is, a bound itinerary atop his desk lists where he's going to be week to week, day to day for the next two years.

He came to TD at the urging of President and CEO Ed Clark, whom David Peterson describes as "arguably the most cerebral and smartest banker on the street." Peterson credits Clark with protecting TD from much of the turmoil that consumed major bankers before and into the recent recession, simultaneously engineering the bank's segue into the U.S. marketplace. "Ed is a very bright guy. Ed's brilliance brought him to the conclusion that Frank would be a wonderful vice-chair. Frank is not a banker by disposition, but he is a brilliant leader, he is very well liked and he does a lot of the speaking and social things," which of course he thrives on. "It's not just that he is a pretty face; he's substantive. He also shows the ephemeral side of leadership, the passion side, the vision side. They went together. I've seen guys with lots of vision and no execution. I see guys with execution and no vision. But he is in a sense the complete package." Peterson says McKenna can create client interface because he can get an audience with anybody in Canada, and increasingly, since his time as ambassador, he can open doors because of his networking achievements in the U.S.

Peterson explains how a traditional, conservative banker and a flamboyant politician get along so well. First of all, Clark is said to be very interested in public policy, which is what essentially drives McKenna. So they have that in common. "Frank is very respectful of Ed and Ed is very respectful of Frank, so they are not stepping on one another's space. I mean, Ed's the banker and Frank brings leadership skills. He brings cachet. Clients love him," says Peterson. And McKenna has developed a Rolodex like few others: it contains the direct coordinates for the likes of Bill Clinton, George W. Bush and Tony Blair. "Nobody is saying, 'Who's that rube from New Brunswick?' They're saying, 'Boy, that guy's good.'"

For his part, Ed Clark had been courting McKenna for years, even before McKenna's appointment as ambassador. In fact, Clark had made overtures to McKenna two or three times before the Washington opportunity arose, but at the time there was a conflict because McKenna sat on the board of directors for the Bank of Montreal. "I'm not sure that I understand the job," he reports saying at the time, "and I don't think I could do it anyway."

FRANK McKENNA ·

But the connection between Clark and McKenna dates back to McKenna's days as New Brunswick premier, when Clark was heading Canada Trust before that company's 2000 merger with Toronto-Dominion Bank. "He called me up and said 'I'm going to be in Toronto,'" Clark recalls. Clark agreed to an appointment in his Toronto office—a meeting that he never forgot. "He thrust himself into my office and said, 'I want to do business. What would it take to move jobs to New Brunswick?'" Clark was persuaded to situate between sixty and seventy people at a call centre in Saint John. In early 2009, the call centre employed more than 275 people and is on track to reach 400 soon.

"I was quite struck," reflects Clark. "He was so unusual for a politician. He delivered everything he said he was going to deliver. He had an eye for business." He told Clark, "You're in the business of making money, and I'm into creating jobs."

From that point, "I sort of watched his career," says Clark. "I just knew he would fit at TD. Most politicians have such huge ego needs that they can't sit in a meeting without saying, 'Isn't this all about me?' Of course Frank has ego needs. We all have ego needs." But he says McKenna can sit in a meeting and learn as he goes. "He has an inquisitive mind. He'll listen but he can also be opinionated."

One of the things Clark seems to like most about McKenna is what he calls his "typical Maritime charm," which allows McKenna to be blunt with people when he needs to be—but they'll still come away liking him. "It is a huge asset and he has it in spades," says Clark. "There are very few people [at his level] in Canada that everybody likes, but everybody likes and respects Frank. And it's not like he just smiles and agrees with everybody."

When the ambassadorial appointment came in 2005, Clark says he simply parked the notion of having McKenna on his team at TD, "but I kept my oar in with him." (One who had been touting McKenna to Clark along the way was Wallace McCain.) When the ambassadorial stint ended prematurely and McKenna was being stalked for the national Liberal leadership, Clark said that as a Canadian he felt it would be phenomenal to see him run, but it would also be phenomenal should he choose to come and work at TD. "I understand in human terms why you would not want to run for that job," says Clark. "When it was clear he was not running, I called and said, 'I'm here, let's cut a deal.'" Canada's business elite had learned about McKenna's skills as a director on countless corporate boards, so it was no surprise to Clark that McKenna would be effective at TD board meetings. "Everybody says he's the best board member they've ever had."

The role at TD was built for McKenna. There was no deputy chair prior to his appointment, so he and Clark were able to shape the job as they went. Not only does McKenna represent the bank when Clark is unable to do so; he also has a multiplicity of roles in dealing with TD Securities and commercial clients as well as in instilling leadership within the ranks of the company. "Internal staff love to hear him talk."

McKenna's message is simple and explicit: leadership matters. "Compare Mugabe to Mandela," says Clark. "For everything in life, people can make a difference"—starting with having the right value system.

There is no such thing as a typical or an uneventful day for McKenna in his life at TD Bank. In the hours before we met in his office he'd already put in more than a full day's work: he met with a deputy minister from Ottawa who was seeking advice because of trouble moving some major projects along; then he had a call with a multi-billionaire entrepreneur who wanted to work out collaborative relationships with several Atlantic Canada universities; then he met with a group of Norwegian investors looking at a billion-dollar investment in Atlantic Canada; then he took a call from a headhunter offering the presidency of a college; then a call from another head-hunter seeking a character reference on a prospective employee; then a call from an accountant closing out the year-end for McKenna's Glenwood Kitchen company. The evening before, he had given a speech in Toronto on financial literacy—one of about a hundred speeches he gives annually.

From his two-year schedule he randomly picked an upcoming Monday. At eight, he was to meet the president of Grant Thornton; at nine he had a meeting with Liberal MP Dominic LeBlanc; at ten, he had an internal bank management meeting; at eleven a strategy session, and at four in the afternoon, he was set to address a private event being held at Massey College. It goes on and on and on. "Yeah, it's just relentless," he admits.

It doesn't hurt that McKenna is on board while TD initiates its U.S. market expansion strategy, symbolized, for example, by the newly branded TD Garden sports and entertainment complex—previously known as the Fleet Center—which serves as the home of the NHL Boston Bruins and the NBA Boston Celtics. "It's truly astounding to me how he did that in one year," says Clark, referring to McKenna's relationship inroads during his one year as ambassador. "If someone had been there for ten years they wouldn't have his contacts. You can send him anywhere." McKenna is very useful to a company which has more branches in the U.S. than it does in Canada.

When they attend events together, Clark treats McKenna as though he were the senior company official. "He's the rock star and I'm not. He's Canada's political rock star. We're both secure with that situation. He's not inappropriate about it, and I love it." Importantly for the bank, Clark says, people from all political stripes recognize that McKenna was a fantastic ambassador for Canada, a guy who's known as a Liberal but a relatively non-partisan Liberal. TD's clients, after all, do come from all political stripes, and the bank cannot be a political institution. "We're very careful about it." As for McKenna's likely tenure at TD, Clark says the job is his as long as he wants to be there.

Clark, McKenna and the bank's chief economist, Donald Drummond, were hailed in the May 14, 2009, edition of the *Globe and Mail* as the triumvirate driving TD to have a more profound effect than any other bank on provincial and federal government policies across Canada. The story characterized TD as "a lobbying juggernaut" that has significantly and positively raised the profile of the bank. Not named in the triumvirate is retired Canadian Armed Forces General Rick Hillier, who is said to be working hard as an ambassador-cum-consultant for TD. He is a friend of McKenna's; the two forged ties when they worked on Canada's victim relief efforts after Hurricane Katrina in New Orleans.

No one, of course, knows more about McKenna, including the most recent version of him, than his wife, Julie. But although they've been married for thirty-seven years, it's really only been in the past ten years that they've actually lived together the way most couples think about living together, and she's finally gained a clear insight as to what makes him unique. "I never saw him the ten years he was premier," she says. Clearly Julie is enjoying this new existence as a couple.

She's had a chance to watch what Frank does and what it is that makes him successful. "I don't know if I had noticed it before. He just has an ability to network people and connect them together. So it's not just meeting people. He meets people and then he connects them to the people that they need to be connected to in order to be successful. Sometimes I look at him and I think, 'How do you do this?'"

She says he can be in an airport and run into someone who wants to connect with someone McKenna knows or has encountered, usually to do with a business matter or idea. Two weeks later, voila! The two people are inevitably connected, according to Julie. She has never met anybody else who can do that so reliably and effectively.

While Frank's TD role is still very public, it has so far provided the McKennas with much more private time, Julie feels. They seem to have more flexibility to choose what they want to participate in. When she was the wife of a premier, she says, she didn't have much time for herself or for just the two of them because of his lifestyle and schedule, and because the children were mostly her responsibility. In that respect, she was almost a single parent. Being premier was his show. Being a mother was her show.

"This time, this is a really nice lifestyle," she says of being in Toronto and out of the public eye. They still get to participate in a wide range of different and exciting things in Canada and around the world. "We do a lot of different things, interesting things, without the kind of public scrutiny." And, interestingly, the two are more involved in social, business and political events in New Brunswick since Liberal premier Shawn Graham took office after defeating Progressive Conservative Bernard Lord. While Lord was premier, Julie says, McKenna viewed himself as being in a divorced relationship with his home province.

In the downtown Toronto TD head office, McKenna's office is on the same floor as that of vice president James Dodds. The two have been working together for three years as the result of a search McKenna initiated shortly after arriving at the bank. Before that, Dodds had spent a couple of years doing business development for TD. McKenna wanted somebody to play a variety of roles that Dodds likens in political terms to that of a chief of staff. He was seeking someone with both a financial and political background who also happened to be from the Maritimes; anyone but McKenna would have thought that the odds of such a person working within the bank were slim to none. It says a lot about the TD human resources system that Dodds was identified right away as a native of Halifax who for five years was director of operations for what was then known as the Progressive Conservative Party of Canada. In spite of the fact that, as Dodds puts it, "I bleed blue," McKenna was more interested in a political mind than a partisan mind. "I remember when Frank was interviewing me, he was joking when he asked if I thought a Tory could work for a Liberal." The answer has evolved into a resounding yes.

In the immense amount of time they've spent travelling together on planes, trains and automobiles, Dodds and McKenna's talk always turns to politics; they agree on 90 per cent of the issues they tangle over. "Inevitably every discussion goes back to a political one. He just loves to talk about politics," says Dodds, "and I just love to talk about politics." As for being blue or red, when it comes to McKenna, Dodds has turned colour-blind. He freely admits that he would change political stripes for his current boss. "I've said, 'Frank, for what it's worth, you'd be the only Liberal that I would vote for." Apparently Dodds is not alone in Conservative circles. "A lot of Tories say officially or unofficially that McKenna is the greatest political leader the Conservatives never had."

"I do a variety of things for him," says Dodds, most of which involve business development and dovetail into those high-profile public events involving world leaders such as Bush, Clinton and Blair. TD has emerged in Canadian banking circles as the one interest specializing in such ambitious events, standing-room-only affairs staged in major Canadian and U.S. cities, as part of its business development strategy. Dodds is responsible for the logistics and planning of these events.

The bank has also staged more than two dozen by-invitation business development events in a special function room at the TD tower in Toronto, where the likes of Michael Ignatieff and other political and business leaders from across Canada have been invited to speak to specially invited groups of existing or potential TD customers.

"THE GREAT THING about the mandate Frank has with the bank is that it's broad-based," says Dodds, adding that McKenna is involved in everything from being the bank's ambassador for business development, to U.S. expansion, to coordinating strategies in the Middle East, to "everything in between. The only time McKenna's not working on a deal is when he's sleeping," says Dodds.

And when it comes to connecting people, Dodds says it is in McKenna's nature to do just that, always working a room, always remembering people's names and their context. His personality and ability to connect people has actually emerged as a cornerstone of TD's business development strategy. The more widespread McKenna is, the more widespread Dodds is. McKenna averages three days on the road per week and Dodds is often with him for 60 per cent of the time.

Dodds is the latest in a string of people who have worked alongside McKenna in a characteristically unorthodox, risk-taker mode. While McKenna was premier of New Brunswick, that role was played by friend and confidante Francis McGuire, and in Washington it was taken by Minister of Advocacy Colin Robertson. So Dodds is, in a sense, McKenna's latest sidekick or foil. As a duo, they have pushed the envelope as far as it can be pushed within the typically conservative environment of a major Canadian bank, especially TD, which Dodds describes as "very conservative."

For Dodds, unorthodoxy comes from his political training and his time on Parliament Hill. "My role is to get the job done and execute, even if that means rolling the dice a bit." The two must have developed an early understanding about where the line is drawn concerning risk-taking and the role Dodds is designed to play. "Everyone's told me he's incredibly loyal, that once you've got his confidence he does not micromanage or interfere"—which has been Dodds's experience. "And with the amount of stuff coming through our office, you really need that kind of leadership approach."

Loyalty—to friends, the Liberal party, business associates and, inevitably, his roots—is extremely important to McKenna. His devotion to his home province of New Brunswick has even found its way into his relationship with TD. He is clearly responsible for the fact that the latest TD annual general meeting was staged in April of 2009 in the Bay of Fundy port city of Saint John. Several hundred delegates attended what was the first major chartered bank AGM ever staged in New Brunswick. While there, at McKenna's urging, the bank donated half a million dollars to Harbour Passage, the city's waterfront development initiative.

McKenna finds greater purpose as Deputy Chair at TD Bank because he's not on some kind of corporate merry-go-round with two dozen different companies. He still does as many or more things during the course of a day as he did during his days as premier or during the eight-year bubble, but he has a renewed home base and a focus. He openly admits to people at the bank, from Ed Clark through the ranks, that although he's enjoying himself, it's still not the same level of intensity, commitment and satisfaction that he had in public life. On the flip side of the coin, he also admits that, at some point in one's life, one has to be realistic.

"You can't be an adrenaline junkie all your life," he says. "And it's dangerous, too. I said when I left Washington, and I guess I said when I left Fredericton, that a person like me that gets so obsessive and so passionate about the stuff you're doing, you've got to be really careful that you don't fall into the vortex. It's a narcotic and you've got to watch you don't get addicted to it." Politicians like him have a different kind of metabolism and a different DNA than other people, but they still have to watch for the precipice.

VI · The Public Good

TWENTY-ONE

Starfish

*"I just know that any one of his friends could phone
Frank tomorrow and say, 'Hey, Frank. I need help.
My mother is sick in China.' He'd think of something."*

FORMER ONTARIO PREMIER DAVID PETERSON

FRANK MCKENNA CAN'T exactly pin down when it became clear to
him that helping people should take precedence in his life. He
didn't bottom out and suddenly realize he could redeem himself by
helping people, like some kind of repentant addict. There was no
epiphany, no eureka moment, no instance where he sat up in bed
and said, "Julie, I've had a vision." And he didn't make a conscious
decision to change his brand from that of politician to humanitarian. Not that it would work anyway, if you believe David Peterson's
claim that, no matter what, a politician never gets rid of his or her
brand as a politician.

It's simply become clearer to McKenna in the last few years that
his public persona does not truly match where his keenest interests

lie. He has learned more succinctly since his time in Washington that his brand as politician could never be as valuable as some other form of brand. Thanks to Washington and its aftermath, his perspective has expanded to such a degree that he can see well beyond the realm of politics. And the longer he operates and functions outside of the inner political circle, the more certain he is that he can overcome what Peterson describes. He can in fact free himself of the political brand for something just as meaningful.

The matter of giving is something he's not really comfortable talking about, because he feels it comes across as vain or self-promotional. The best explanation he can muster is that his view of the world stems from his meagre upbringing as a member of a large family on a small farm in rural New Brunswick, not to mention that although there were already as many as ten souls under the McKenna roof, his mother Olive would often take in relatives for lengthy periods as a result of some crisis or another in some part of their extended family.

To be clear, however, the McKennas of Apohaqui did not have a lock-hold on generosity. "It was a given that family would help family and neighbours would help neighbours," he says. "In the farming community, people were constantly helping each other. Sometimes a neighbour's help might be necessary to finish a crop, or to raise a new barn if the old barn burned." He believes that helping one another is part of the "rural DNA." When he moved to the Miramichi, now designated a New Brunswick city (although it is really an amalgamation of a series of small communities that retain their local names and personalities), he continued to feel this sense of closeness and mutual reliance. At the family home in Cap Pelé, friends and neighbours still help one another. Even in the Toronto urban enclave where the McKennas, Petersons and McCains live so near to one another, there is a definite sense of sharing and mutual reliance.

FRANK McKENNA ·

Remembering the night he drove McKenna half an hour in the wrong direction as the then premier tried to catch some sleep, former aide Nat Richard says that the flip side of McKenna's toughness and high demands is that he can be "awfully thoughtful." Richard recalls that even at the height of pressures or campaigning, McKenna would always have his eye on calling people, sending cards or visiting people in the hospital.

One anonymous observer talks about how McKenna is prepared to cast aside what others think and to overlook people's shortcomings if he believes there is more to their story than meets the eye. In three examples, McKenna put his name and credibility on the line by associating himself with people who were not exactly riding the crest of a rave wave.

Even before things were at their worst for former federal Liberal leader Stéphane Dion, McKenna was among a group of New Brunswick party diehards who were determined to do their part to help clear Dion of his accumulated campaigning debts. With the man most would consider to be the most unpopular U.S. president of modern times, McKenna has come out in full public association with George W. Bush by hosting him in a series of public events in North America and by inviting him to be the keynote speaker at the annual 2009 Fox Harb'r business networking event. And he has stuck by former prime minister Brian Mulroney no matter how much of a public kicking Mulroney has taken over the Karlheinz Schreiber affair.

McKenna took what was nearly a public stand on behalf of Mulroney when he agreed to introduce the former prime minister at the annual Toronto fundraising dinner for their alma mater, St. FX. The event was held on November 13, 2007, nearly at the very moment when Mulroney was again seeing headlines blow up concerning his involvements with Karlheinz Schreiber and the supposed Airbus affair. Many others would have avoided any association with the former prime minister at the time. McKenna's acceptance of the invitation demonstrates that, even with all of the upheaval of Meech Lake in their wake, he is totally comfortable demonstrating that he will stand with Mulroney.

In fact, McKenna has grown weary of the entire Mulroney-Schreiber scandal. "I also happen to believe that whatever the facts are in the Schreiber case, it is old news in a country that has more important issues. I do not believe that we should continue to devote large resources to tarnishing the name of a former prime minister. Canadians are in possession of enough facts to make their own judgment." He also believes Canada is wasting its credibility as a nation by continually retracing Mulroney's steps, and that, first and foremost, Mulroney deserves better treatment as a former prime minister than what he has been afforded. "Whatever his weaknesses were, he had considerable strength and he was our prime minister." McKenna says that if he were prime minister, he would can any notion of an inquiry "in a heartbeat."

Especially troubling to McKenna is that Mulroney was denied an achievement in Meech that he had a right to enjoy. He goes so far as to say that what hurts him more than anything else about the whole Meech saga was what Mulroney, let alone the country, did not get out of it in the end.

A STRONG SENSE of family and community have certainly played a role in forming McKenna's social conscience. And so too have friends and others he would consider heroes. All have influenced him.

McKenna believes that South African leader Nelson Mandela, whose conviction that the positive force of forgiveness and reconciliation is what mentally got him through nearly three decades of incarceration until his celebrated release in 1990, is a leadership fig-ure like no other, a man to be admired and emulated. "I think that the serenity and the sense of perspective [is what] I get from him," McKenna reflects. "The ability to have been in jail—I think it's about twenty-seven years of his life—and to be subjected to the amount of persecution that he faced, and to be able to leave incarceration with such equanimity and serenity and balance and sense of purpose and vision." McKenna says that Mandela's life teaches the great lesson that people can overcome any adversity. "There are other lessons, too. Forgive your enemies. Never close doors." In McKenna's view, the unification of South Africa undertaken by Mandela was a staggering job. "And you could only do it with somebody who had saint-like qualities, and that was the role that he played."

In a more deeply personal way, Fernand (Fern) Landry left an indelible mark on McKenna. He was "one of the most impressive human beings that I have ever met," says McKenna. "He was a franco-phone with such a brilliant mind that he was able to lead his class at the University of New Brunswick Law School and complete a mas-ters degree at Harvard, entirely in English." Serving as a key deputy minister in McKenna's government, Landry and his wife, Aldéa, who served as deputy premier, were instrumental in helping McKenna navigate his way through the "always tricky" waters of linguistic relationships between French and English in Canada's only officially bilingual province.

"Fern was a model of patience and tolerance. He taught me the virtue of being less impulsive, being more patient with other views and learning the art of compromise. He also provided great perspec-tive, the importance of taking a long view and not being distracted by momentary setbacks or being overly concerned about short-term political ups and downs. Fern was one of the kindest, gentlest and wisest people that I ever knew. He was a very soothing balm to my rougher edges."

Then there is his friend Dr. Paul Farmer, an anthropologist and physician with a history at Harvard University and Brigham and Women's Hospital in Boston, who turned his life toward international health and social justice through Partners in Health, the organization he co-founded in 1987. In the Tracy Kidder book *Mountains Beyond Mountains: The Quest of Dr. Paul Farmer*, Farmer is revealed as an individual who is dedicated almost beyond belief to the causes he pursues, including relief efforts in such countries as Haiti, Rwanda, Russia, Malawi and Peru.

McKenna says that by watching and learning over the past ten years from people like Farmer and Bill Clinton (through the Clinton Foundation and the Clinton Global Initiative), it is clear to him that life is about more than title and position. He has discovered that there are people doing very important things in the world that have nothing to do with leading a political party or running a government.

"I don't need flashbulbs going off all around me," he says. "It is not about being in the limelight." McKenna was exposed to what power really looks like during his year in Washington versus what power looks like at home in Canada. How much more interesting could the prime minister's office possibly be than his time in Washington and his life since? Could he not make a tangible difference through other channels?

Because of their close connection over the years, McCrea has a perspective on the kinds of personal things that affect McKenna and how he tends to respond. She recalls that his reaction to 9/11 was not just utter disbelief like everyone else's, but also a desire to do something to help. He has also shared the fear he experienced during Julie's bout with breast cancer several years ago. Perhaps, although he hasn't said it, there is a connection between that episode and his recent life choices.

So it becomes increasingly clear what has motivated McKenna to make the choices he's made about his life since first turning down the leadership run in 2006. He is carefully modest in discussing a concept of giving that he and Julie call "Starfish."

McKenna does not recall where he first heard this simple story, one of those fables he loves to tell and retell. However, it is one he has never forgotten and likely never will. Its lesson is one that has inspired him toward the fulfillment of a dream.

Once a man was walking along a beach. The sun was shining and it was a beautiful day. Off in the distance he could see a person going back and forth between the surf's edge and the beach. Back and forth this person went. As the man approached he could see that there were hundreds of starfish stranded on the sand as the result of the natural action of the tide.

The man was struck by the apparent futility of the task. There were far too many starfish. Many of them were sure to perish. As he approached, the person continued the task of picking up starfish one by one and throwing them into the surf.

As he came up to the person he said, "You must be crazy. There are thousands of miles of beach covered with starfish. You can't possibly make a difference." The person looked at the man. He then stooped down and picked up one more starfish and threw it back into the ocean. He turned back to the man and said, "It sure made a difference to that one!"

One gets the sense that, once the idea is out there and more public than just within the family unit, his comfort discussing it, if not promoting it, will come to be second nature to McKenna, as with his other charitable interests. For now, though, the Starfish idea has to be drawn out of him. Julie, on the other hand, is a bit more comfortable with the subject. She describes how she and her husband have talked about the development of a Starfish foundation.

Central to it is the involvement of their entire family. "We want our grandchildren particularly to be more aware of what's going on in the world and just how privileged they are," says Julie.

Frank says that he and Julie were becoming a bit frustrated that their children and grandchildren were not understanding the worth and value of acting charitably. It's not that they weren't capable of acting charitably or of being altruistic, "but we sensed with them and with others that the lack of connection between the beneficiary and the benefactor was creating a real gulf, and we found in our own personal lives we tended to give to organizations we know," primarily Atlantic initiatives that they could see and touch and get up close to, and know exactly where their money was going. It's not that the mainstream, well-known international aid organizations aren't good organizations, but the cliché of how much money goes into administration always seemed to be in the backs of the McKennas' minds. Starfish becomes for them a way to think of giving in a relationship that is more personal and direct than simply writing a cheque.

McKenna's vision for the development of his own foundation began to really and truly crystallize with his work on behalf of another one. On September 13, 2008, in the aftermath of Hurricane Gustav, tropical storm Hanna and Hurricane Ike, he boarded a sixteen-seat military-style helicopter to fly to Gonaïves, Haiti's fourth-largest city, and from there on to the capital city of Port-au-Prince. On board were film star and social activist Matt Damon, Haitian-born rapper and social activist Wyclef Jean, and TD's James Dodds. The men had volunteered to help distribute food with ONEXONE (pronounced one-by-one), a charity that McKenna has chaired since March 2008. Matt Damon has also committed himself to the charity, which recently partnered with Wyclef Jean's own foundation, Yéle Haiti, which assists his fellow Haitians in the areas of education, health, environment and community development.

As the helicopter moved through the humid Caribbean air, what they saw completely stunned them. More than five hundred people had been declared dead and nearly fifty thousand homeless as a result of the string of natural disasters, all made worse by the dearth of emergency preparedness. And the evidence of the disaster was inescapable. Thousands were literally living on their rooftops to escape the devastation of flooding and to avoid the threat of looters. McKenna was nearly in tears. "Haiti was eye-opening for him," says Dodds. "It was like nothing he had ever seen before. It moved Matt Damon, too."

The victims were not thinking about work or school or money; they were thinking about moment-to-moment survival. "It was one of those things," said Dodds, where "you are so overwhelmed that you tune it out until you're home in your comfy bed and you begin to think about it." Dodds said that for all of them, the sense of devastation in Haiti lingers, especially the notion that just an hour or so by air from the U.S. mainland such absolute poverty exists. Months after Frank McKenna returned home, Julie says, he is still affected by the Haiti trip. "He found the whole thing very moving."

"I've never in my life witnessed the devastation that I saw in Haiti," McKenna says. The trappings of a normal civil society were almost totally non-existent, owing to the government's constant instability, which he says made it impossible to deal with the horrible level of poverty and lawlessness that are so rampant in the country. The cumulative effect of four hurricanes within the period of a month became a tipping point for the already ravaged nation. "I have witnessed poverty in a number of places around the world, but nothing of this magnitude."

ONEXONE was founded by Canadian Joelle (Joey) Adler to celebrate the life of her late husband Lou Adler. Having admired McKenna before she even met him, Adler—together with Rogers Communications' Edward Rogers—had asked him to chair ONEXONE. "I remember knowing about Frank when he was premier and also when very often he would be asked to comment during federal matters," says Adler. "There was something that drew me as a person to him." Always a political junkie, she was not disappointed when she finally had the chance to meet him, in contrast to the disillusionment she was feeling about politicians in general. "He's one of those guys that's respected and loved." His involvement has been good for the foundation and has definitely heightened his humanitarian sensibility.

Still riveted by what he'd seen in September of 2008, McKenna followed up on his first Haiti experience by developing a continuing commitment to the country. In March of 2009, he joined Bill Clinton and United Nations Secretary-General Ban Ki-moon to promote the development of an anti-poverty action plan for what is classified as the poorest country in the entire western hemisphere. Rhyming off a litany of problems that have pushed Haiti further and further toward poverty and violence over the decades—political, environmental, economic and social—he made a plea for governments and business to rally behind the Clinton Global Initiative and other forces to help right the country. "Clinton saw us [Damon, Jean and McKenna] in Haiti and had a team down there the next day." Next thing McKenna knew, Clinton was announcing at a global initiative function in New York City that his new number-one project was going to be assisting in Haiti. "Because he saw us on TV," says McKenna.

In broader global economic terms, McKenna said that people in developed nations may be undergoing challenges because of the economic crisis that emerged late in 2008, but that there is no comparison to what's taking place in Haiti. "We have to realize that whatever pain we're feeling, it is miniscule compared to the misery of people who are living on less than a dollar a day," he said in a news release publicizing the March mission with Clinton.

Putting things further in perspective, he speaks about factories which have as little as two hours of electrical power per day unless supplemented by generators. Haiti, he believes, could become as much a valid Caribbean tourism destination as the neighbouring Dominican Republic or other island nations that have made tourism the backbone of their economies. Just as he did with NB Works in the 1990s, McKenna talks about employment as being a major part of the fix. "There is no better form of aid than a job," he says. "If people could actually make investments here that would make sense for them and create jobs here, that's an extremely beneficial form of aid."

This is the same type of philosophy professed by famed primatologist Dr. Jane Goodall. Her worldwide Roots & Shoots campaign, like other projects seeking to create change in the developing world, promotes putting people to work, introducing micro-credit systems to Third World nations and denouncing "aristocrats appearing before the beggars" as a pitiful form of providing relief.

A new generation of compelling voices has entered the aid dialogue, including economist and author Dambisa Moyo. A native of Zambia now working at Goldman Sachs, Moyo argues that the rich world and Africa should create new ways of helping poor countries to become more independent. She uses the example of Ghana to illustrate how some countries have successfully tapped the bond markets for funds, and she espouses the virtues of micro-finance, venture capital and opening up trade links.

In late April 2009, McKenna and Dodds flew to Rwanda to join Matt Damon, Edward Rogers, Joey Adler and Judith Irving of New Brunswick's industrialist Irving family. There, they visited several relief projects first-hand. Damon, who had just wrapped production on a new Clint Eastwood film about Nelson Mandela, said in an interview from Kigali that he would unequivocally become involved in anything that McKenna asked him to, because he trusts McKenna implicitly. As a Hollywood celebrity, he's met enough "BS artists" and enough genuine people to be able to tell the difference, and also to be highly scrutinizing. "We've been in enough situations, and the integrity the guy has—you can't fake it."

Damon and others who are giving to the Rwandan relief effort are very important players in bringing about change, but according to Adler, "the single most important person on the trip is McKenna. A lot of people might have just lent their name to something like this, but Frank brings the experience to guide, to do media, to promote [the ONEXONE] brand and give extra help to a country which needs moral support and a foundation."

In Rwanda, the entourage met with President Paul Kagame to discuss opportunities for future development in the war-ravaged country. Kagame told them that his country and its people are thankful for the forms of philanthropy they are receiving, but that they do not want to perpetuate a culture of dependency—a philosophy that closely mirrors McKenna's own.

In spite of what Rwanda went through during its genocide, Adler believes that now, with reformation and leadership from the likes of President Kagame, it is like a country in its infancy and can serve as a blueprint by which other African countries can grow. Adler thinks

ONEXONE should concentrate its energies and resources on a single country where they can make a pronounced difference rather than spread the organization thinly over too many initiatives. She spoke about ditches being dug for the laying of fibre optic cables, about hospitals which now have computers and cellphones and about a president who is driving the development of environmental policies. Kagame, she claims, does not want handouts for his people; he wants partnership and development for his country, which Adler believes is fully behind him.

McKenna admires the goals and aspirations of ONEXONE and thinks about Starfish in comparative philosophical terms—the project realistically admits that you can't save everyone in Haiti, but if you can take one village and make life better, then you have something for other villages to emulate. He uses the example of creating a model village through the provision of medical care, finding fresh water solutions, bringing into play agricultural solutions and establishing ideas such as micro-finance. "And then with that seed of that village, maybe it will go somewhere, maybe it won't. But if it succeeds, then all of the other communities can say, 'Here's something that we can emulate.' So it's that idea of, as an individual, recognizing that you may not be able to save the world, but if you can save a piece of it, sometimes that helps."

From visiting Haiti and spending more time closer to causes he believes in, McKenna has learned how people can really contribute outside of political office or a "vanity appointment." In a sense, he has rediscovered the importance of something that has always been there in his own personal value system. Some people have been on the ground, largely unheralded, working in Haiti for twenty to thirty years, "just getting things done," as McKenna puts it. More than any other angle on his future, this is what he's spending his time thinking about. "I've felt that energy again with some of the ONEXONE stuff." Deep down, McKenna seems aware that he can't be a Bay Street banker, corporate director and business networker and still be an effective benefactor to the extent that he fully intends.

McKenna wants to spend more time developing Starfish. He talks about his participation in a 2008 U.S. meeting on international aid, with talk leaning toward new ways of delivering help. He mused then and during this interview about the not-so-crazy notion of establishing technologies in parts of Africa where children could be connected to North American children. It wasn't long ago that the idea of community computer access sites (CAP sites) in Canada hadn't even been dreamed up yet. Now there are CAP sites everywhere, providing technology access to adults and children of income and class levels that would otherwise provide them with no direct interactive technology exposure. So why not a CAP premise for communities in Africa? Eventually, a child or a family in North America could be communicating with and contributing directly to the welfare of an individual child in Africa. "So it's a person you're giving money to, not just an organization."

The McKennas have gone about their family philanthropy in a very quiet and unassuming way. "A number of us have January birthdays," says Julie. "I do, Frank does, my son-in-law does, and one of my grandchildren." So the McKennas decided to forego both Christmas and birthday gifts a year or so ago, channelling their energy instead toward charitable work during a visit to the poverty-riddled Caribbean country of Jamaica.

Through a friend, the McKennas found a kindergarten that provided them with a list of things needed by its poorer students. In a sense, the McKennas had exchanged their traditional Christmas gift lists for this list. The family arrived with suitcases full of craft supplies and books and arranged with the school to come and deliver the items on a specific day. Included in the visit were three of their grandchildren who were old enough to understand what the project was all about. The adults and young people at the school had no inkling who the McKennas were: they were just some people who had come to visit with stuff the students really needed. The McKennas saw first-hand exactly what the need was in Jamaica, and what it meant to fulfill part of that need.

If these ideas sound unstructured, McKenna admits that in fact they often are. His life-altering visit to Haiti with Matt Damon and Wyclef Jean literally came together over the course of hours, not weeks or months of planning. Jean had spoken to ONEXONE and Damon and McKenna and they all just agreed to do it. "And then people at the bank here all got into it and they started checking on security issues. We found a plane, got a bunch of people to throw money in the hat and we were gone, literally within a day."

Whatever form Starfish might finally take, McKenna says it will involve the belief that people should not allow the magnitude of a challenge to overwhelm them. "Even though we cannot 'boil the ocean,' we can solve individual problems and sometimes create the catalyst for success in a family or a community. Every building block is important, no matter how small."

Any potential prime minister of Canada might purport or aspire to such thinking, but bureaucracies and politics and partisanship have every potential to derail and dissolve individual dreams. Within the life he has chosen over politics, McKenna can manage his idealism and dreams according to his own agenda and in his own time. And he can pass·those dreams and ideals on, as is his ultimate dream, to his grandchildren.

TWENTY-TWO

My Canada II

*"I would like to be somebody who would be seen
as a Canadian patriot who could help broker
national resolutions to issues."*

FRANK McKENNA ON HIS FUTURE AS A CANADIAN

WHETHER INSIDE OR outside political office, McKenna naturally finds
it impossible not to think and talk about the directions in which his
country is headed. In his "My Canada" lecture of 1998, he focused on
Canada alone. Today, however, his focus is much more on Canada's
place in the world. Even with so much information at hand—his
1970 thesis on the Canadian constitution, the "My Canada" lecture, a
2006 federal Liberal party policy discussion paper he wrote, copies
of speeches, the public record, news clippings and the political lessons
he has learned and related, as well as stories and anecdotes from
dozens of individual viewpoints, including his own—there still
seemed much to extract about the future from his ever-open and
ever-curious mind as we sat down in his TD Wellington Street office

in Toronto and exchanged calls and emails over a number of months. As stated in this book's introduction, it seems you can ask McKenna anything and he will always answer.

It became clear in our exchanges that four overarching themes preoccupy his mind: the challenge of stimulating greater leadership in Canada and internationally; his developing humanitarianism; what he intends to do about both as a private citizen rather than as a political leader; and Canada's long-term relationship with the U.S. To his way of thinking, these themes are inextricably linked to one another and to virtually every major issue that confronts Canadians.

McKenna is very preoccupied with the development of Canadian leadership in general, whether it be what Canada's existing leaders, governments and institutions are doing on domestic policy matters or what they are doing—or what they're not doing—to help people around the world to help themselves. Over the last few years, McKenna seems to have discovered his own way of addressing these matters.

The need for daring and skilled leadership is at the core of McKenna's vision of Canada's future as a world leader. And he longs for a role in it all. Although he has turned down traditional political leadership at the national level, it is not as though he has given up on playing some kind of critical role in the future of the country.

"The trouble is, there's always a gap between what you would like to be and what you are, and what you would like people to think of you and what you are. I would like to be somebody who would be seen as a Canadian patriot who could help broker national resolutions to issues," he says. However, in the face of being seen as a non-partisan Canadian patriot, there is the lingering issue of his Liberal party affiliation, a leftover of that political brand which David Peterson characterized as being unshakable. And in the absence of a team of publicists and marketing suits to pigeonhole McKenna into a new image, since his resignation as premier in 1997 it has been up to him to figure out how to define himself professionally, realize his goals and brand himself anew. He is the only spin doctor he's got.

Being a Canadian patriot does not mean remaining exclusively Canada-centric. McKenna has proven that through his work with ONEXONE. "I would like to be more involved in international extreme poverty issues and/or U.S.-Canada issues. I would like to perhaps have more involvement on an international stage at a modest level. But within Canada, I would like to continue to help introduce people to opportunities, to support my region [of Atlantic Canada] and to help political leaders to overcome challenges and just be a contributor to the maturity of our country."

Meanwhile, in his role at one of the country's largest financial institutions, McKenna has kept a constant watch on the global economic crisis and its implications for Canadians. Just as he expressed in his "My Canada" lecture, he has clear policy viewpoints about the direction the country should take in areas affecting the direct well-being of Canada's citizenry—economics, education, the knowledge economy, health care and security.

More important than McKenna's viewpoints on specific policies, though, are his broader objectives of leadership and humanitarianism: all sorts of domestic and world conditions can and do change so rapidly in this day and age that leaders need to be open-minded, flexible and ahead of the future. No sooner is the ink dry on a policy paper or on the pages of a political biography than the game has changed. Initiatives and policies surrounding the arts or health care or education or industrial development or security are not constant. The only constants are the need for leadership and helping people.

McKenna's number-one lesson in political life is that having a fixed political policy or viewpoint, or being dogmatic, is just plain wrong. Former Newfoundland premier Clyde Wells's dogmatism over Meech Lake killed the accord and his reputation. McKenna's open-mindedness through the evolution of Meech is what helped right the problem and saved his reputation.

Dogmatism is what will haunt the reputation of Prime Minister Stephen Harper. McKenna says that he supports a number of the initiatives the Conservatives finally introduced in 2009 to help Canada weather the global economic crisis after the blunder of the *Economic and Fiscal Statement of 2008*, which nearly toppled the government. Nonetheless, he adds, "If I had criticism it would be the sheer magnitude of the number of initiatives that were introduced more for political reasons than as part of an overall stimulus package." In that regard, even though the economic crisis was not of Canada's or Stephen Harper's making, McKenna says Harper's tactics smack of the American approach to earmarking bills which pass through Congress and the Senate, all for the sake of partisanship and garnering local constituency votes. This is no time to be playing partisan games, which is exactly what Harper was doing late in 2008.

In the matter of health care, for example, again McKenna believes that a fixation on one policy or position will not serve Canadians well. He says that Canada is overly preoccupied with a system that is publicly funded to a greater degree than any other country in the world. Even the more socialist countries of the world, such as the Scandinavian nations and France, have health care systems more mixed than Canada's. What McKenna would truly hate to see is an extreme shift to that of the U.S. model—there, according to McKenna, things are pretty much a shambles. "The United States is so ideologically dug in that they cannot move off privately delivered health care and privately funded health care, no matter how costly and wasteful it is. And as a result, they are paying twice as much per capita as any other country in the world." Having studied the numbers, he says this dramatic waste of resources continues to leave some 45 million Americans with no health care coverage whatsoever, with companies suffering competitively as a result. Health care, he believes, is the United States' Achilles heel, and this is reflected in the risks that President Barack Obama took to change the system by declaring in July 2009 that U.S. health care reform would be achieved by the end of that calendar year.

So what would having renewed and greater leadership do for Canada? For one thing, studying and listening to what's going on in the world rather than being driven solely by ideology is to be recommended. Rather than trickle toward the U.S. ideology on health care, it's McKenna's belief that Canada should pursue a health care system which is publicly funded but which has "the scope" for private sector products and activity to emerge. He also believes that the provinces should be allowed to do more experimentation at the service delivery level, where people on the health care ground floor know what's going on. "The trouble is that the people that are mainly operating the file at the national level have never run a health care system. All they do is transfer money and make the rules. The people who actually run the systems are at the provincial capitals and I think they've got a very different set of priorities."

So it's not as though McKenna does not have policy points of view. After all, he is respected enough to have been asked by organizer Tom Axworthy of the Liberal Party of Canada to prepare a paper on Canada-U.S. relations as a tool toward a policy renewal process. Among the many issues addressed in that paper was McKenna's concern with Canada's lack of a branded identity, very much lost since the Lester B. Pearson era, when the country was known as a peacekeeping nation. McKenna envisions waging a campaign much as he had begun in the U.S. This is one issue that is not going to morph depending on other world conditions. The Canada brand challenge will always need work and investment. "We have an enormously compelling story to tell and should tell it more forcefully."

Telling Canada's story clearly and succinctly would mitigate what McKenna refers to as an underdog image on the international stage. "We are a pretty undeveloped personality," he says. There is a dichotomy in this, he believes. "I think that the bounty that we have in Canada, whether it's democratic institutions or financial institutions or natural resources, puts us really in the top echelon of countries in the world. But I think we are punching below our weight. Right now, I don't think the country is doing terribly. I don't think it's doing as well as it should be doing, but I don't think anybody in the country feels a profound sense of malaise. But by not moving ahead, we're falling behind."

McKenna can't understand why leaders in the country don't do more to respond to this challenge. "We could be a major world player. We could be a wealthier and a more prosperous and a more generous country than we are. We could do all of those things." Again, one feels here that McKenna's mind is at work in the international rather than just the domestic theatre. He feels regretful that the country is quite content just rolling along in the same old way, as though it has not yet met its calling.

He points out different areas in which Canada might be resourceful, a source of strength and light. The Scandinavian focus on foreign aid is one approach to emulate. Another is on the trade front. "Canada could be an example to the world by opening its borders to trade from Third World countries," he believes. "There are many who believe that trade is a better way to lift Third World nations from their cycle of poverty than direct foreign aid." It's in the expression of these views that one can see how the combination of new leadership and a sweeping humanitarian point of view can take something like the economy and shake it up. "In many respects," he adds, "Canada is one of the best-equipped countries in the world to offer such openness. As a trading nation, it may be very well in our national interest to adopt such a course. This would have considerable influence in our relationship with the United States."

McKenna's view on Canada playing a cornerstone humanitarian role is driven not just by his having witnessed human deprivation and suffering in Haiti, Rwanda and elsewhere. It is founded on the unembroidered facts and statistics measuring Canada's progress in the area of humanitarian aid. He quotes World Food Program director Josette Shiner as saying that Canada was exemplary in removing from its foreign aid policy the requirement that products be sold from the giving country, which would not allow the receiving country to build capacity. "She advised me that Canada has been a leader in untying its aid," says McKenna. "And, ironically, we have probably received more orders for Canadian products since we made this change than before."

"ON THE OTHER hand, what we are doing is very meagre in terms of the quantum of need and the efforts of some other members of the international community. We are a wealthy country. Much of the rest of the world is not." McKenna recites statistics showing that at least 80 per cent of humanity lives on less than ten dollars per day, and over one billion people live on less than one dollar per day. Nearly a billion people are unable to read a book or sign their name. More than eight hundred million go hungry every day. More than eight million die every year because they are too poor to stay alive. "The gap between rich and poor people gets bigger and bigger. In 1820, the ratio was approximately three to one. The ratio is estimated at seventy-five to one at the present time. What would it take to really make a difference? McKenna quotes Jeffrey Sachs, an American economist and director of the Earth Institute at Columbia University, as saying that 1 per cent of the income of the rich world would end extreme poverty.

MCKENNA BELIEVES THAT Canada and most other rich nations are going in the opposite direction from what the developing world needs. Aid from the world's richest countries fell 13 per cent over the last several years. Canada's performance leaves a lot to be desired. "We are now giving 0.28 per cent. That is half of what we gave in the 1990s. We are giving far less than countries that are not as wealthy as we are—including Denmark, Norway, Germany, Netherlands, Sweden, Ireland, France, Finland, Luxembourg, United Kingdom, Switzerland, Austria, Belgium, Spain and Australia. We should and we can do better. This is a country that has spawned such illustrious world leaders as Norman Bethune, Stephen Lewis, Lester Pearson, Roméo Dallaire, and Dr. Moses Coady. We live in the reflective glory of these great leaders. Unfortunately, we are not putting our money where our mouth is."

McKenna not only wishes that Canada would put more money where its mouth is internationally, but also recognizes that institutions and individuals must likewise do more. And he has found a way to make that happen, to bring his twinned focus on humanitarianism and leadership concerns together under one institutional umbrella. Toward that objective, McKenna has deepened his personal commitments of mental capital, time and money toward the university that helped shape who he is.

In June of 2009, he was elected chairman of the St. FX board of governors, further cementing his ties to his alma mater, which have included his acting as honorary advisor to the university's Expanding Futures capital campaign and as honorary chairman of the Coady International Institute. The institute is named for Dr. Coady, who was instrumental during the 1920s in pioneering the practice of popular education and community organizing dedicated to improving the lives of disadvantaged people. After Coady accepted the appointment in 1928 as director of the university's extension department, he spent the next two decades driving what became known internationally as the Antigonish Movement, which became the home base for cooperatives and credit union development in the Maritimes and internationally.

Current university president Dr. Sean Riley explains that the mandate of the Coady Institute is unlike anything linked to academic institutions elsewhere in North America. More than five thousand institute graduates work today in more than one hundred and twenty countries. Graduates who have spent from six to nine months at the institute include senior staff from a women's organization in Zambia, community development workers in Egypt and operators of a micro-financing network that helps more than a million poor women in India. The idea is to provide executive development for existing community leaders. The institute's philosophy sounds incredibly close to that of Goldman Sachs economist Dambisa Moyo.

"And this is where it all circles back to Frank," says Riley. "Frank himself represents this multi-talented leadership dimension," which is why he approached McKenna during the fall of 2008 about the idea of forming the Frank McKenna Centre for Leadership Studies, a new entity that will bring together an interdisciplinary group of faculty to support quality leadership studies aimed at the public, private and not-for-profit sectors. McKenna agreed, and made a substantial personal donation to the centre. That donation forms the base of a multi-million-dollar campaign funding both bricks and mortar and an endowment fund, with the emphasis on the latter. McKenna did so, according to Riley, because he believes that institutions have a role to play in building leadership, and because he sees leadership as part of the diet and the DNA of St. FX. He also agreed because the project will be designed to have a transformative impact over the long term, having both domestic and international implications.

Riley insists that the McKenna Centre will not create a new silo of programming within St. FX. Rather, it will inject leadership content into courses through the experiences of guest lecturers, or "visiting minds," across the entire spectrum of the university, impacting virtually all programs and departments. Riley says the university hopes to be the standard-bearer for "Leadership R Us." The trick will be for the Centre to play two roles: to infuse leadership into everything the university touches and then to "provide a new dimension of energy behind the activist university," which takes its form in the Coady International Institute. In that vein, the Centre becomes a near-perfect vehicle for McKenna to drive home his dreams of helping people in need, wherever they may be.

"Simply put," McKenna says, "we may be unable to help develop democratic institutions in countries around the world or even invest enough money in food aid. However, if we can build capacity through developing their leaders, we will allow them to take the future into their own hands. What is true for developing countries is also true for aboriginal communities and mainstream students at home in Canada. Many of the most astute business minds or scientific minds are handicapped by the lack of development of leadership skills. I fully intend to stay involved with the project and presumably would be helping to attract some of the speakers and staff. The physical infrastructure of the centre is far less important to me than the programming."

It is in this kind of package that McKenna envisions a maturing of Canada as nation that is generous internationally but also takes care of some of its domestic affairs, such as the state of progress of Aboriginals.

Alongside what he sees as a pressing need for leadership and an increased humanitarian role for Canada around the world, one other concern echoes time and again for McKenna: the nature of Canada's relationship with the United States of America. And in dealing with the U.S., there is one issue that trumps all others: security.

"Canadians should avoid an antiquated concept of sovereignty when it comes to security matters," he wrote in his 2006 Liberal party policy paper. "A mature and confident nation must recognize the mutual self-interest of perimeter security." He believes that Canada's actions on security should not be mistaken as a question of holding sovereignty. He also warned that, should a major event occur, such as another 9/11 or worse, with linkage to laxness in Canadian security, it would have "a profound impact" on trade between the two countries and consequently on Canada's national wealth. "We must commit to the highest possible standards of technology and security. These standards must exceed standards that Americans view as acceptable. We must be the safest partner in the world." Still mindful of what happened on the day he began working as Canadian ambassador to the U.S., McKenna suggests that Canada should reopen the debate on ballistic missile defence. He still believes that demonstrating cooperation on BMD could help erase all or part of the deficit in Canada-U.S. relations following Canada's refusal to support the Iraq war.

Sovereignty, though, is one issue McKenna feels need not be driven by relations with the United States. Canada "must become relevant on the world stage in its own right," he says. "It must pursue social and economic policies that are right for Canada. It must not engage in endless hand-wringing by juxtaposing itself against the United States. Our pride and our self-esteem should be a manifestation of our nationhood. It has nothing to do with our relationship with the United States. We need more respect for ourselves. We need more confidence in ourselves. We need a much more elevated sense of self-worth." He quotes Michael Ignatieff: "The besetting sin of Canadian foreign policy is a kind of airy and empty moral perfectionism that just does not deal with the world we live in."

Using security cooperation as one of a number of tools, McKenna believes, an enhanced relationship with the U.S. will help shape Canada's influence elsewhere in the world. "Of all nations in the world, we are the most uniquely positioned to exercise such influence over the U.S. It will be a mark of our confidence and maturity as a nation to deal with our American neighbour in a respectful and businesslike manner without allowing a lack of confidence or moral superiority to colour the strength of the relationship. Canada is a wealthy and highly admired nation. We must accept the responsibilities incumbent with this status. We should start by 'getting it right' with the only neighbour we have."

And it is with McKenna's clarity of thought about the final pillar of Canada's future in the world that we see the irony of his shortened time in Washington. It leaves us curious—that attribute that he so looks for in leaders—to keep an eye on McKenna as he resolves his own leadership quest in what will be the closing chapters of his life.

One thing McKenna has proven is that he practises what he promises and what he preaches. He swears that, if called upon, he could still recite the words of "Clancy of the Mounted Police," in which author Robert Service is clearly writing about the principles of honour and determination and commitment—leadership, one might say. This theme is captured wholly in just the first four lines of the poem, which McKenna performed as a child at Apohaqui Superior School:

In the little Crimson Manual it's written plain and clear
That who would wear the scarlet coat shall say good-bye to fear,
Shall be a guardian of the right, a sleuth-hound of the trail—
In the little Crimson Manual, there's no such word as "fail."

FRANK McKENNA ·

APPENDIX

FRANK MCKENNA'S LIST of corporate interests during the period 1998 to 2005:

Acier Leroux, as a director and member of the Corporate Governance & Compensation Committee; Air Canada (ACE Aviation Holdings Inc.), as a director and member of the Audit Committee; NBTel, as a director; Amec North American Advisory Board, as a board member; Bank of Montreal, as lead director, chairman of the Conduct Review Committee, member of the Audit Committee and member of the Pension Fund Society; Barrett Corporation, as a director; Canwest Communications Corp., as a director, chairman of the board, member of the Audit Committee and chairman of the Executive Compensation Committee; The Carlyle Group Canadian Advisory Board, as a board member; Datacom Wireless, as a director; Duke Energy Transmission Advisory Board, as a board member; FNX Mining, as a director; General Motors of Canada, as lead director; Kinek Technologies, as a director; Major Drilling Group International, as a director, chairman of the board, member of the Corporate

Governance Committee and chairman of the Nominating Committee; Marsh Canada Limited Advisory Board, as a board member; MINACS, as a director and member of the Governance and Nominating Committee; Noranda Inc., as lead director and member of the Audit Committee and chair of board governance; Shoppers Drug Mart, as lead director and member of the Audit and Compensation Committees; United Parcel Service, as a director; Zenon Environmental Inc., as lead and chair of corporate governance.

ACKNOWLEDGEMENTS

MY GOOD FORTUNE to write this book came about because of the endless patience and resourcefulness of Frank McKenna's assistant Ruth McCrea and the imagination of McKenna loyalist Francis McGuire. Both are incredible people to whom I owe so much. I would like to acknowledge the trust, professionalism and vision of publisher Scott McIntyre and the assistance of all his creative associates in Vancouver and Toronto, in particular Chris Labonté, Peter Cocking, editor Barbara Berson and copy editor Peter Norman, from whom I have learned much. My agent, Rick Broadhead, is a wizard. Author David McNally and Dell Publishing provided the permission to include an excerpt from his work *Even Eagles Need a Push: Learning to Soar in a Changing World*. Author Philip Lee has kindly permitted the periodic use of his 2001 biography, *Frank*, as a point of reference. It was an amazing privilege to interview so many outstanding personalities in both Canada and the United States; thanks to all of them, with special thanks to Colin Robertson, Bernie Etzinger, Nat Richard, Roger Noriega, James Dodds, David Peterson and Peter Hogg. Two of the most gracious interviews I've ever conducted were those with former prime ministers Brian Mulroney and Paul Martin, the latter taking the personal time to write the foreword. Thanks, as always, to Tim Gordon, General Store Publishing House, and to Dan Soucoup, Nimbus Publishing, for the previous opportunities they have given me.

To Frank and Julie McKenna, I cannot thank you adequately for allowing me to examine your lives so that readers can better understand what it is you are both made of. And finally, to my partner Charlotte Stewart, for her unrelenting patience, for the many ideas she contributed to this effort, for the way in which she challenged me and for her constant support and love.

INDEX

Page numbers with suffix "a" refer to the Appendix.

McKenna, Frank, New Brunswick
premier (1987–97), *xvii*; advanced
technological infrastructure, 146;
courted Canada Trust, 255;
encouraged call centres, 234, 255;
F-troop loyalists, 163–64; landslide
victory (1987), 19, 28–29, 239;
love of fables and stories, 52–53;
Meech Lake Accord, 35–47; NB
Works, 32–34; reflections on
experience, 223–25; relationship
with Nat Richard, 24–26;
relationship with Paul Martin,
ix–x; relations with border states,
218; social welfare concerns, 31–32,
34; ten-year pledge and resignation
(1997), 51–53, 248; work habits
and energy, 24
McKenna, Frank, in private sector
(1997–2005): business experience
relevant to ambassadorship,
79–80; Carlyle Group, 64–65, 204;
corporate interests, 63–69,
295–96a; dissatisfaction with
private sector, 75–76; Fox Harb'r
networking program, 65–67; "My
Canada" speech, 58–62; non-profit
activities, 68; relationship with
Gotlieb, 204; transition to private
life, 53–57
McKenna, Frank, in private sector
(2006–present): on BMD issue,
292; on Canadian sovereignty,
292–94; humanitarian interests
and work, *xvi–xvii*, 267–81, 283,
284, 288–89; interest in current
Canada-U.S. relations, 292–93;

interviewed on *The Hour* (2009),
237; limited effectiveness in U.S.
relations, 209; ONEXONE chair,
276, 284; on policy flexibility,
284–86; promotes leadership,
283–84, 286, 290–92, 293–94;
relationship with Bill Clinton, *xv*;
relationship with Ed Clark, 253–56,
257–58; relationship with George
W. Bush, *xv*; relationship with
James Dodds, 259–62; as St. FX
board chairman, 289–90; Starfish
foundation, 273–74, 279–81; TD
Bank Deputy Chair, 242, 253–63
McKenna, Frank, U.S. ambassador
(2005–6): advocacy, 172–75,
199–200; ambassadorial style of,
123–28, 142, 159; appointment
negotiations, announcement, and
formalities, 17–18, 73–80, 81–82,
94–97; asymmetric relationship
with U.S., 78–79, 194–95; attitude
toward diplomats, 74–75; BMD issue,
85–89, 90–93, 206, 211, 212; on
Bush administration, 98–100; on
Byrd Amendment, 152; Canadian
American Business Council speech,
140–42; credentials ceremony,
94–97; cultivated future leaders of
America, 136; Devils Lake issue,
156–59, 160–62, 174–75; dispelled
U.S. myths about Canada, 178–87,
193–94, 195–96; Dobbs interview,
180–84, 185–86; drive-by
diplomacy, 129–30; Empire Club
speech, 109–12, 113–14, 115–17;
as entrepreneurial ambassador,

media relations: BMD issue, 86, 89;
   Devils Lake issue, 157–58;
   dispelling U.S. myths about
   Canada, 180–87; and early
   successes of embassy, 167; Empire
   Club speech, 110–11; FM's skill
   with, 78, 79, 135, 161, 176–77, 207;
   Henry Champ's views, 188–92
Meech Lake Accord, 39–47; Bourassa's
   reaction, 45; distinct society
   clause, 36, 43; dogmatism about,
   285; emotional effects on FM,
   35–36, 45–46, 270; first round
   (1987), 39–42; and FM's Liberal
   leadership decision, 228, 239–42;
   Hogg's analysis, 42–45; Peterson's
   analysis of, 46–47; second round
   (1990), 42, 43. *See also* Quebec
Memoirs (Mulroney), 39–40, 46
Mendenhall, James, 153
Mercer, Rick, 135
minority governments, 88, 166, 212,
   238–39
Monahan, Joe, 8, 10, 14–16
Moreno, Luis Alberto, 135–36
Mother and Papoose (sculpture), 134
Moyo, Dambisa, 277–78
Mulroney, Brian: as bilateralist,
   217–18; on FM and Meech Lake,
   39–40, 42, 45, 46, 239–40; FM's
   support of, 269–70; and Gotlieb,
   203; Meech Lake Accord, 35–47;
   similarities to FM's background, 36
Murray, Patty, 218
"My Canada" speech (1998), 58–62,
   119, 200
Myers, Rick, 98

Nash, Steve, 196
Naylor, Thomas, 132, 133, 135
NB Works, 32–34
Netanyahu, Benjamin, 99–100
New Brunswick: Acadian community,
   37, 41, 114; broadband infrastruc-
   ture, 146, 178; culture of mutual
   help, 268; as knowledge-based
   economy, x; in national news, 28;
   public opinion on Meech Lake
   Accord, 39; site of TD annual
   general meeting, 262; socio-
   economic disadvantages, 32, 62.
   See also McKenna, Frank, New
   Brunswick premier (1987–97)
Newman, Don, 28–29, 54, 192–93,
   241–42, 247–48
New York City, 111–12, 146–47, 195–96
New York Times, 88, 117, 133
9/11 Commission Report, 182
Nixon, Richard, 65
Noriega, Roger, 91–92, 102–3, 156–57,
   177–78
North American Aerospace Defense
   Command (NORAD), 85
North American Free Trade
   Agreement (NAFTA), 170, 217
Novak, Robert, 116

Obama, Barack, 55, 100, 118–19, 209
Office of the Prime Minister (PMO), 82,
   86, 189
ONEXONE, 274–76, 279, 281, 284
O'Niell, Tip, 179
O'Reilly, Bill, 180, 184–85
Ornstein, Norman J., 114
Otis, Marion, 9

United States Constitution, 109
Université de Moncton, fundraising
    for, 68
University of New Brunswick, 20, 68

Wallin, Pamela, 146–48, 216
Warren, Jake, 192
Washington Advocacy Secretariat,
    170–71, 175–76. *See also* advocacy
Webster, John, 73, 74
Weinberger, Caspar, 65
Wells, Clyde, 39, 40, 41–42, 43, 285
Wetmore, George Ludlow, 158–59
Wilkins, David: at Canadian American
    Business Council, 140; on FM's
    refusal to seek Liberal leadership,
    229; at Fox Harb'r, 66, 67–68; on
    Paul Martin's criticism of U.S., 117;
    refused South Carolina governor-
    ship, 245–46; relationship with
    FM, 108–11, 114–15, 116–18
Wilson, Michael: as ambassador to
    U.S., 133, 138, 177, 189, 193, 204–5;
    softwood lumber agreement,
    152–53, 155
workfare programs, NB Works, 32–34
World Trade Organization, on Byrd
    Amendment, 152
Wyeth, Nathan, 132

Yéle Haiti, 275

Zambia, aid efforts, 290
Zoellick, Bob, 91–92

ABOUT THE AUTHOR

HARVEY SAWLER was born and grew up in Hamilton, Ontario, but has lived most of his adult life in Atlantic Canada. After dropping out of high school, he ventured into journalism: among his first assignments were man-on-the-street interviews on the morning after the 1972 Canada-Russia hockey series and, days later, covering Prime Minister Pierre Elliott Trudeau on the election trail in rural Prince Edward Island. From writing and reporting, he moved on to spend nearly thirty years in arts and tourism marketing and product development, emerging as a respected Canadian tourism consultant. Since returning to writing in 2000, he has produced seven books, including *The Beer Bandit Caper*, *Twenty-First Century Irvings*, *Last Canadian Beer: The Moosehead Story*, *On the Road with Dutch Mason* (with co-author David Bedford), and the novels *The Penguin Man*, *One Single Hour* and *Saving Mrs. Kennedy*. He lives at Bellevue Cove, PEI, with his partner, Charlotte Stewart. He has two daughters, Shannon and Vanessa, and two inspiring grandchildren, Maddie and Alex.